Multilingual Baseball

Also Available from Bloomsbury

Corpus Approaches to the Language of Sports, edited by Marcus Callies and Magnus Levin
Sports Discourse, Tony Schirato
How Language Shapes Relationships in Professional Sports Teams, Kieran File

Multilingual Baseball

Language Learning, Identity, and Intercultural Communication in the Transnational Game

Brendan H. O'Connor

BLOOMSBURY ACADEMIC
LONDON • NEW YORK • OXFORD • NEW DELHI • SYDNEY

BLOOMSBURY ACADEMIC
Bloomsbury Publishing Plc
50 Bedford Square, London, WC1B 3DP, UK
1385 Broadway, New York, NY 10018, USA
29 Earlsfort Terrace, Dublin 2, Ireland

BLOOMSBURY, BLOOMSBURY ACADEMIC and the Diana logo are trademarks of Bloomsbury Publishing Plc

First published in Great Britain 2023
Paperback edition published 2024

Copyright © Brendan H. O'Connor, 2023

Brendan H. O'Connor has asserted his right under the Copyright, Designs and Patents Act, 1988, to be identified as Author of this work.

For legal purposes the Acknowledgments on p. x constitute an extension of this copyright page.

Cover design: Elena Durey
Cover image © Game on. Rearview shot of a team of baseball players running onto the field. Yuri Arcurs / Alamy Stock Photo

All rights reserved. No part of this publication may be reproduced or transmitted in any form or by any means, electronic or mechanical, including photocopying, recording, or any information storage or retrieval system, without prior permission in writing from the publishers.

Bloomsbury Publishing Plc does not have any control over, or responsibility for, any third-party websites referred to or in this book. All internet addresses given in this book were correct at the time of going to press. The author and publisher regret any inconvenience caused if addresses have changed or sites have ceased to exist, but can accept no responsibility for any such changes.

A catalogue record for this book is available from the British Library.

A catalog record for this book is available from the Library of Congress.

ISBN: HB: 978-1-3502-9852-1
PB: 978-1-3502-9856-9
ePDF: 978-1-3502-9853-8
eBook: 978-1-3502-9854-5

Typeset by Deanta Global Publishing Services, Chennai, India

To find out more about our authors and books visit www.bloomsbury.com and sign up for our newsletters.

For Jenn and Ellie
and
In memory of Yordano "Ace" Ventura

Contents

List of Figures	viii
Acknowledgments	x
Introduction	1
1 Language Socialization and the Professional Development of Latin American Prospects	27
2 English, Spanish, and the Afterlives of Latin American Prospects	65
3 Non-Native Spanish Speakers Challenging Linguistic and Racial Divides in Major League Baseball	105
4 Forging Transnational Connections through Language Brokering and Language Learning in Asian Baseball	137
Conclusion	175
Notes	191
References	199
General Index	211
Index of names	221

Figures

1	Mike "King" Kelly in a Chicago White Stockings jersey, c. 1880–6	7
2	Team photo of the 1869 Troy Haymakers including Esteban Bellán of Cuba, the first known Latino player in the US major leagues	10
3	Entries for the Bender family with Mary Bender's Anishinaabemowin (Chippewa) name from the 1905–9 Indian Census Rolls	11
4	Baseball card of Charles Bender, 1905	13
5	Detail of a cartoon depicting Charles Bender with stereotypically Native features and Plains Indian ceremonial dress, 1910	13
6	Detail of a cartoon from *Cleveland Plain Dealer*, "Ki Yi Waugh Woop! They're Indians," 1915	14
7	Colin Simpson of the Class A Spokane Indians sports the team's home jersey with "Spokane" in the tribe's Salishan language and a redband trout–inspired pattern	16
8	Connecticut-born Blue Jays outfielder George Springer shows off the "La Gente del Barrio" home run jacket after his leadoff home run	18
9	Bulletin board with national origins of Royals' Dominican academy players	30
10	Example of Royals DR Academy essential questions	35
11	Lead educator Johan Febrillet leads pitching prospect Luis Polanco through a lesson on English verb tenses at the Royals' Dominican academy	36
12	Three academy players pose in front of the logo celebrating the Royals' 2019 Dominican Summer League championship	43
13	Infielder Yosmi Fernández signing his first professional contract with the Kansas City Royals, February 8, 2021	49
14	Whiteboard from mental skills meeting, Oakland A's instructional league, September 2021	52
15	Diamondbacks minor league pitcher Michel Gelabert in the Billings (MT) Scarlets' dugout, June 2020	73

16 Elvin Liriano and a Tri-City Dust Devils teammate converse with Washington State University students on a campus visit during the 2015 season   93
17 Alex Bregman sitting between Spanish-speaking teammates José Altuve and Carlos Correa in the dugout, June 14, 2018   115
18 Interpreter Hyunsung Kim, Larry Young, Félix Tejada, a Japanese umpire, and Carlos Rey on a day off at the 2013 World Baseball Classic in Japan   144
19 Yordano Ventura brandishes the Dominican flag during the Royals' World Series victory parade, November 4, 2015   187

Acknowledgments

My deepest gratitude to everyone who shared their insights on language diversity in professional baseball with me, especially Nick Additon, Zak Basch, Dave Bush, Deron Dolphus, Parker Dunshee, Dan Feinstein, John Foster, Michel Gelabert, Emily Glass, Kevin Goldstein, Richard Guasch, Eric Johnson, Hyunsung Kim, Jacky Bing-Sheng Lee, Elvin Liriano, Jill Long de Mercado, Juan Mosquera, Robert Puason, and Luis Victoria.

I owe a special debt to Jeff Diskin for his steadfast support and gracious hospitality in the Dominican Republic. On the Dominican side, thanks also to Johan Febrillet, Jorge Guzmán, Jesse Levy-Robinett, and all the players and staff at the Royals Dominican Academy, especially Yosmi Fernández.

Many thanks to Morwenna Scott, Laura Gallon, and the team at Bloomsbury Academic, as well as Kim Greenwell and Richard Feit at acad/edit, who streamlined early drafts, and Louise Chapman and the team at Lex Academic, for expert indexing. I'm grateful to Amanda Pascarelli, Chip Colwell, and the team at SAPIENS for publishing my initial article on multilingual baseball and allowing me to use snippets in this book. Ben Lindbergh fulfilled a dream by hosting me on the Effectively Wild podcast and jump-started a couple of relationships that proved fruitful—thank you. Elly van Gelderen and Norma Mendoza-Denton responded to queries on some of the finer linguistic details, sparing me the embarrassment of getting (those) things wrong. Early conversations with Oscar Mancinas helped me think through the scope of the project and convinced me that it was worth pursuing. Of the friends I've shared baseball with over the years, three stand out: José Lugo, Philip Stevens, and David Varner. Although they were not directly involved in this book, I'd like to recognize them for being an important part of the story. A profound bow to Dan Dorsey Roshi for endeavoring to keep me on the way in trying times.

Jeff Diskin, Deron Dolphus, John Foster, Hyunsung Kim, Jacky Bing-Sheng Lee, Elvin Liriano, Adam Schwartz, Philip Stevens, and Luis Victoria read and commented on chapter drafts. I'm grateful to all of them for their valuable suggestions and fact-checking. George Gmelch and Ray McDermott also took the time to read chapter drafts and responded encouragingly.

The Global Sport Institute at Arizona State University provided seed grant funding to support the completion of the manuscript. Thanks to Director of Research Scott N. Brooks and everyone at GSI. Eileen Díaz McConnell generously shared her research funding, which helped considerably as I was developing these ideas. The College of Liberal Arts and Sciences at ASU granted me sabbatical leave in fall 2021, allowing me to conduct most of the research represented here. As always, I'm grateful to my colleagues in ASU's School of Transborder Studies for their friendship and support.

Among the many teachers who have guided my linguistic explorations are some who have passed on but whose influence is everywhere in the book: Jane Hill, Richard Ruiz, Deborah Schiffrin, and Ron Scollon.

I relied heavily on several online repositories of baseball statistics and commentary, which I gratefully acknowledge here: Baseball Reference (baseball-reference.com), FanGraphs (fangraphs.com), My KBO Stats (mykbostats.com), and CPBL Stats (cpblstats.com). A hat tip, also, to all the baseball researchers and analysts who have kept an obsessive record of the game, making my work possible.

Thanks to the following people and institutions for permission to reproduce images: Billings (MT) Gazette/Lee Enterprises, Carlisle Indian School Digital Resource Center, Yosmi Fernández/MB Baseball Academy, Getty Images, Eric Johnson, Hyunsung Kim, the National Baseball Hall of Fame and Museum, and the Spokane Indians.

My brother and closest baseball buddy, Kieran O'Connor, has been an enthusiastic booster of this project and a constant source of encouragement and inspiration. Not that I ever doubted his love, but he proved it in 2015 when he bounced back from the Blue Jays' defeat in the American League Championship Series to will my beloved Royals to a World Series victory.

Endless love and gratitude to my mom, Catherine, my sisters, Meghan—who, as a child, endured a rainout at Shea Stadium, followed by an unceremonious beer baptism—and Mairin—a Yankee gal who resisted all attempts to make her a Mairin-ers fan—along with my nieces, nephews, and in-laws.

It almost goes without saying, but it all started with my dad, Gary, who, at Veterans Stadium in Philadelphia on May 27, 1990, made all of us—even Mom—stay to the end of a John Smoltz no-hit bid that ended with one out in the bottom of the ninth. That's what it's all about.

For my wife, Jenn—my best friend and the first reader of this book, for love that hopes and endures all things—and my daughter, Ellie, bilingual baseball *aficionada* and Jackie Robinson superfan—I have no words. You'll never know, dears, how much I love you. This is for you.

Introduction

La Bendición: A Bilingual Blessing

On October 17, 1971, the Pittsburgh Pirates triumphed in Game 7 of the World Series, clinching an improbable comeback against the heavily favored defending champions, the Baltimore Orioles. The Pirates had quietly made history a month and a half earlier, when manager Danny Murtaugh filled out a lineup card with "all brothers out there on the field," as first baseman Al Oliver put it: the first all-Black and Latino starting nine in Major League Baseball history, twenty-four years after Jackie Robinson shattered professional baseball's color line.[1] Murtaugh, a white man with "a reputation for treating Black players with fairness," claimed to have seen Pirates, not Blacks, when setting the lineup. While the significance of that moment may have been slow to dawn on the players, manager, and media (Markusen, 2006), the impact of another moment in late October was both immediate and lasting.

Amid the raucous celebration in the Pirates' locker room, the Pittsburgh broadcasting legend Bob Prince introduced Puerto Rican–born Roberto Clemente—one of the "brothers" in the historic September lineup—as "the greatest right fielder in the game of baseball." Few would have argued with that assessment. Clemente had just become the first Latino to be named most valuable player of the World Series, crushing a home run in the fourth inning of Game 7 to seal the Pirates' victory. Revered as a player and humanitarian, he would die just over a year later in a plane crash while delivering emergency supplies to Nicaragua. He apparently intended to use his status to confront the corrupt Somoza government about the mismanagement of earthquake relief.

On that happy day in October, though, Clemente began his postgame interview with what his biographer called "one of the most memorable acts of his life, a simple moment that touched the souls of millions of people in the Spanish-speaking world" (Maraniss, 2006). He addressed Prince and an estimated thirty-seven million viewers:[2]

Thank you, Bob. And before I say anything in English, I would like to say something for my mother and father in Spanish. *En el día más grande de mi vida, para los nenes, la bendición mía, y que mis padres me echen la bendición de Puerto Rico.*

[On the greatest day of my life, for my kids, my blessing, and that my parents would send me their blessing from Puerto Rico.]

According to Latino sports media platform La Vida Baseball, "these were the first words spoken in Spanish live via satellite on US network TV."[3] I have not been able to confirm that claim; whether or not Clemente's Spanish words were "the first," the gesture was indisputably a watershed moment for the visibility of Latinos and Spanish speakers in US baseball. The greatest Latino player of his generation—and still the greatest Puerto Rican player of all time by a wide margin[4]—began his celebratory interview by reaching out to his family in Spanish, sending an unmistakable message that Spanish speakers belonged in the major leagues, even as nonwhite players were still chipping away at the game's legacy of racist exclusion.

Clemente acted bravely and powerfully in choosing to use Spanish in such an unprecedented way and at such a visible moment. But what happened next was also telling. Clemente's teammate Steve Blass, who had just pitched a complete game masterpiece, holding the Orioles to four hits and one run, leaned into the frame and interrupted with his own message for Clemente's parents: "Mr. and Mrs. Clemente, we love him, too!" The interviewer, Bob Prince, recovered gracefully, building on Blass's jubilant interjection and affirming Clemente: "We understood you."

Once things quieted down, Blass was apparently mortified by his "spontaneous and joyful" interruption; from a distance of five decades, I find it touching and prescient (Maraniss, 2006, p. 264). A bilingual ballplayer who was perfectly capable of conducting interviews in English decided to use Spanish at a particular moment for a particular purpose and audience. Two English speakers (Blass and Prince) reacted not with derision, mockery, or incomprehension but with follow-up utterances[5] which, while in English, presumed that Clemente's use of Spanish was meaningful and appropriate to the context. In other words, Blass and Prince treated bilingualism as an unexceptional feature of life in professional baseball. This was, to borrow a phrase from physicist Frank Wilczek, a "radically conservative" move in light of the history of baseball and the United States (Wilczek, 2021).

This book focuses on multilingualism and language diversity in contemporary professional baseball. Before diving into the place of language in the modern game, however, it's worth taking a step back to consider how different languages and their speakers have shaped the history of baseball—especially in the United States, where attitudes toward language, race, and culture in the national pastime have always been mixed up with broader social and political currents. Putting contemporary multilingual baseball in the context of the game's history allows us to appreciate how much has changed—thanks, in no small part, to the efforts of pioneers like Roberto Clemente—as well as how much of the modern landscape, to quote catcher-cum-philosopher Yogi Berra, is "déjà vu all over again."

Uncovering Baseball's Multilingual Past

Baseball, like the United States, has always been multilingual. But US professional baseball, like the country, has often preferred to think of itself as monolingual. American monolingualism has never been the case in *descriptive* terms—that is, "how things are"—but has historically been touted as a national ideal in *prescriptive* terms, or "how things should be." This is perhaps the defining linguistic contradiction of the United States and one that is mirrored in the national pastime. It is a land of staggering linguistic diversity, both before and after European colonization, whose overriding language ideology—not enshrined in federal law, though not for lack of trying (Adams & Brink, 1990)—is something like the attitude of willful ignorance expressed in the well-worn quotation: "If English was good enough for Jesus Christ, it's good enough for me." The statement is of spurious provenance, and it sounds like a joke, but members of Congress, past and present, have used it to advocate for English-only policies and against bilingual education, according to the late language policy scholar Richard Ruiz (who noted that Jesus was almost certainly multilingual, for what it's worth) (Ruiz, 2016b).

Successive waves of immigrants to the United States have learned that "linguistic assimilation into English has been universally held as a panacea and mandate for all groups"—put differently, as a "cure" for the "problems" of pluralism and a requirement for belonging (Wiley, 2000). As immigration intensified in the nineteenth and early twentieth centuries, American Indian nations were simultaneously undergoing "linguistic pacification" as the federal government forcibly placed children and youth in boarding schools, seeking to stamp out Indigenous languages and lifeways "so as to literally clear the path for the takeover of Native lands" (McCarty & Nicholas, 2014). Becoming acceptably American required that immigrant groups' diverse languages and cultural practices be "ironed out" over time (Ruiz, 2016a); manifest destiny demanded that Native American languages be erased, the better to imagine the West as empty space, ripe for an expanding English-speaking empire (Wolfe, 2006).

In part because of these ideologies,[6] information about multilingualism in early baseball is hard to come by. Nevertheless, the evidence suggests that a high degree of language diversity characterized baseball from the beginning. The popular notion that early professional baseball was exclusively "a game for poor immigrants and high school dropouts" (Eig, 2010) may be a myth (Riess, 1980), but some of the first nationally recognized baseball superstars were, in fact, from bilingual[7] immigrant families. The mighty Henry Louis Gehrig— Lou Gehrig, the Iron Horse—was nearly named Heinrich after his German-born father; his birth certificate shows that "H-e-i-n" was quickly corrected to "Henry"—"a giant step toward assimilation" for the family, penniless residents of a predominantly German area of Manhattan (Eig, 2010). Lou Gehrig spoke only German until he entered school at the age of five. His even-mightier Yankees teammate Babe Ruth was born in Baltimore, Maryland, to US-born parents but is also supposed to have spoken German as a child with his immigrant grandparents.[8]

Catcher Moe Berg was no Ruth or Gehrig on the field, but he deserves a spot in the multilingual baseball Hall of Fame. His parents hailed from a Jewish area of Ukraine; when Moe's father immigrated to New York City in 1894, he spoke Yiddish, Russian, and Hebrew and had learned to read English, French, and German (Dawidoff, 1994). Moe capitalized on his multilingual upbringing to major in modern languages at Princeton, where he studied another seven languages (Dawidoff, 1994, p. 31). During the Second World War, he famously undertook several clandestine missions for the US Office of Strategic Services— the future Central Intelligence Agency—in Europe, where being a polyglot was presumably an asset.[9]

Language and Race in the History of Segregated Baseball

Another contributing factor to language diversity in early baseball, beyond the presence of players from immigrant families, was the lack of a firm "color line" banning Black players (i.e., of African descent) and, eventually, other players of color from professional leagues. The exact circumstances are debated, but the laughably named "gentlemen's agreement" took effect in the last decade of the nineteenth century. Prior to that, nonwhite ballplayers endured racist taunting from fans, players who refused to participate in integrated games, teammates who deliberately sabotaged them, and demeaning depictions in mascots and journalism, but they were not excluded wholesale from the major leagues (Burgos, 2007). After the establishment of the color line, historian Adrian Burgos, Jr., has argued, "Latinos were the main group used to test the limits of racial tolerance" in professional baseball. That is, since their "racial" identity was less defined, compared to Black players, the status of Latino players was somewhat unclear, which meant that teams could, and did, use them to "test the limits" of inclusion (Burgos, 2007, p. 12). As Jeffrey Powers-Beck has documented in detail, American Indians also occupied an in-between position that allowed some Native players to participate in otherwise segregated leagues during the first half of the twentieth century (Powers-Beck, 2004).

The ambiguous status of Latino and Native ballplayers in early US baseball points to the fact that "race"-based identities are not preordained but made—hence the quotation marks around "race."[10] Predominantly white professional leagues excluded Black players without question—though, even then, at least one light-skinned African American player managed to "pass" as white (Morris & Fatsis, 2014)—but the malleability of race meant that the issue was less straightforward with regard to early Latino and American Indian players, notwithstanding the vociferous racism directed at them. For such players—"ethnic" but not Black, or not definitively Black—*language* played a crucial role in what social scientists call "racialization," or the process of sorting people into racial categories and thereby "making" race (Omi & Winant, 1994). Of course, this phenomenon is not limited to baseball. Language has historically been crucial in determining who is "American enough" or "white enough" to participate fully in US society (Hill, 2001). These debates and distinctions are not just academic. Legal historians have shown that changing understandings of "race" and whiteness informed changes to US immigration law, including the definition of "national origin" and eligibility for citizenship (Ngai, 2017).

Within early professional baseball, judgments about language and culture shaped views of who was eligible to play in segregated leagues, making it possible for team owners to "gerrymander" the color line, as Burgos, Jr., puts it. This racial and linguistic ambiguity also allowed players to present themselves strategically to gain entry. The mother of Ted Williams, one of the greatest hitters in MLB history, was born in El Paso, Texas, near the US-Mexico border, and had a Mexican surname (Venzor). Williams was raised in San Diego, California, and visited Tijuana occasionally with his mother but "did not grow up in a Spanish-speaking barrio in San Diego or in a household where Mexican culture was dominant" (Burgos, 2007, pp. 149–50). He never identified as Mexican American or Latino, nor did others treat him as such, as opposed to contemporaries like Melo Almada and Lefty Gómez, whose names, phenotypes (i.e., appearance), and language background led to "strict scrutiny" on racial terms but did not, however, lead to their exclusion from MLB (Burgos, 2007, p. 150). Still, things might have gone differently for Williams, as he acknowledged in citing "prejudices" that would have followed his mother's name in California, especially during the Great Depression when thousands of Mexican-origin residents were deported (Burgos, 2007, pp. 149–50).

Four Stories about Language, Race, and Ethnicity in Early Professional Baseball

To illustrate some of the contradictions of language, race, and ethnicity in the early history of professional baseball in the United States, I'll present the stories of four players, two of whom were connected to upstate New York, the birthplace of baseball and, not entirely coincidentally, my birthplace.

King Kelly: Ethnic Difference and "Inherited" Accents

Hall of Famer Mike "King" Kelly was born in 1857 in Troy, New York, to Irish parents who had apparently immigrated in the 1820s or 1830s, just prior to the Great Hunger. My own ancestors joined the migrant stream not long after, settling in the same area and fighting for the Union in the US Civil War, as Kelly's father did. Kelly's family, like most fleeing "British misrule" (his words) at the time, was destitute; when his father was not serving in the army, he may have been, at various times, a papermaker, a saloon keeper, and/or a laborer (Rosenberg, 2004). Like some of the modern-day players from poor or working-class backgrounds in Chapters 1 and 2, King Kelly took pains to emphasize his family's commitment to education, writing that, while Irish immigrant parents "may not have had the advantages for an education themselves . . . they know the value of education, and feel that their sons and daughters shall receive their share of it in this great country of ours" (Kelly, 2006) (Figure 1).

It is impossible to say if King Kelly's parents were Irish-English bilinguals or if Kelly was exposed to the Irish language as a child. The 1860 US Census record for the family notes only that both of Kelly's parents were born in Ireland and that his mother, Catharine, was an illiterate adult, bearing out Kelly's description of her as lacking formal education (Rosenberg, 2004, p. 15). The Census Bureau did not ask about language use or ability until 1890;[11] based on my ancestors' turn-of-the-century census records, older family members' first language was commonly listed as "Irish," though what census takers understood this to mean is unclear, since by the 1920s and 1930s, Celtic languages like Irish and Scots Gaelic were being conflated with English in census tabulations (Stevens, 1999).

The details of the language ecology of King Kelly's childhood are murky. What is clear, however, is that his immigrant background led people to *hear* his language differently, filtering his American English through the lens of ethnic difference: "Quotes attributed to [Kelly] frequently suggest that he spoke with a bit of an Irish brogue, despite being American born. If so, it was obviously an inherited trait" (Appel, 1999). As was also the case with early Latino and American Indian ballplayers, journalists represented Kelly as a kind of ethnic caricature, using stereotypically "Irish" features in reporting his speech, as in the following excerpt from 1886, where Kelly supposedly teased Irish Catholic fans in St. Louis by pretending to be an Irish Protestant unionist:

> So yer Kerry Patchers, eh? Well, this is the twenty-fourth of May [Queen Victoria's birthday]. God save the Queen! I'm coming up yer way tonight and start an Orange lodge. I expect all of yez ter join up. Let me hand in your name! (Appel, 1999, p. 86)

For good measure, the story stated that Kelly also whistled "The Boyne River," a classic unionist marching tune. It's hard to know what to make of this. Did Kelly actually speak that way? Was he deliberately stylizing his speech—that is, "putting on" an accent he had learned to perform from his parents and other Irish immigrants? (Coupland, 2001). Or was the newspaper account less

Figure 1 Mike "King" Kelly in a Chicago White Stockings jersey, *c.* 1880–6 (Brown Brothers/National Baseball Hall of Fame and Museum). Reproduced with permission of the National Baseball Hall of Fame and Museum.

a reflection of Kelly's speech and more a reflection of the "hearing practices" of the (presumably non-Irish) pressmen who wielded the discursive power to transform Kelly into a stereotype (Rosa & Flores, 2017), at a time when the racial identity of Irish Americans was, itself, unsettled? A piece of Civil War–era campaign literature dating to Mike Kelly's childhood sought to spread fears about a possible "amalgamation . . . of Irish and negroes," the latter of whom were sometimes called "smoked Irish" (Ignatiev, 2012). Lamentably, the outcome was not a political amalgamation but an increasingly tense racial context where Irish American ballplayers, among others, asserted their whiteness in explicit contrast to Black players, helping to codify racial segregation in the professional game.

Esteban Bellán and Vincent Nava: Racial Ambiguity and Linguistic Mockery

Cuban-born third baseman Esteban Bellán arrived in Troy, New York, in 1868—an immigrant, like young Mike Kelly's parents, but one who came to the United States under vastly different circumstances. Bellán's parents hailed from the Cuban elites, who began sending their children to private Catholic institutions in the United States during the island's struggle for independence from Spain out of "a desire to place the next generation beyond the purview of Spanish colonial authority" (Burgos, 2007, pp. 18–19). Bellán started playing baseball as a high schooler at the Rose Hill campus of St. John's College in the Bronx (now Fordham University) but was soon drawn to the professional game and became the first Latino player in the first nationwide "major league," the National Association, when he appeared with the Troy Haymakers from 1869 to 1871 (Burgos, 2007, pp. 18–20). While Bellán was still with the Haymakers, the team's representative at the National Association's annual meeting nonetheless supported a resolution to bar clubs with "colored men" from the league—one of the first decisive moves toward the color line. In any case, Bellán subsequently returned to Cuba, one of a handful of baseball-loving Cubans educated at US institutions who helped to build the island's baseball culture (Burgos, 2007, pp. 18, 22) (Figure 2).

Bellán was the "right kind" of Latino—upper class, educated, not Black—and had the additional good fortune to arrive in the United States at a time when professional baseball was still loosely organized and regulated. It is instructive to compare his case with that of Vincent Nava, who, though he debuted in 1882, twelve years after Bellán, was the first *brown* player in professional baseball, according to Burgos, Jr. (as opposed to the first Latino). Nava's mother was from Durango, Mexico, and he grew up in California as the adopted son of a white

English immigrant, whose surname (Irwin) he borrowed when breaking into the National League. Afterward, his team, the Providence Grays, apparently decided to publicize his birth name (Nava) in order to market Vincent as an ethnic curiosity (Burgos, 2007, p. 38).[12]

With Roberto Clemente's postgame interview in mind, Nava's story brings forth two important points about the visibility of racial and linguistic difference in professional baseball. First, no one at the time knew or acknowledged that Nava was of Mexican origin. The Grays emphasized that Nava was "Spanish" or a "Spaniard," setting the stage for later efforts to assert the whiteness or "Castilian" heritage of Cuban players—in other words, downplaying the African, Indigenous, or *mestizo* roots of Latinos and painting them as essentially "European."[13] Teams and journalists exploited Latinos' racial ambiguity, especially where lighter-skinned players were concerned, to muddy the question of inclusion and exclusion in professional settings. At various times, Nava was called a Cuban, an Italian, and a Spaniard; he was also suspected of being a white-passing African American. Ambiguous race talk went both ways, however. Burgos, Jr., compiled a list of labels that late nineteenth-century sportswriters used to refer to Black players whose presence in organized baseball was increasingly called into question—Cuban, Spanish, Portuguese, Mexican, Italian, Arabian, Indian, and, yes, Irish (Burgos 2007, pp. 35, 51). Writing about African American players as though they might be Latino, since Latinos were not unambiguously white *or* nonwhite, allowed the press to maintain "plausible deniability" as the color line was still hardening.

A more important point, for my purposes, is that mocking early Latino players' *language* was used to mark them as *racially* different and raise doubts about their suitability for organized baseball. Burgos, Jr., quotes an 1883 newspaper parody of the Grays' coach supposedly trying to communicate with Nava, his "Spanish protégé": "Hi, Senor! Quito offi il firsto basilo et makadagio towardso secondo basilo liki hellio!" (Basically, get off first base and make a dash toward second like hell.)

This comes across as a very early example of what linguistic anthropologist Jane Hill termed Mock Spanish—that is, limited uses of Spanish or "Spanish-like" elements by US English speakers that subtly or "covertly" denigrate Latinos, especially Mexicans. It does make use of certain features of the Mock Spanish register, like highly generative -o suffixation ("towards-o," "helli-o") (Hill, 2008). But it does not otherwise resemble contemporary Mock Spanish usages; it sounds vaguely Romantic, but some of the elements come across as more Italian ("il," "makadagio") or French ("et") than Spanish—to my ears, anyway. This suggests that it was written by someone with little direct contact with Spanish or Spanish

Figure 2 Team photo of the 1869 Troy Haymakers including Esteban Bellán of Cuba (standing, far right), the first known Latino player in the US major leagues (National Baseball Hall of Fame and Museum). Reproduced with permission of the National Baseball Hall of Fame and Museum.

speakers and little sense of how Spanish differed from related languages. In its way, it's perfect: the vague, Esperanto-like tone reflects the uncertainty around the racial identities of players like Vincent Nava—then, as now, understood with reference to different ways of using language.

Charles Albert Bender: "Speaking Indian" in Public

Hall of Fame pitcher Charles Bender—nicknamed "Chief," like virtually every other Native American ballplayer of the early 1900s—was the son of a German immigrant father and a Chippewa (Ojibwe/Anishinaabe)[14] mother and grew up on the family's allotted homestead, following the provisions of the 1887 Dawes Act, on the White Earth Indian Reservation in Minnesota. As with King Kelly, the linguistic environment of Charles Bender's childhood is easy to imagine and difficult to reconstruct (Figure 3).

Charles and his family were "métis," or mixed-race residents of the reservation, and possibly less likely to participate in Anishinaabemowin-speaking networks and churches as a result (Kashatus, 2006). The federal obsession with quantifying Indians' racial "purity" as a condition for tribal enrollment had already taken hold. Charles was identified as "1/2" Chippewa on census documents (US Census Bureau, 1900) and, at age thirteen, was recorded as "half" blood on his intake documents for Pennsylvania's Carlisle Indian Industrial School (Carlisle Indian Industrial School, 1896b). Still, Bender's mother is listed in the 1905–9 Indian Census Rolls with her "Indian name," "Pah shah de o quay," alongside her English (married) name, Mary Bender (US Census Bureau, Indian Census Rolls [1905–9], p. 580). The 1900 US Census records only that Mary could speak English—that was the sole question about language—and that she could not read or write, which suggests that she did not attend English-language schools as a child (US Census Bureau, 1900). The 1940 Census was the first time non-foreign-born residents were asked about their mother tongue but only as a supplemental question. By then, Mary had passed away, and Charles's mother tongue was not recorded (US Census Bureau, 1940). If Charles was given a Chippewa birth name, it does not appear in the Indian rolls or census records, but he was supposedly known by the Chippewa nickname "Mandowescence" in childhood (Kashatus, 2006, p. 5).[15]

Based on the available evidence, whether he spoke or understood the language with any degree of proficiency, it seems almost certain that Charles Bender was exposed to Anishinaabemowin while growing up on the White Earth Reservation and it is entirely possible—though far from certain—that his mother was a first-language speaker of Anishinaabemowin. What is certain is that, when Charles arrived at the Carlisle Indian School in 1896, he entered an educational setting in which Native children were systematically and deliberately forced to adopt English as "the habit of the tongue and mind" and to forget what they knew of their mother tongues. The Carlisle School's 1895 annual report,

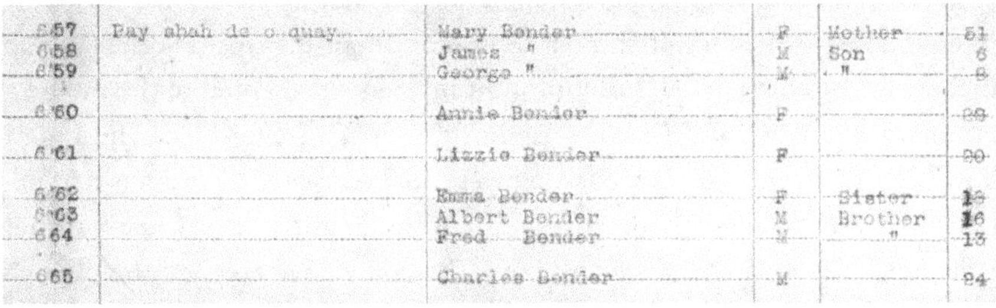

657	Pay shah de o quay	Mary Bender	F	Mother	51
658		James "	M	Son	6
659		George "	M	"	8
660		Annie Bender	F		28
661		Lizzie Bender	F		20
662		Emma Bender	F	Sister	18
663		Albert Bender	M	Brother	16
664		Fred Bender	M	"	13
665		Charles Bender	M		24

Figure 3 Entries for the Bender family with Mary Bender's Anishinaabemowin (Chippewa) name from the 1905–9 Indian Census Rolls (US National Archives).

written by no other than Richard Henry Pratt of "kill the Indian to save the man" fame, laid out the policy plainly:

> The use of the English language is made compulsory in the school, and further pushed through bringing into one school children from many tribes, and then, from time to time, sending pupils into English-speaking families by the outing system—by which multiplicity of means, English soon becomes the habit of the tongue and mind with most students. (Pratt, 1894–5)

Pratt went on to comment that the school had the "greatest difficulty . . . with those [students] who have previously made some progress with reading some Indian vernacular"—in other words, that it was more difficult to assimilate students who were literate in their mother tongues.

Along with the "linguistic pacification" of tribal nations by way of compulsory English for Native youth, baseball was promoted at Indian boarding schools as an "important vehicle in the assimilation process," a civilizing endeavor through which Indian boys could learn "Anglo-American values of teamwork, sportsmanship, and individual achievement" (Kashatus, 2006, p. 25). This attitude didn't just apply to American Indians; Horace Wilson, the first American baseball "missionary" to Japan, was a teacher who might have seen the principles of baseball as conducive to understanding Western mathematics (Nakagawa, 2014). Later, during the Japanese colonial expansion, the occupiers of Taiwan and Korea saw baseball as a means to encourage cultural assimilation and diminish ethnic conflict (Morris, 2006). For Bender's part, his Carlisle student card noted his "excellent character," though, according to his file, he was once suspended for "treachery to the baseball team" under unknown circumstances (Carlisle Indian Industrial School, 1896a).

The devil's bargain promised by residential institutions like Carlisle—adopt white ways and gain acceptance in mainstream US society—was a bait-and-switch for Charles Bender and his classmates (who had relatively little say in the matter, in any case). After pitching a shutout in the 1905 World Series, Bender famously told a newspaper, "I do not want my name presented to the public as an Indian but as a pitcher" (Powers-Beck, 2004, p. 72). Nevertheless, he and his fellow "Chiefs" in professional baseball were always treated as Indians first and baseball players second; their racial and ethnic identities overwhelmed their on-field exploits for journalists and fans. They may have escaped the outright exclusion that Black players faced, but they were never allowed to forget that they were racially suspect (Figures 4 and 5).

Figure 4 Baseball card of Charles Bender, 1905 (public domain). Image provided by Carlisle Indian School Digital Resource Center.

Figure 5 Detail of a cartoon depicting Charles Bender with stereotypically Native features and Plains Indian ceremonial dress, 1910 (Hugh Doyle/public domain). Image provided by Carlisle Indian School Digital Resource Center.

Even Bender's triumphs served as opportunities to depict him as an ethnic curiosity and to reinforce views of American Indians as backward and clownish. Compare the faithful rendering of the young pitcher on a 1905 baseball card with a cartoon that appeared in 1910 to commemorate one of his finest moments, a no-hit victory for the Philadelphia Athletics over the Cleveland Naps (who would be renamed the "Indians" in 1915—more on that shortly). Bender is shown dancing on the head of the Athletics' elephant mascot with a goofy grin and oversized crooked nose that anticipate Chief Wahoo, the Sambolike character in Cleveland's future logo. He is also wearing a Plains Indian war bonnet, despite being from a tribe that wore no such regalia, an image that paints Native peoples as homogeneous and undifferentiated.

As with non-native players like King Kelly and Vincent Nava, though in different ways, *language* was also essential to the dirty work of racializing the few Native ballplayers who succeeded in the early major leagues. This sometimes took the form of what linguistic anthropologist Barbra Meek (Kaska) has analyzed as "Hollywood Injun English"—that is, ungrammatical, mocking, or childish representations of American Indian English such as you might hear in old Western

Figure 6 Detail of a cartoon from *Cleveland Plain Dealer*, "Ki Yi Waugh Woop! They're Indians," 1915 (Public domain).

movies (Meek, 2006). A newspaper clipping from Bender's Carlisle file[16] exhorts readers to "take off [their] fuzzy-wuzzys" for Bender and his fellow "big chief," New York Giants' catcher John Meyers (Cahuilla, future chief of the Mission Indian Agency of Southern California), as "heap big Americans" who put the lie to the truism that "the only good Indian is a dead Injun" (Salgado, 2008) (Figure 6).

Sometimes, however, media coverage of Native ballplayers veered into mock representations of American Indian languages—which players like Bender and Meyers probably heard and may have spoken as children—rather than mockery of Indian English. A 1915 cartoon from the Cleveland *Plain Dealer* attempted to comment humorously on possible consequences of an "Indian" takeover of baseball, inspired by the team's recent name change from the Naps[17] to the Indians.[18] Along with the expected tropes—a war bonnet from the Plains, a grinning Indian holding a baseball bat and saying "Heap big stick!"—the cartoon imagines a fanciful encounter between an "Indian" player (with long hair and face paint) and a non-Indian umpire.

In the cartoon, subtitled "Will it come to this?," the player appears to be arguing a call with the umpire, who is walking away from him and holding his hand up. The player says "Wukwog-o"; the umpire responds, "When you talk to me, talk English you Wukoig!"—to which speech bubble the cartoonist appended an arrow and an explanation: "That last word is in Indian." Just above that scene, the cartoonist pictured Cleveland fans' "new rooting lingo," also presumably "in Indian": "Slkro-wow Wahooooooo," "Kiok-ilk wek-oo," "Wahoo Zoea-erk." Like the war bonnet, these caveman-like representations of "Indian" language elided distinctions between different Native nations and ways of speaking, reinforcing a narrative that all Indians were essentially the same and lumping distinguished players like Bender and Meyers in with mascots like Chief Wahoo.

Making Bilingualism Visible

In the preceding stories, when bilingualism in baseball was made visible, it often had the effect of reinforcing racial stereotypes (e.g., "speaking Indian" or speaking *like* an Indian), playing on doubts that certain players belonged in organized baseball (e.g., the use of Mock Spanish in reference to Vincent Nava) or suggesting that dialect and accent variations were immutable features of ethnic groups, rather than learned behaviors (e.g., Mike Kelly's "Irish brogue"). Visibility, as Bryan McKinley Jones Brayboy has commented of representations of American Indians in schools, is not always a positive thing; it can be problematic, since some forms of visibility can "trap" groups of people in outdated or racist frames, like insects in amber (Brayboy, 2003).

The cartoonish depiction of "speaking Indian" is a case in point. Prior to the arrival of Europeans, "nearly 300 distinct, mutually unintelligible languages" belonging to over fifty language families were spoken in the territory of the present-day United States and Canada, and "many more have disappeared with little trace" (Mithun, 2001). If Charles Bender and John Meyers had any knowledge of their heritage languages (Anishinaabemowin and Cahuilla, respectively), they would have spoken tongues from two unrelated families with different histories and grammars, intertwined with distinct cultural, social, and religious practices. "Speaking Indian," as the cartoonist would have it, makes Native North American languages visible in a problematic way by flattening distinctions among them and makes actual American Indian languages and their speakers *invisible* by implying that all Indian speech is homogeneous gibberish. A similar process of erasure, though with different implications, was at work in the early twentieth-century US Census, when Celtic languages, such as Kelly's parents or grandparents might have spoken, were collapsed into a catch-all category that made them synonymous with English (Irvine & Gal, 2000).

However, as the opening anecdote about Roberto Clemente was meant to suggest, the main message of this book is not that language diversity has been, or still is, seen as a problem in professional baseball (Ruiz, 1984). Rather, I seek to shed light on the *importance* of bilingualism in today's transnational game and to document the myriad ways that baseball people, including players, coaches, teachers, scouts, interpreters, and staffers, encounter and deal with diverse ways of speaking and use language strategically to form relationships and pursue opportunities.

Here, then, in the vein of Clemente's speech, are two recent counterpoints to the examples of linguistic mockery and derision in the previous section. First, on the topic of "speaking Indian": beginning in 2015, the minor league Spokane (Washington) Indians baseball team, in consultation with the Spokane Tribe of Indians, adopted the tribe's name for themselves in the Spokane language[19]—not as a one-off tribute but as the team name on their primary home uniforms. The team undertook this change with the tribe's blessing, ensuring that the name was written properly—*Sp'q'n'i?*, even though the final symbol, representing a glottal stop, is not used in English orthography—and, instead of a Plains Indian war bonnet, worked with the tribe to add culturally appropriate symbols to their jerseys and marketing materials, such as a redband trout (Harwood, 2018) (Figure 7).

This is not to say that all Spokane or Native people endorsed the team's continued use of the "Indians" name. But the story of "the first Native American language to be featured on a professional sports team's primary jersey" does

Figure 7 Colin Simpson of the Class A Spokane Indians sports the team's home jersey with "Spokane" in the tribe's Salishan language and a redband trout–inspired pattern (James Snook/Spokane Indians). Reproduced with the permission of the photographer and Spokane Indians.

provide a stark contrast with early representations of Native players and languages in professional baseball, suggesting that visibility does not have to be a trap.[20]

In a related development in 2016, MLB worked with a Texas-based, Latino-oriented advertising agency to create a campaign called "Ponle Acento"—"Put an accent on it"—that encouraged players with Spanish surnames to include acute accents and tildes (the diacritic on the Spanish ñ) on their jerseys. While the movement started as part of MLB's broader effort to reach out to Latino and Spanish-speaking fans, it was championed by players like Adrián González (Mexican American) and Robinson Canó (Dominican) as a way to highlight linguistic and cultural diversity and celebrate the presence of Latinos in MLB. As Burgos, Jr., and others noted, it was also a long-overdue corrective to a tradition of "exaggerating [the] malapropisms and mispronunciations" of Latino second-language speakers of English like Clemente in the baseball press and a generally "lax attitude" toward spelling and pronouncing Spanish names correctly (Blitzer, 2016).[21] Coverage of the campaign (including its online avatar #PonleAcento) described it as a response to the changing demographics of the game and the outcome of Latino players' being "more vocal" about their preferences.

Ponle Acento displayed changing attitudes toward bilingualism in baseball, but it also tested "the limits of inclusion" for Latinos and Spanish. A 2016 account of the campaign included the tidbit that shortstop Eduardo Núñez, upon being traded to the Minnesota Twins, had asked the team for a tilde on his jersey; he got the tilde but reasoned that requesting an accent over the ú would be taking things too far.

Some of the most impactful developments in recent years are those that have challenged the idea that bilingualism is only "for" certain players or groups of people. In the example of the Spokane Indians' jerseys, the tribe was gratified that the team had decided to use the Salishan name precisely because the team was *not* made up of Native players. Multiple tribal officials and members commented that the partnership was an opportunity to educate outsiders about the Spokane Tribe and language, and even to gain international visibility because of the presence of Latin American minor leaguers.

At the major league level, Latinos have also foregrounded diversity in ways that embrace teammates and staff members from Latino and non-Latino backgrounds. The Toronto Blue Jays' home run jacket, for example, which is ceremonially presented after each Blue Jays homer, was the "brainchild" of one of the team's Spanish-English interpreters, Hector "Tito" Lebron (the right cuff reads "It's a Tito thing"), "to represent the multicultural backgrounds of the team and its fan base" (Hunter, 2021) (Figure 8).

Figure 8 Connecticut-born Blue Jays outfielder George Springer shows off the "La Gente del Barrio" home run jacket after his leadoff home run on July 31, 2021 (Steve Russell/Toronto Star via Getty Images).

The back of the blue suit jacket sports a large Blue Jays logo surrounded by the names of countries represented among Blue Jays players and staff, in both English and Spanish, with "La Gente Del Barrio"—"the people from the hood," roughly—in large lettering underneath. The jacket comes across as an expression of international pride, appropriate to a profoundly international city and a team with a nationwide fan base, as well as a cheeky clapback at people troubled by language diversity in baseball, a topic I explore further in the conclusion.

MLB's Players' Weekend promotion, during which players can choose a nickname for their jerseys, has been another opportunity to showcase the game's linguistic and racial heterogeneity. Besides myriad Spanish nicknames, German-born Max Kepler has been seen representing his Polish father with "Różycki"; pitcher Hyun-Jin Ryu's jersey has featured his name in Korean script; and Jacoby Ellsbury, an enrolled member of the Colorado River Indian Tribes, has reclaimed "Chief" as an emblem of Native pride.[22]

What to Expect from This Book

"Multilingual baseball" is an enormous subject, far too big for one book. I write this with an acute awareness of the book's gaps and shortcomings, with respect for the rich body of scholarship on racial and cultural diversity in baseball, and in the hope that future researchers will address some of the areas I've neglected. The book does not pretend to give a representative or comprehensive picture of bilingualism in baseball. I try to cover a lot of ground in terms of speakers and contexts, but rather than generalizing across many examples, I delve deeply into the stories of individuals who have been involved with multilingual baseball in a range of capacities.

Anthropologists, as Clifford Geertz put it, are more interested in "the world around here" than "the world in general" (Geertz, 1983). We no longer have the luxury of indulging in "grand narratives," or one-size-fits-all explanations for human behavior, so we're left with "object lessons," the "small theories" that make us ask better questions (González, 2010). In this spirit, I approach the people and stories in the following chapters as "local example[s] of the forms human life has locally taken" (Geertz, 1983, p. 16), not as "typical" cases or stand-ins for generic experiences. The book is a collection of detailed snapshots of language diversity in professional baseball at the time I did this research, not the final word on the topic. My goal is to give readers a sense of how the sociolinguistic tapestry of baseball looks to the people who live their lives bilingually, or help others to do so, in the transnational game.

Most of the names in this book will be unfamiliar, even to deeply knowledgeable fans of the game. This is because the familiar names—the players who go on to successful careers in the major leagues—are a miniscule fraction of all the people involved in the sprawling, transnational business of multilingual baseball. This includes the vast majority of players who never make it to the major leagues as well as players in professional leagues outside the United States; it also includes coaches, player-development staffers, English teachers and education personnel, front-office executives, medical and training staff, scouts, interpreters, umpires, and the groundskeepers and kitchen and cleaning staff who maintain team facilities, at a minimum. As a lifelong fan of the game, realizing just how complex the enterprise of professional baseball is and how many people are involved, in different roles and at different levels, has been enlightening and humbling.

Since it isn't possible to cover everything, the chapters in this book inevitably mirror my own interests, preoccupations, and experiences as a white, first-language speaker of English who speaks Spanish as a second language and whose research and teaching, until now, have focused mostly on language, culture, and schooling for Mexican American and Latino youth in the US Southwest. The first chapter, then, looks closely at the experiences of promising Latin American players who sign as teenagers with MLB clubs and go through an intensive, short-term process of "socialization," or social molding, to conform to MLB teams' expectations of behavior—including language use—for "professionals."

The second chapter follows Latin American prospects through their transition to Minor League Baseball in the United States, exploring how players' verbal behavior in English and Spanish changes over time, what this means for their identities, and what happens when players are released, or let go, from MLB organizations.

The third chapter documents cases of Spanish learning among native English speakers in professional baseball and considers teams' incipient efforts to promote a bilingual culture among their players. The fourth chapter takes a wide-ranging look at multilingualism in Korean and Taiwanese baseball, placing the experiences of West-to-East baseball migrants (i.e., players and coaches who went from the United States or Latin America to Asian baseball) alongside East-to-West dynamics (i.e., Korean and Taiwanese bilinguals who leveraged their language ability to work in MLB or other international baseball contexts). The conclusion bookends the introduction with an analysis of "language panics" or language-related controversies, in contemporary Major League Baseball, with an eye to how multilingual encounters are still fertile ground for stoking fears about demographic change, even as the language ecology of the United States—and the US game—has changed dramatically.

Readers who love baseball may already be thinking about how much I left out. There's very little about Japanese baseball, which has inspired many excellent books in its own right (e.g., Whiting, 2022), nor does the book address the early cultural exchanges between American and Japanese teams that helped to seed the Japanese baseball tradition and exposed US players to another face of the game (Guthrie-Shimizu, 2012). The experiences of US-born or raised Latino players who grew up bilingual—like Adrián González, Jesús Luzardo, and Marcelo Mayer, to name just three—are largely absent, a lacuna I hope to correct in future work. Neither do I take up the question of language in relation to the amateur and semiprofessional ethnic baseball cultures that developed in US communities of color during the era of segregation and some of which persist today. Baseball historians and anthropologists have lovingly chronicled the advent of Japanese American baseball in California (Fitts, 2020) and the role of fast-pitch softball leagues in the social cohesion of Mexican American communities (Chappell, 2021). As a final example, I do not broach the subject of how Black/African American English varieties contributed to language diversity in MLB clubhouses during integration.

I have tried to keep the discussion clear and jargon-free. When introducing terms from linguistics or anthropology, I have glossed or explained those terms in the main text or the endnotes. The endnotes also contain information that may be of interest to linguists and anthropologists but is less likely to interest baseball fans or nonspecialist readers.

What to Expect from This Book (for Academic Readers)

While I introduce concepts from linguistics and anthropology as they become relevant to the discussion, rather than presenting them in monolithic fashion, I will say a little about my overarching theoretical orientation. Following legendary linguistic anthropologist Michael Silverstein, who passed away as I was writing this book, I take the *total linguistic fact* to be "the central datum for a science of language" (Moore, 2021; citing Silverstein, 1985). By "total linguistic fact," Silverstein referred to the interplay between *structure*—the formal features of language—*use*—the relationship of language to the social and interactional context—and *ideology*, or the cultural models of language that "circulate," or get passed around, in speech communities. People employ language ideologies to "rationalize usage (and structure)" or make sense of *why* people use language the way they do (Silverstein, 1985).

In plain(er) English, people's interactions and their commentary on those interactions are opportunities to "[get] underneath why people get excited about things in order to figure out what is at stake for them, and why" (Heller, 2011). As for early American anthropologists, "language" and "culture" are not essentially separate things from my point of view. I treat the stories and encounters in this book as "linguistic-ethnographic objects"—language-and-culture mash-ups—rather than analyzing them only in terms of linguistic structure *or* cultural practice (Blommaert, 2007).

Linguistics-savvy readers will notice that I sometimes use terminology that is not currently in vogue—for example, first language (L1), second language (L2), English as a second language (ESL), native language, and mother tongue. Scholars have argued that such labels obscure the flexible and nondichotomous nature of bilingualism—which is to say, the fact that bilinguals mix elements from different "named languages" (like English and Spanish) without paying undue attention to the boundaries of those languages (see, e.g., García, 2011; Wei, 2018; Mortimer & Dolsa, 2020). According to this line of critique, the uncritical use of labels like L1 and L2 makes it sound as though the distinction between languages is straightforward and bilinguals simply switch back-and-forth, rather than drawing fluidly from a "repertoire" or communicative toolkit that includes features associated with different codes (Otheguy, García, & Reid, 2019).

Others have pointed out that what "counts" as a named language, if not entirely arbitrary, nonetheless depends on social and historical processes and not just on facts about linguistic structure (Makoni & Pennycook, 2007).[23] People do not always learn their "first" and "second" languages sequentially, as those terms imply, and it can be difficult to settle the question of someone's "native language" or "mother tongue" (which are not necessarily synonymous). "English as a second language" is dispreferred to "English for speakers of other languages" or "English as a new/additional language," because it might be someone's third or fourth language, not their second.

As an anthropologist, I strive to be attuned to *emic*, or insider, categories—the concepts that people rely on in particular social contexts—as opposed to filtering people's understandings through linguists' *etic* (outsider) categories (Collins, 1992). Thus, when I use labels like "L2" or "native language," I'm not making claims about the mental grammar of bilinguals; I'm doing so because the people in this book talked and acted as though those distinctions were relevant to their experience—for example, between Spanish as a first language and English as a second language, or vice versa. In other words, since baseball people "oriented" to boundaries between languages as socially meaningful, I treat them as meaningful for the purposes of the analysis. Sometimes, as with "ESL," a widely recognized label has the advantage of being less clunky than the alternatives for nonspecialist readers. All the same, I try not to use such labels naïvely or uncritically and, where appropriate, take advantage of opportunities to point out their limitations for understanding language-in-use—for example, in the discussion of Taiwanese language diversity in Chapter 4.

A final comment on emic and etic categories: one of the challenges of writing this book has been balancing my critical tendencies, as a linguistic anthropologist and educational researcher, with what I found to be a very different worldview among baseball people. Academics tend to focus on systemic inequities and persistent forms of disadvantage and discrimination—linguistic and otherwise—because many of us believe that a deeper understanding of injustice could point the way to remedies for it. It's not that baseball people are unaware of structural issues that make the diamond uneven, as it were; indeed, many I encountered were outspoken about the need for social change. But succeeding in professional baseball demands a different mindset.

Baseball people, by and large, propound a sincere, even touching belief in the possibility of self-improvement through hard work and are often quicker to look for individual-level explanations (like someone's personality or work ethic) than structural ones. Baseball might not be a pure meritocracy, but most of the people in this book regarded it as much closer to a meritocracy than we'd be justified in regarding the US educational system, for instance. Again, in many cases, it wasn't that they saw structural inequalities as unimportant, but that dwelling on those issues was not seen as productive for a player's on- and off-field development. In a merciless industry where failure is lurking around every corner, the determination to overcome all obstacles and succeed at all costs is a prerequisite for making it even to the lowest levels of the professional game.

Speaking Baseball Language

My observations and encounters in the world of multilingual baseball brought forth a consistent theme—one that echoes the historical contradictions of language diversity in the United States and the national pastime. On the one hand, people told me, baseball language is universal. Knowledge of the game "transfers everywhere," I was told: "The languages and cultures can be so different, but when you step on the baseball field," everyone's speaking the same language. "At the end of the day . . . we are all playing baseball, which is a language in and of itself." For international players, even if there's "a lot of discomfort away from the field . . . there can be a lot of comfort on the field" because of the shared language of baseball.[24]

On the other hand, the voices in this book attest that baseball language is different everywhere. It's not just the presence of different languages and ways of speaking, though I've focused on that in this introduction, but the existence of different norms for communication and behavior across transnational contexts. Latino teenagers are faced with the daunting task of understanding what it means to talk and act like a "professional" from the point of view of an MLB team; US import pitchers in Korea confront bewilderingly different expectations for interacting with umpires; coaches learn to modify their speech to work successfully with interpreters; English and Spanish speakers recognize that bilingualism can strengthen their relationships with teammates and coaches, and so on.

One of the beauties of professional baseball is that migrant streams converge in complex ways, so that speakers of different languages and backgrounds are "thrown together" in unexpected configurations to pursue the short-term common goal of winning baseball games as well as their individual goals of achieving long-term professional success (Massey, 2005). At times, this leads to conflict. At other times, however, it prompts players and others to explore language as a "tool for conviviality" or a resource for acknowledging and living with difference (Illich, 1973). Roberto Clemente's groundbreaking use of Spanish was one such moment. I'll offer a final anecdote that complements Clemente's interview and sets the tone for the discussion to come.

One day in December 2018, in a raucous locker room in La Romana, Dominican Republic, a shaggy, bearded white man was awarded a ceremonial necklace—a comically large chain with his team's logo, a giant "T," suspended from it—by his cheering teammates.[25] Like the Blue Jays' home run jacket, the necklace went to the hero of the day, and on this occasion—a teammate announced in Spanish—it was Hunter Pence, a 36-year-old outfielder, erstwhile San Francisco Giant, and, at the time of his heroics, a member of the Toros del Este of the Dominican Winter League. The league is the province of up-and-coming Dominican prospects, Latin American baseball lifers—and in Pence's case, out-of-work veterans from Major League Baseball.

It wasn't exactly Game 7 of the World Series with a history-making lineup, but you couldn't have told the difference from the scene in La Romana. Pence had hit a game-winning home run with the Toros in the hunt for the playoffs. As the team clamored for a speech, the newly bedecked hero, only a little reluctant, tried to mount a flimsy plastic chair, shouting, "Let's go, let's go—whoop!" One foot fell off, and he made a second, successful attempt at standing and gestured with his arms to quiet his adoring teammates. He waved his hands in front of him, as if to downplay his accomplishment: "OK, OK, hey. *Eso juego no es* much *importante*," which roughly translates to "That game isn't too much important."

Taken out of context, Pence's utterance could have been mistaken for Mock Spanish, but there was no hint of mockery. He flashed a self-deprecating smile, and his teammates sported huge grins on their upturned faces, egging him on. "But—*pero es—es* very important to improve"—he interrupted himself, appealing to someone off camera: "How do you say 'improve' in Spanish?" "*Mejorar, mejorar!*" came the shouts from all corners. "Constantly improve, get better," Pence continued, churning his right arm. "We got one more game, let's bring it!"

Hunter Pence's linguistic risk-taking—his unapologetically amateurish mixing of Spanish and English and willingness to seek his teammates' support—belongs to a different category than Roberto Clemente's. Clemente risked speaking Spanish in front of a television audience of millions, sending a message that Latinos belonged in professional baseball and the United States. Pence, by contrast, risked looking silly in front of his Spanish-speaking teammates, who probably did not expect much in that area from a "seasonal laborer," in effect, trying to work his way back to the major leagues.

All the same, his efforts to use Spanish, even in a limited way, clearly struck a chord with his teammates, based on their enthusiastic reaction. Language is not just for getting your point across, after all. Hunter Pence's speech may have been a gesture of empathy for his Spanish-speaking *compadres*, an attempt to put himself in their shoes, however briefly, knowing that many of his teammates had been language learners throughout their careers. With that in mind, Chapter 1 takes an in-depth look at the early stages of the process of learning English and "becoming professional" for young Latin American signees with major league organizations.

1

Language Socialization and the Professional Development of Latin American Prospects

"Did you see the baseball fields?"

I had seen them all right, on my descent into Santo Domingo, Dominican Republic, among the tin roofs and half-finished cinder block houses, the swaths of sugarcane, piles of burning brush, and the free-for-all gaggle of cars, motorcycles, and trucks hauling shipping containers down narrow roads—paved, unpaved, pitted with craters—lined with *colmados*, or convenience stores, and fruit and coffee vendors. Even from the air, what Alan Klein called the "international industry" of Dominican baseball, a potential means of escape from the "economic straitjacket" of island life and a matter of national pride, was evident (Klein, 2006).

The person asking the question was Jeff Diskin, the senior director of professional and community development for the Kansas City Royals, who had invited me to observe the team's English and educational programs at their Dominican academy in San Antonio de Guerra, just east of Santo Domingo, and in whose hands my life now rested as we barreled down the aforementioned roads in a white rental pickup. Over the next few days, I would get to see some of those baseball fields up close—not just the immaculately groomed diamonds at the pro academy where the Royals' elite Latino prospects trained but scrappy neighborhood fields where younger kids played in the evenings, public fields that MLB teams had paid to rehabilitate, and the fields at amateur academies where middle and high school–aged boys dreamed of signing with MLB clubs.[1] I played a memorable game of wiffleball in the front yard of an orphanage that the Royals support as a community-service endeavor. A skinny boy who looked to be about four whistled a line drive past my left ear and into the makeshift outfield. I was starting to believe the stories I had heard about Dominican academy teams' making mincemeat of the utterly overmatched high school and college teams from the United States that showed up to play them from time to time.

I had met Jeff the previous month at the Royals' spring training facility in Surprise, Arizona. I had interviewed him and Jorge Guzmán, the Royals' former assistant director of Dominican operations, about the team's mandatory English program for young international players. They were generous and forthcoming, but Jeff insisted that I ought to see what was happening in the Dominican Republic if I really wanted to understand the place of language learning, and education more broadly, in young players' professional development. I didn't take much convincing; this was a rare opportunity to gain firsthand knowledge of a setting that is usually off-limits to people who don't work in professional baseball.

In this chapter, I will explore multilingual baseball from the perspective of English learning as professional development for teenaged Spanish-speaking prospects from Latin America, incorporating insights from education and player-development personnel, ESL teachers, scouts, and players. The key concern of the chapter is the role of English learning in making young amateur Latino players into *professionals*—that is, young adults who not only speak English functionally but have been socialized to conduct themselves in ways that are consistent with MLB teams' beliefs about what it means to be professional. Structurally, this chapter loosely mirrors the journey that Latino prospects dream of making when they sign contracts with major league clubs. It starts with a discussion of prospects' socialization—the way they're molded, and mold themselves, to conform to MLB clubs' expectations—at pro academies in the Dominican Republic and then moves to their experiences after coming to the United States.

It All Starts Here: Becoming Professional in the Dominican Academy System

International players are eligible to sign with MLB clubs at sixteen, though some Latin American players have been scouted since they were twelve or thirteen, and many have verbal agreements with their eventual teams before turning sixteen, negotiated through their trainers or *buscones*, amateur talent scouts. This is technically illegal but widely accepted, with discomfort, as the way things work in the absence of an international player draft. Even so, criticism has been mounting of the system—a "cesspool" and a "mafia," according to some MLB personnel—which incentivizes scouts to recruit preteens, facilitates "nefarious dealings" between MLB scouts and amateur trainers, and pressures older teenagers to turn to performance-enhancing drugs out of desperation if they are not signed as sixteen-year-olds (Torres & Rosenthal, 2022).

Still, as one trainer who was outspoken in his condemnation of the system observed, teenaged prospects are generally coming from impoverished areas with relatively few opportunities and, once signed, have access to significant advantages, including nutritious food, safe lodging, and education (Torres & Rosenthal, 2022). Klein also criticized a tendency to "demonize" Dominican actors, especially *buscones*, in MLB and US media discourse about the Dominican amateur system and described this tendency as "ethnocentric hubris." The "systematic disparaging of Dominicans and their culture," in Klein's view, has functioned to maintain MLB's control over "the Dominican player commodity chain," pointing to Dominican individuals' corrupt behavior but turning a blind eye to the structural inequality in the system (Klein, 2014).

Behind the Scenes at a Dominican Professional Academy

Teams' Dominican academies, which are clustered in a few areas close to the capital of Santo Domingo, serve as way stations for prospects from around Latin America, who arrive soon after signing and live, train, and attend classes at the academy until they are called up to the team's facility in Arizona or Florida or until they get released. In the meantime, teenaged prospects who have trained for years with a singular focus on getting signed and playing for an MLB organization are faced with the concrete realities of life at the academy. Emily Glass, a Rockies and former Marlins staffer, referred to "the teenage angst of being a professional baseball player. . . . [It's] probably one of the most demanding schedules outside of serving in the military." Players must adhere to a fairly inflexible schedule of stretching, conditioning, on-field drills, individual practice in the batting cage or bullpen, and scrimmages and games with other academy teams, not to mention English classes, high school completion or technical classes, eating, and sleeping—all while living away from their families and being able to leave the complex only rarely.

As Johan Febrillet, the Royals' lead Dominican educator at the time of my visit, put it:

> When you're here at the academy, we have possibly 95 percent . . . control over you. You're here from Monday to Sunday. Sometimes the players are given permission to go out on Saturdays, but they gotta come back on Sundays. But from Monday to Saturday, they have to be here. They sleep here, they eat here.

So in other words, we control what they eat. We know what time they wake up. We know what they do at night. We know if they're sleeping well. . . . We have control over many things.

One of the Royals' Dominican prospects informed me soberly that he had gone five months without seeing his family, who lived too far away for weekend visits. If it sounds draconian, well, that's the price you pay for the slim chance at becoming one of the very best in the world at what you do, with fame and fortune dangling tantalizingly out of reach. A bulletin board in the academy classroom informed the players IT ALL STARTS HERE over a photo of the academy, with arrows drawn to Royals players who had started at the academy and gone on to appear in the major leagues and the dates of their MLB debuts. A second bulletin board featured maps of current academy players' countries of birth (Dominican Republic, Cuba, Venezuela, Nicaragua, Mexico, El Salvador, Aruba) with lines connecting each country to a photo of the academy (Figure 9).

The Royals' and Astros' academies are located off the main drag in San Antonio de Guerra, down a well-paved side road. As you approach, the academy is largely hidden by tall hedges to the left, but you can glimpse the back wall of the main building, which features the Royals logo flanked by the logos for the

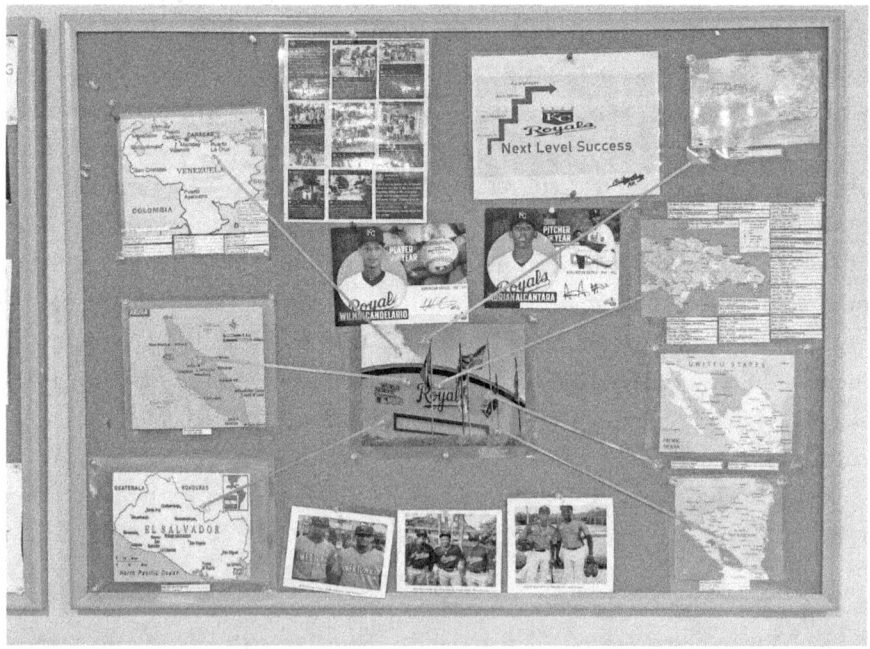

Figure 9 Bulletin board with national origins of Royals' Dominican academy players. (author)

team's two championship seasons, 1985 and 2015. A row of flags with American and Dominican flags, a Royals flag, and several other flags representing academy players' countries of origin—Venezuela, Mexico, Nicaragua—stands in front of the wall. At the entrance, private security guards wave you through the sliding gate, exchanging greetings with staff. One of the guards doubled as a barber; as we were leaving one day, I saw him giving three players haircuts with an electric razor behind the guardhouse.

The academy itself feels a bit like a midrange chain hotel, albeit one with unexpectedly stunning landscaping. On the ground floor, doors from a breezeway open onto the cafeteria, the classroom (aka the "sixth tool room"— see later), the main lobby (used only for visitors), a conference room, and a computer lab where students can complete Rosetta Stone coursework and virtual high school assignments. The computer lab was nicknamed the "Fifty-First State Room" and was decorated with information about the United States, including photos of Joe Biden and Kamala Harris, a map showing the location of the Royals' minor league affiliates around the country, and a larger close-up map of Surprise, Arizona, home to the Royals' spring training and instructional league activities, indicating the locations of restaurants, pharmacies, stores, and so on in relation to the team's facility. Down a short set of stairs are the training room, the clubhouse (where players shower and dress), and the equipment and coaches' rooms, which were under construction when I visited. The second floor houses dormitory-style rooms where the players sleep summer-camp style, about ten to a room, in wooden bunk beds with royal-blue sheets, many of them draped over the bedframes to provide a semblance of privacy.

The regimented nature of academy life has to do, in great part, with the physical and material exigencies of player development. Succeeding at a professional level means "outworking the competition," as baseball people say, in order to fulfill one's promise as a ballplayer.[2] I visited at a relatively relaxed time during the off-season, but even so, the daily schedule was demanding. Breakfast started at seven o'clock, followed by an all-player meeting, stretching, base-running drills, defensive drills by position (catchers/infielders/outfielders), batting practice in the cage and on the field (for position players), and side sessions in the bullpen (for pitchers). The team's analytics staff used high-speed cameras to document players' performance throughout practice to supply players and development staff with video data.

After the morning's activities came lunch, then one-on-one or small-group English classes or Rosetta Stone English practice, bookended by strength and conditioning work and injury rehabilitation, for some. Fall games against other academy teams would start the following week, further crowding an already packed schedule and complicating the educational staff's efforts to preserve time for English classes. Johan recalled an afternoon game that had gone into extra innings so that he had to hold class after dinner—a thankless task, given the probable attention span of a seventeen-year-old who has just played a five-hour baseball game in the sun and lost (said Johan).

Beyond the physical training and mental conditioning associated with player development, however, the structure of the academy seeks to make players who were formerly amateurs into *professionals*. "Professional," in academy-speak, doesn't just mean that the players are getting paid by the organization but refers to the task of socializing sixteen- and seventeen-year-old players into new identities as professionals—of leading them to see themselves as different kinds of people. Academy life involves a comprehensive effort by the team to "resocialize and implant a new habitus," a set of desirable mental and physical characteristics, into newly signed prospects, transforming *potencia* ("potential"; "raw ability") into on-field performance through "a fusion of disposition and bodily discipline" (Klein, 2014, pp. 54–5). Johan, the lead educator, spoke with admiration of prospects' success in suddenly having to become "adult people":

> These players go through . . . a lot of challenges as human beings because they're young, but they gotta live a life of an adult person. You know, being away from home at age sixteen, seventeen, not being with your parents the way you used to, having to interact with different people from different countries, different cultures . . . understanding each other, supporting each other. Those are a lot of things that our players managed to accomplish at a very young age. And I think that they deserve to be, you know, recognized for that and to understand that it's hard, what they have to go through. And many of them . . . go through it in a very successful way, I would say.

Latino signees undergo what anthropologists call a "breached initiation"; they skip over the usual adolescent rites of passage and are shoved somewhat rudely into adulthood, having to adapt to a different way of life and shouldering adult-like responsibilities, including securing their family's financial future, beginning with how they handle their signing bonus (Mendoza-Denton & Boum, 2015). In this way, their developmental pathways resemble those of other immigrant youth from the "1.25 generation"—that is, those who arrived in the United States as teenagers—though their circumstances differ dramatically. For both groups, stepping into "adult" roles does not mean that youth *feel* like adults, at least not right away (Diaz-Strong, 2021). Attaining the feeling of being an adult, rather, is a gradual, uneven process for Latin American prospects, as for their immigrant age-group peers, and one in which language learning plays a central role.

"They're Always Baseball Players First": Baseball ESL as Workplace English

When I asked about English education or other educational opportunities for young Latino players, baseball people frequently reminded me that "they're always baseball players first," to quote Jeff Diskin, and that teams' educational efforts had to be understood within the larger context of player development. The goal of player development, of course, is a successful career in professional baseball—and, by extension, a worthwhile return on investment for the organization. MLB teams' Dominican academies owe their existence to the ugly but undeniable economic realities of the transnational game. As Alan Klein writes, US teams established footholds in the Dominican beginning in the mid-1980s when they realized that it was more cost-effective to move their scouting and training operations abroad in light of the "investment opportunity" that Latin America represented: "For what a top ... draft choice would cost in the United States ... one could sign 100 Dominican prospects and be reasonably assured that half a dozen would become Major Leaguers" (Klein, 2006, pp. 124–5).[3]

Kevin Goldstein, a prospect analyst and former Houston Astros executive, remarked, "They wouldn't be giving these kids English classes if there wasn't a good business reason for it." Such comments might come across as cynical. However, they prodded me, as someone primarily interested in *language* development, to focus my inquiry more squarely on the place of language and cultural socialization in players' *professional* development, understood in a baseball-specific way.

Jeff said:

> We look at ourselves more as professional development. . . . So we talk about class and school, and it's all true. But our ultimate goal is to help these guys achieve their ceilings and help them have success on the field. And I think we all know if you're not happy with your job . . . [it] can make everything miserable. And the language barriers, obviously, when players, young men come here, if there's struggles or issues, it can cause problems. So if we can help alleviate those, it'll help them feel better about themselves and also help them [in] the job that they do.

"Achieving their ceilings" is baseball talk for fulfilling one's innate potential, a frequent topic of conversation where teenaged prospects are concerned, since merely possessing "tools"—the physical raw materials for baseball success—does not guarantee that a sixteen-year-old will develop to his full potential as a ballplayer by his early twenties. A major goal of the process of professionalization for newly signed prospects, from the Royals' perspective, was giving them what the team described as the "sixth tool" (in addition to the traditional five tools of baseball—hit, hit for power, run, field, throw) that would lead to "next level success": education, which encompassed both schooling and the Spanish sense of *educación*, or social and moral development.

Personnel from other teams affirmed that prospects' English education was tied to teams' and teachers' beliefs about what English skills would be necessary in the specific, rather restricted, contexts in which young professional players spend most of their time. Jill Long de Mercado, the president of Higher Standards Academy (HSA), which contracts with MLB teams to provide English classes and cultural education, told me that her organization treated ESL for Latino prospects as a form of "workplace English." Jill commented that her company had done extensive observational research to understand exactly what kind of English would most benefit their learners:

> We developed our own curriculum based on years of research, of going to practice . . . doing intense work, intense observation work. Just, you know, putting in the time. On the field, in the meetings, in the weight room, looking at all aspects of the player and what they need, because it's workplace English, what we do.

In the DR, I got to sit in workplace-oriented English classes in the Royals' academy classroom. The walls were hung with posters of baseball phrases and key verbs, photos of graduates from previous years' high school completion and technology classes, and "DR Academy Essential Questions" intended to prompt reflection on becoming professional, such as "How can learning English help you as a professional baseball player?" and "Why is it important to be a good teammate?" (Figure 10).

In one session, a pitcher and catcher worked together to identify English slang terms for areas of the strike zone, using an online quiz that the Royals had created with images and descriptions of different pitch locations—"elevated" and "buried" for pitches above and below the zone, "down and in," "down and away," and so on. A distractible but motivated infield prospect from the previous class stood with me behind the quiz takers, trying to call out the locations before they

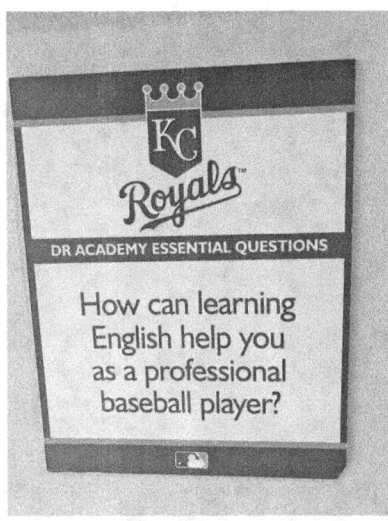

Figure 10 Example of Royals DR Academy essential questions (author).

could. I told them, half-jokingly, that they would need this vocabulary to be able to argue effectively with umpires about balls and strikes (Figure 11).

Johan also showed me several videos of lessons incorporating what is known as "total physical response" in language teaching, meaning that prospects had to engage their whole bodies in the learning process. For example, a baseball verb simulation activity required pitchers to act out verbs like *land* (bring your weight to rest on your front foot) and *pivot*. For a Marco Polo–type activity, players were blindfolded and scattered around one of the baseball diamonds. They then had to group themselves with like teammates (batters with batters, pitchers with pitchers) by calling out baseball verbs associated with either batting or pitching. It was goofy, to be sure—but, said Johan, it was also "a great moment for [the players] to *be*," a momentary respite from the serious grind of academy life. Other "workplace English" materials I reviewed at the Royals DR academy covered body parts and injuries (with a gruesome compilation of video clips of baseball players injuring themselves) and specific in-game situations like hitting a cutoff man, laying down a sacrifice bunt, and so on.

"Helping Them Function in the United States": Baseball ESL as a Transitional Skill

Off the field, English is seen as necessary for players to function independently in the United States once they have left the academy and have more freedom

Figure 11 Lead educator Johan Febrillet leads pitching prospect Luis Polanco through a lesson on English verb tenses at the Royals' Dominican academy (author).

and responsibility. An assistant general manager for the A's told me that the latter dimension of English becomes crucial when international players reach the upper minor leagues—AA and AAA—and are expected to live without the intensive support provided by team personnel at lower levels.

Jill and others described English learning and "life skills" in the same breath, asserting that English was a means to an end—namely, that players needed "functional English" so that they wouldn't hit significant speed bumps in their baseball development as they adjusted to life in a different country. When I asked her about Higher Standards Academy's philosophy on English education for ballplayers, she replied:

> It's good for their player development, obviously, to be able to speak English and communicate better, but there's also a huge aspect of just helping them function in the United States. So much of the very initial stuff . . . is just, here's how to order a pizza [or] do your laundry. . . . There's a whole, . . . "We're teaching you English," but then there's also, for lack of a better word, functional English that you're teaching them as well . . . almost like life skills.

Food came up repeatedly in stories of players' initial forays into English learning. At first, this seemed too obvious to bear mentioning. Food is a staple of "basic" or beginner-level language instruction; even someone who claims to have forgotten their high school Spanish probably remembers a few food terms. In the field of education, culturally significant foods are often treated as a superficial manifestation of "culture" in the classroom, an innocuous complement to a "heroes and holidays" approach to teaching diversity (Au, 2009). On closer consideration, however, I realized that players' early experiences with food in the United States were critical milestones in their English learning *as athletes*. As teachers like Jill emphasized, understanding the language socialization of professional baseball players means understanding how they encounter language as athletes—which is to say, people for whom food and nutrition are of paramount importance and for whom a lack of access to the proper foods could have deleterious physical and professional consequences.

Thus, in addition to equipping players to succeed in the workplace, English was treated as a transitional skill, a tool that players would need so that their physical and mental development would not be interrupted on their way to the major leagues. As Jill said:

> Everything that we do in classes [is] transitional skills, . . . so when we start out, we start with the basics on what they need. . . . When they come to us at a novice, low novice speaking level, we're starting out with what they need for success upon immediate transition to the US, which is food. So they've got to be able to describe what their likes and dislikes are, they've got to be able to go to Chipotle and order their food. Because this is what they have access to—financially, and traveling with a team, looking for some type of comfort, something that resembles home, so [Chipotle and] Panda Express become an extension of [that], something to keep them going.

When I spoke with Michel Gelabert, a Cuban-born minor leaguer in the Arizona Diamondbacks' system, he was in a posture I myself remembered well: flat on his back on his sofa, yawning away, with his twenty-month-old daughter napping on his chest. I offered to call back later so that they could both sleep, but he said that we would have a better chance of talking while the baby was still asleep. Michel didn't bat an eye at communicating in English, unlike certain other L1 Spanish-speaking players who were relieved to find out I spoke Spanish. Even in his exhausted state, he spoke comfortably about his first days in the United States, laughing off his missteps with the grace of someone who had emerged on the other side as a proficient English speaker:

> I remember the first restaurant I went [to] was Chipotle, and I literally went, like, by signs. [laughing] I was like, "I want *that*" [pointing]—I didn't know how to

say *rice*—"and that, and that, and that," like that. Yeah, after that, the first couple things I learned was greetings. Like, *hello, goodbye. Good afternoon, morning,* and *food*. I was like, "I need to be able to talk about food, 'cause I need to eat!" [laughing] "I want chicken. I want rice."

Another Spanish-speaking player I interviewed claimed that a teammate ended up eating nothing but hamburgers for every meal—for how long, I don't know—because he didn't have enough English to order anything else.

"I'm Not Trying to Be a Safety Net": Socializing Novice Professionals

Talk about food was not the only "transitional skill" that educational staff associated with English learning. Luis Victoria, now the coordinator of minor league operations for the Oakland A's, who previously worked at the Royals' Dominican academy, commented that he wanted players to see how their efforts to learn English would translate into an ability to *defenderse* upon moving to the United States—to stand up for themselves, whether in reading a contract or speaking on their own behalf. As Luis said, he wanted them "to know that they're successful, know that everything they're learning, they can put it into practice and it's working":

> I'm not trying to be a safety net. . . . You need to know how to read a contract and read what's in front of you. If you're gonna sign it, you know what you're signing, right? Or talk about yourself so somebody else doesn't talk about you. . . . So that's the thing, like I don't do everything for them, but . . . I still want to make sure that they're getting the right input in Spanish if they need to. It's like, "Hey, try it first. You know, see where your English development has evolved to. You *have* the skills, so *use* it."

With respect to this discussion of workplace English and transitional skills, a near constant dilemma for educational and player-development staff working with Latino prospects was how much to help. In other words, staff wrestled with how to give young *peloteros* the skills they needed to "defend themselves" professionally without making the players dependent and, therefore, unable to function independently when they come to the United States. This was directly related to the role of Spanish and English in players' communication with coaches, teammates, trainers, and others: staff were committed to providing adequate support in Spanish but also worried that too much support would discourage players from relying on their emergent English bilingualism.

Anthropologically, we might frame this as a question of novices and experts. Classic work on language socialization described it as a process in which cultural novices—that is, newbies or rookies—are socialized *through* language as they are socialized *to use* language in certain ways. Those two aspects of socialization are related but not synonymous. Language can be used to get people to understand how they're supposed to act in specific contexts, whether covertly or overtly (indirectly or directly). On the other hand, "coaching" novices on *how* to speak and communicate dovetails with other types of cultural expectations (e.g., how you wear your uniform and how you behave on the field) but is distinct from them. Recently, however, anthropologists have pushed back on the figure of the "novice" in descriptions of linguistic and cultural socialization (Berman & Smith, 2021). "Novice" isn't a genetic trait. A novice is made, not born, always defined as a novice *according to someone else*. This implies that we need to look closely at how certain people *come to be seen* as novices within particular social, economic, and cultural structures.[4]

Educational and player-development staff were aware that Latino prospects were not novices "by nature," as it were, but were made into novices due to the circumstances of professionalization after signing with MLB teams. Staff also understood that players' language socialization into English was a key area in which their novice status became visible. While prospects might have appeared as experts in other contexts, their identities as English learners—as one dimension of "becoming professional"—helped to solidify their identities as novices at the academy and even in the United States.

Jeff Diskin spoke sensitively about the issue of Latino players' being made to feel inferior, or even infantilized, within US organizations. That is, Latino prospects were novices because they were made to be novices within the system of MLB teams' professional development. Jeff reflected on a yearly program that he and his staff had developed called Embracing Diversity, in which the Royals selected around a dozen US-born players from the minors (players considered to be prospects) for a trip to the Dominican Republic. The trip was often the highlight of the American players' minor league experience, according to Jeff. They got a glimpse of "a completely different model" of player development and a completely different way of life. It was also impactful for the players' Dominican-born teammates, who acted as guides and language brokers, reversing their usual roles and upending the deficit-based thinking that Jeff and his team explicitly sought to counter through this experience:

> We're constantly putting our Latin players in a position of feeling inferior. You know, we do this for you, we do that for you. We get you a translator,[5] we help

you get set up in apartments. We do all this, but down there [in the Dominican], they're in charge. That's who the [American] guys look to if they got questions about this, they got questions about that. So it's good [for] our Latin guys in that perspective.

Personnel tasked with players' educational and professional development felt they had to walk a fine line between providing *enough* support for young players facing a daunting learning curve—in terms of language, culture, and baseball—and providing *too much* support. This dilemma is familiar to bilingual educators who seek to push learners into their "zone of proximal development" or slightly out of their comfort zone, without leaving them "submerged" in a linguistic and cultural situation they cannot deal with on their own.

Zak Basch, at the time the minor league coordinator of the A's, described this as the "biggest cultural challenge" of his job, commenting that he was committed to supporting players in certain ways (e.g., making sure someone picked them up from the airport when they arrived in the United States) but sometimes struggled to know how much support was enough: "If I do everything for them, they'll never learn." But, as Jeff's comments and the foregoing discussion suggest, this dilemma is baked into the system of international player development, which *requires* Latino prospects to be made into novice "professionals" in order to be remade as potential major leaguers.

English Learning and Becoming Professional

In one sense, "becoming professional" involves learning enough "workplace English" to deal with language diversity or "language barriers," in Jeff's words, in order to "achieve [one's] ceiling" as a ballplayer. These instrumental discourses about English—as something that is necessary to survive as a professional ballplayer—point to *one* dimension of becoming professional, but they don't tell the whole story (Kelman, 1971).

The other key dimension of professionalization has to do with players' growing into the adult-like roles they are expected to shoulder at the age of sixteen or seventeen. At the Royals' academy, I observed a meeting where the education staff planned orientation activities for the new international class, who would sign at the January deadline and arrive soon afterward for four days of intensive onboarding. The staff were reviewing the schedule from last year's orientation and talking about changes they wanted to make. A Google Doc projected at the front of the classroom read, "We need to create an orientation process for our newly signed Latin prospects that more closely resembles our orientation process for our American players," reflecting staff's concern that international signees not be at a disadvantage relative to draftees from the United States.[6]

The very first activity on the first day of orientation was "distribution of class attire" or getting players into the official clothing they would be expected to wear for the duration of orientation and at all subsequent team activities, an outward symbol of their new status as professional athletes. The theme for day one was "Royals organization," and one of the conversation prompts for the first small-group session, to be facilitated by coaches and education staff, was "What are some responsibilities and behaviors that amateur players can do but professional players should not do?" The team thought it was important for new signees to begin thinking about the long-term impact of their present actions, for their own good and because their comportment would reflect on the Royals organization. As professionals, the players were newly exposed to public scrutiny and had to get used to having "eyes on them" at all times, as the staff put it.

Johan commented on prospects' transition from *having* baseball role models to *being* role models for others, and he touched on a theme that came up in the previous section: the need to equip players to function independently and make good decisions without "coddling" them:

> Of course, down the road, players have to decide for themselves, they gotta make their own decisions. 'Cause we don't want to tell 'em what to do, but we can help them . . . to learn how to think for themselves so that they could be leaders in the future too, that they can lead others and be examples for people in their neighborhood, society, because they also become, you know, models for other people and they gotta understand that.
>
> They have, "Oh, my favorite baseball player is this person, my favorite role model is this." But once you become a professional player, you gotta understand that that's what you're gonna be for some other people who are behind you. And that's why you gotta be careful with what you do on and off the field.

I commented that that seemed like a lot of responsibility for a sixteen-year-old, and Johan laughed in agreement:

> Oh yes. That's why I always say we gotta bear with them sometimes. . . . [In contrast to] normal things that we expect from sixteen-year-old kids, these kids, they gotta come to the academy. They gotta learn how to live here far from home. They gotta adapt to new rules, to the life of an adult. They've gotta share space and their lives with people who are coming from another country who are completely different from them in many ways. And somehow, they have to turn into adults at a very young age, and they gotta learn how to be responsible, how

to be accountable for their actions. And also, most important, to understand how their decisions right now will affect their lives one year from now, two years from now, four years from now.... Not to be shortsighted; but think about the future and how the decisions you make play an important part in your life when it comes to ten years from now.

Some of these "decisions" had to do, predictably, with what players posted on the internet. The Royals even had a secret group of veteran academy players with the tongue-in-cheek name "the FBI committee" whose job it was to monitor their teammates' social media activity and bring any problematic material to the team's attention. Other key decisions were financial, as the team strove to educate prospects about when and how they would receive their signing bonuses and salary payments, what was withheld from their paychecks and why, and how to discern wants and needs to avoid burning through their income too quickly.

Other "professional" expectations were organization specific and reflected the Royals' desire to instill a common ethos in everyone associated with the team, from front-office administrators to the youngest Latino prospects. In the Spanish version of the team's 2019 minor league handbook for players, I found a diagram called "Vistiendo el Uniforme con Orgullo"—wearing the uniform with pride—that laid out dos and don'ts for minor leaguers, from the unremarkable ("Shirts should always be tucked into pants") to the extremely specific ("Sunglasses are not permitted on the cap . . . or blocking the Royals logo"; "Cleats must be 75% blue"). This diagram was paired with another image, apparently of the same player, accompanied by a list of values that if embraced would lead to success in the major leagues—character, composure, care, and so on (Figure 12).

As I read it, the pairing reinforced the point of the nitpicky uniform expectations, from the team's perspective; wearing the uniform properly on the outside was an indication that the individual player had internalized the values associated with professionalism and success. In front-office speak, it was evidence that someone "trusted the process." This "process," while it applied to US-born and international players in the Royals organization, was seen by some as especially crucial to the socialization of Dominican players, due to perceptions of their relative lack of education and preparedness.

Potencia and Educación: Responding to Deficit Views of Dominican Ballplayers and Dominican Spanish

Like Johan, many Latin American staffers made sense of prospects' language socialization by comparing the young ballplayers' experiences to the staffers'

Figure 12 Three academy players pose in front of the logo celebrating the Royals' 2019 Dominican Summer League championship (author).

own English socialization during their playing days (for former players) or otherwise. Such discourses often highlighted the relative socioeconomic—and, by extension, sociolinguistic—disadvantage of prospects, especially Dominican prospects, though not always. Contrasts between contexts of language socialization could be used to affirm the resilience and adult-like status of young Dominican *peloteros*. On the other hand, they could be used to portray Dominicans and the DR as backward and uneducated in relation to other people and countries. Dominican prospects, then, were seen as especially in need of "cultural remediation" at academies, intended, in Klein's view, "to erase undesirable traits and forge new, more desirable ones" (Klein, 2014, p. 55).

Juan Mosquera, the Oakland A's international scout for Latin America, reflected that the transition to the United States had been somewhat easier for him as a relatively well-educated Panamanian who had some familiarity with US people and culture prior to playing in Minor League Baseball (MiLB):

> I played for the Cardinals in the minor leagues, and since I was a person who came from a place where there was internet, where there was a computer, where my school had given me some English, and at least I knew how to say, "How are

you?," you know? So the impact was a little calmer. In Panama, we had gringos and Americans because of the Panama Canal. I'd been going to McDonald's for many years. For me, a pizza wasn't anything new either. So it was fine.

Juan, who came across as compassionate, knowledgeable, and experienced, sounded a theme that I heard from other educational and player-development staff: that players' psychological and intellectual development—in the context of learning English—was even more important than their physical and on-field development. Learning English, to this way of thinking, was just one dimension of a long-term process of socializing or shaping players to adapt culturally, and at a young age, to a professional situation for which their lives to that point had not prepared them.

While English might be necessary to function in the baseball workplace and to make a successful transition to life in the United States, English education was also seen as contributing to the overall personal development of players who, quite often, had chosen to focus primarily on baseball at the expense of school from an early age. Juan brought up the apparent contradiction between the Dominican Republic's status as a hotbed of baseball talent and its relative lack of educational opportunity, particularly where baseball players were concerned. Because of this situation, said Juan, much of the *potencia* or inherent talent of the country was in danger of being lost:

> The education they're giving to Dominicans today [in MLB organizations] is going to have a positive impact. . . . I expect that they're going to have even more because there's so much talent and seeing at the same time so much is lost because of the intellectual [dimension] that they don't have. So the Panamanian in this case . . . has a lot of intellectual [potential], but unfortunately, they don't have that same [physical] potential that a Dominican player has.

Though I took Juan's use of "intellectual" to mean something like "mentally prepared," some of the discourse I encountered in the course of my research came uncomfortably close to reinforcing stereotypes about the supposed physical superiority of human bodies that have been racialized as intellectually inferior—a stereotype that has dogged African Americans in the United States and one that has also been applied to Indigenous Taiwanese baseball players vis-à-vis Han Chinese, to give another example (see Chapter 4) (Morris, 2006). Certainly, "the classic image of the non-white athlete as 'raw talent' who lacks discipline and method" did not originate in baseball or even in sports. As Niko Besnier wrote, these are enduring colonial images that may nonetheless be reinforced or challenged by practices in professional sports (Besnier, 2015, p. 857).

I heard Dominican prospects compared, in their presence, to horses and race cars. These metaphors were not negative, necessarily, but they conjured up animals and high-performance machines whose innate "horsepower" had to be harnessed through *educación*—that is, the "intellectual" development provided by the organization—to close the oft-mentioned gap between *potencia* (potential, but also power) and results. As a Cuban-born pitcher in MiLB put it to me, some believed that young Dominican players had a tendency to "limit themselves" by failing to recognize the academic preparation that was needed to make the most of their *potencia* on the field: "Some Dominicans didn't study. . . . Or like, they don't have the academic preparation to adapt themselves and understand that they need this language and [all] the rest of it, and a lot of times they limit themselves."

Beliefs about the relative mental "preparedness" of, say, Colombian versus Dominican ballplayers, since I also heard Colombia mentioned in contrast to the DR, cannot, perhaps, be disentangled from beliefs about Afro-Latino bodies and other kinds of bodies. (Cuban voices provide an interesting counterpoint; while many Cubans are of African descent, the country also has a relatively strong system of education and high levels of literacy compared to the Dominican Republic.) These beliefs are also related to language ideologies about which variety of Spanish is more "proper." It's not Dominican Spanish. In fact, a Spanish-speaking staffer told me in an aside that many young Dominicans have not even been properly educated in Spanish—much less were they ready to learn English, was the implication. This could be understood as encoding negative attitudes about Dominican Spanish—that it doesn't count as "real" Spanish, for example.

Still, there is no escaping the fact that the system for developing amateur baseball talent in the Dominican can result in the neglect of formal schooling for players as young as twelve or thirteen (though, as Jeff noted, many young Dominican men also drop out of high school for non-baseball reasons and start working). When baseball, rather than schooling, becomes the primary focus for middle-school-aged youth, concerns about players' level of literacy or preparation in academic Spanish are not merely the expression of language ideologies but also a reflection of real dilemmas that face English teachers in academy or affiliate settings. Kevin Goldstein, the former Astros' executive, commented:

> In the Dominican, a lot of these kids are dedicating their life to baseball at twelve or thirteen and therefore not getting a full education, and so . . . the first year or two of the English classes at the complex in the Dominican are

actually *Spanish* classes. Because you need to get them fully literate in Spanish before you start teaching them English. . . . You know, they can read and write, but their full literacy is not where you need to be a [learner] of English, and so there's actually . . . a whole process of teaching these kids Spanish before you teach them English.

As I understood him, Kevin did not mean that Dominican prospects needed to be taught their own language but that their single-minded focus on baseball from an early age sometimes resulted in gaps in academic Spanish and Spanish literacy that had to be remedied as a foundation for successful L2 learning. Johan said that the diagnostic process used for placement in English classes at the academy included assessing players' Spanish literacy skills in addition to gauging their English proficiency.

Eric Johnson, who taught English for the Padres' and Rockies' minor league affiliates, commented that even well-meaning team personnel who had positive relationships with the players and had spent time in the Dominican sometimes held what he called "a real deficit view . . . intellectually" of his ESL students. "Deficit view," in education, refers to viewing people in terms of what they lack as opposed to the strengths they bring to a classroom or a baseball field. When I asked Eric what he meant, he said that talk about young Dominican ballplayers echoed a familiar refrain from his work in bilingual education with local school districts:

> Interestingly, it's very parallel to the stuff that I hear in local school districts when they talk about immigrant parents. . . . It's that deficit discourse: "When you're talking to *them*, you need to know that . . . they probably didn't go to school, they don't know how to read or write, very low literacy, they don't know . . . a lot of Spanish, so expecting them to learn English is hard"—though, I mean, you've heard the same things; that's not a new trope.

A "trope," as Eric used it, is a repeatable figure of discourse, such as a metaphor that is reused and becomes familiar in certain contexts. Thus, in pointing out that a deficit framing of Latinx immigrants—including parents and baseball players—as uneducated, as not speaking Spanish properly, being unable to learn English, and so forth is "not a new trope," Eric was making the point that this type of talk is bigger than baseball. As with many of the examples in this book, talk in baseball contexts is "recursive" with talk in other domains of language use or social contexts—not to say that it's the same, but that it does reflect common presuppositions about languages and their speakers (Irvine & Gal, 2000).

Deron Dolphus, who went from teaching ESL for the Marlins to working in a bilingual school elsewhere in the DR, remarked on the irony of others' criticizing Dominican players' intellectual ability without taking into account structural factors such as the lack of resources for literacy development in many areas of the country:

> So you say, "Oh, you need to read this," but okay, where are the books for me to improve my reading skills? We have the internet . . . but then again, you have power outages, wi-fi is weak. Then trying to find the right books and the right articles for them to read. . . . The only schools that have those books are the rich schools, and they usually bring those books from the United States. . . . But your poor schools, you're not going to get that type of resource or the books that you need in order to teach these things. Because in a lot of the school system, they have teachers, but some are not qualified. And then some of 'em don't have the knowledge to teach what's in the books.

Even among Dominicans, baseball players had a reputation of being especially difficult to teach, according to Johan Febrillet. Prior to working at the Royals' academy, Johan had been an English teacher in a postsecondary setting in the DR, where some of his colleagues voiced negative beliefs about ballplayers as language learners. This did not discourage Johan from pursuing an opportunity with the Royals; on the contrary, he told me, it inspired him to embrace the challenge of teaching "unteachable" students, and it strengthened his conviction that he could have a significant impact on players' lives:

> One of the things that got me motivated to do it was that I would hear a lot of teachers saying it's too difficult. It's hard to deal with baseball players. That was everything I was getting from so many colleagues and teachers who had had the opportunity to work for [baseball] academies. . . . That inspired me even more to give it a try. When I heard it's a challenge, it's extremely difficult, it's not the same as we do here in the School of Languages or the university, then that got me going to say, "Okay, that's where I want to be. . . . And I think I can impact the lives of baseball players . . . as an educator."

Given widely voiced beliefs about the supposed educational deficiencies of Dominican prospects, I was curious to hear whether Johan thought that his being Dominican mattered to his students at the academy. He affirmed that it did and went on to detail the difference between "judging" and "understanding," as he put it, taking an anthropological perspective on the issue. Rather than resorting to cultural stereotypes as an explanation for players' behavior, he argued, being from the Dominican Republic allowed him to appreciate the social and economic factors that had shaped the players' upbringing prior to life at the academy—and, in so doing, to adjust his pedagogical strategies to reach players more effectively:

> If you're Dominican . . . you can say that possibly you understand 75 percent or 80 percent of the things that [Dominican] players or people in general have to go through . . ., especially if they're coming from, you know, some of [these] areas in the country where the level of education is not that high, where they have economical needs, where the backgrounds are not the best ones, I would say.
>
> So when you receive players as a Dominican leader who understands the culture here and the education system, I think you can, instead of *judging* players because of their behavior or because of their level of education before they come to the academy, instead of *judging*, you start to *understand* . . . the players and why they behave the way they do. That helps you to come up with strategies that would help you get to them.

In one sense, "receiving players as a Dominican leader" simply meant that Johan sought to understand where they were coming from so he could modify his teaching approach to meet the students' needs. In another sense, given Johan's experience as an educator in the DR, he could anticipate the kinds of "judgments" to which Dominican players were subjected and address those judgments proactively through his work in the classroom.

"Cuando Dios Quiera": Language Education for Uncertain Futures

On my last afternoon in San Antonio de Guerra, I was pressed into service, willingly, as an English conversation partner for some of the more advanced speakers at the Royals' academy. Johan gently reminded me that "advanced" didn't mean what it would in a university foreign language classroom but "advanced" relative to prospects who were still learning English letter names, numbers, and basic baseball terminology. After leading a few group sessions, I spent a leisurely half hour chatting one-on-one with Yosmi Fernández, a quietly charismatic and self-possessed infielder from Santiago, DR. He had only come to the academy in February 2021 but was already among the more proficient English speakers I had encountered there, speaking a little hesitantly but clearly and with evident determination.

Yosmi shared some of his strategies for making rapid progress in English. At night, when his teammates were playing video games or sleeping, he would watch Netflix shows with English audio and subtitles, reading along as he listened. He also listened to songs by English-speaking artists—the rappers Drake and Lil

Baby, among others—and talked on the phone regularly with a friend from Santiago who had gotten a certificate from an English school in the DR and was now living in Boston, saying that they had adopted each other as English conversation partners.[7] In addition to the Rosetta Stone software that the team provided for English enrichment, Yosmi had downloaded the Duolingo app on his phone for extra practice. Unlike teammates who enrolled in the virtual high school completion program offered at the academy, Yosmi had stayed enrolled in his old high school virtually and was on track to graduate early. He expected that English would be useful for making friends and navigating everyday life in the United States but also believed that the language would benefit him beyond the baseball diamond because "English is everywhere."

Yosmi showed me a photo of his signing day at the amateur academy in Santiago, not even two years ago—sitting at a table, contract in front of him, pen in hand, decked out in a Royals jersey and cap, and beaming at the camera (Figure 13).

Jeff Diskin, who had visited that same amateur academy on a trip to Santiago earlier that day, mentioned that the academy's walls were decorated with photos

Figure 13 Infielder Yosmi Fernández signing his first professional contract with the Kansas City Royals, February 8, 2021. The caption reads, in part: "Congratulations on this achievement after years of work!" (Yosmi Fernández/MB Baseball Academy). Reproduced with permission of Yosmi Fernández and MB Baseball Academy.

of players who had signed, including several who were now at the Royals pro academy. The photos represented inspiration for younger amateurs, the culmination of a childhood dream, and the beginning of a major league dream, as well as a dream from which many prospects ultimately awake to confront uncertain futures. I asked Yosmi when he thought he might end up at the Royals' facility in Arizona, the next step for prospects at the Dominican academy. "Cuando Dios quiera," he said, looking to Johan for help. I stepped in with the English equivalent: "God only knows."

Afterward, I recounted this conversation to Jorge Guzmán, sharing my impression that Yosmi was an "awesome kid," and Jorge shook his head as if it pained him to agree. "He *is* an awesome kid. And he had *such* a hard year this year. He got, what, ten hits in over a hundred at bats or something?[8] And he's got all the tools! Have you seen him run? Have you seen him field?" he asked, turning to another staffer. "And he's got all the makeup, everything you could want. And he signed for three hundred [thousand] or something"—not top-of-the-class money, but a significant chunk of the team's international bonus pool, nonetheless.

Jorge underscored a bitter truth about prospect development in and out of the English classroom, and one that was at odds with the conventional wisdom about young Dominicans: that they were at risk of wasting their talent if it could not be harnessed through the process of professional socialization in and through language that I've described in this chapter (Schieffelin & Ochs, 1986). Yosmi wouldn't fail to maximize his *potencia* because of a lack of academic preparation, intellectual aptitude, discipline, or commitment to English and professional development. It reminded me of what Jeff had said about the strict interpretation of the education department's mandate: to remove any off-the-field obstacles that might interfere with players' ability to reach their ceilings. If things didn't turn out the way Yosmi and the team hoped, it would be because he was trying to do "the hardest thing to do in sports," as Ted Williams put it: "Hitting a baseball . . . a round ball, round bat, curves, sliders, knuckleballs, upside down, and a ball coming in at 90 miles to 100 miles an hour" (Berkow, 1982). I'll be rooting for him.

"Until Somebody Actually Gets Here": Becoming Professional across Borders

On a sunny late September day at the Oakland Athletics training facility in Mesa, Arizona, nineteen-year-old prospect Robert Puason stepped to the plate in a simulated game situation. This was the A's instructional league, an opportunity for young international players and recently signed draft picks from US high schools and colleges to get additional on-field experience—and, just as important, to spend time with the team's training and development staff—after the Athletics' short-season minor league affiliates had ended their seasons.

As I watched from beside the visitors' dugout, I asked Dan Feinstein, the A's assistant general manager for major league and international operations, if it was possible to predict how well different Latin American players would adapt to life in the United States. "We try to get to know these kids as well as we can," Dan said. "Our area scouts know them. And they have a *pretty* good feel for it? But until somebody actually gets here. . . ." Dan trailed off, but the implication was clear: though the A's, like the Royals, prided themselves on their robust education program at their Dominican complex, you couldn't really know how someone's process of acculturation would go until he arrived in Arizona.

Puason, a long-limbed middle infielder from Guaymate, a small community in the eastern Dominican Republic, signed with the A's in 2019 for a bonus north of $5 million. Despite his sky-high potential or "ceiling," he had scuffled somewhat in his first year in full-season professional baseball, accumulating 139 strikeouts against only 24 walks and 65 hits in 337 plate appearances for the A's low-A affiliate in Stockton, CA. A well-respected independent prospect analyst also noted Puason's inconsistency as a defender—specifically, that he tended to follow-up spectacular plays with head-scratching errors—an observation that an A's staffer echoed at that morning's meeting in debriefing the previous day's game: "Puason finally made a play!"[9] He said it sarcastically but not without affection.

I had had a chance to observe Puason off the field at the mental conditioning session earlier that morning, where the player-development team's affection for him came through clearly. "Bobby" (as nearly everyone called him) had an awkwardly endearing way about him, sitting a little nervously with his knees squeezed together and hugging his elbows, as though he weren't quite sure what to do with his long frame. The session facilitator was a universally revered, ostensibly retired member of the A's organization described to me by the then director of minor league operations as one of the great minds in the history of player development.

Six players sat in a row at a long table in the front of the room facing the facilitator and educational coordinator, with an additional player behind them and a constellation of three or four other coaches and staffers sitting on tables and in chairs around the perimeter. As everyone was getting settled, the facilitator broke the ice by teasing Bobby and Junior Pérez, another Dominican prospect to Bobby's left, about their relative draft position for the team they had both played for in the Dominican winter league—a team, not coincidentally, affiliated with the A's.[10] The facilitator spoke halting but passable conversational Spanish, reflecting his time scouting and working with prospects and their families in the Dominican Republic.

The point of the session, which I saw outlined in English and Spanish on a whiteboard upon entering the classroom, was how players could stay positive and keep their focus on their approach (i.e., practicing and sticking to their plan) rather than obsessing about their results. The top of the whiteboard read "*Cosas que podemos controlar*"—things we can control. To the right was a longer Spanish reflection on how players might productively deal with the disappointment and failure that are a constant part of baseball: "*Entre el estímulo y la respuesta hay un espacio y en ese espacio está tu libertad para elegir tu respuesta*"—between the stimulus and response there is a space and in that space is your freedom to choose your response (Figure 14).

As a bilingual staffer commented later in the meeting, players are incredibly results-focused and, at this stage, unable to escape baseball. Addressing the players, he said that they think about signing, about getting out of the Dominican Republic, and then "live on the field"—far from home, pressured to succeed in

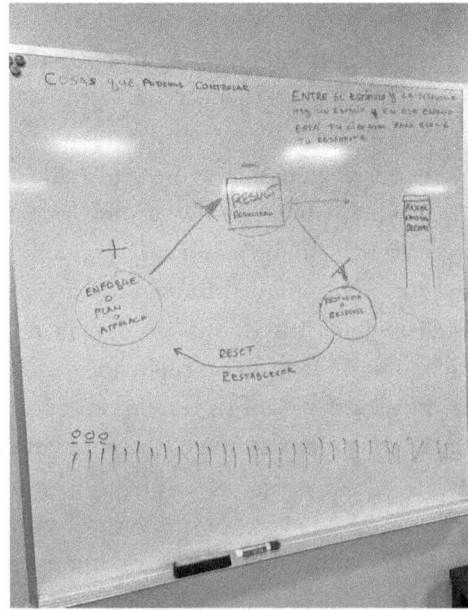

Figure 14 Whiteboard from mental skills meeting, Oakland A's instructional league, Sept. 2021 (author).

the crucible of professional baseball, supporting their families financially, and living and dying with every at-bat or fielding chance.

Bobby, an eager and engaged participant, was the first to volunteer an answer when the facilitator asked if anyone had used the approach they had discussed in the previous session. That session had emphasized having a good plan of attack and, following a positive or negative result, focusing not on the result but on the players' *respuesta* (response) to that result in order to *reestablecer*—to "reset" before their next plate appearance or chance in the field. Bobby said that he had committed an error in the field but had been able to "erase" his error with a good play the following day—perhaps the play the scout had applauded during the staff meeting.

Later, during that afternoon's situational drill, Puason turned on a choice offering from the pitching machine and yanked it over the right field wall. Teasing followed, as the coach leading the drill urged Bobby to celebrate by running the bases (not standard protocol for a drill), and Bobby obliged with a sheepish trot that petered out around third base. As he walked back to the dugout, the facilitator from the morning session called to him through the fence, appealing to the educational coordinator for help: "Do you know what it means if I say 'It leaves a good taste in your mouth?' How do you say, 'leaves a good taste in your mouth' in Spanish?" "*Que deja un buen gusto en la boca?*" Puason looked confused, and the mental skills coach and interpreter collaborated to expand: if you eat something good and after you're done eating it, you still have a good taste in your mouth? Do you feel like that after the *jonrón?* That there's still a good taste? Bobby then understood but joked in English that the home run wasn't a big deal because he didn't see himself as a power hitter: "Not really, I don't have that much power. Just line drives."

It would have been easy to miss just how much was going on in this interaction: the way the coach's encouragement to run the bases was "keyed" as a friendly tease, and how the trot and the subsequent exchange around the English figure of speech ("leaves a good taste in your mouth") were meant to support the ongoing mental and physical development of a talented young player who had been struggling recently—not to mention Bobby's quick uptake of the unfamiliar idiom and his humorous disalignment from his coaches, a possible way of saving face and deflecting attention from his challenges (Goffman, 1974).

Prospect "Makeup" and Language Socialization

Multiple A's staffers singled out Bobby Puason as someone who had worked hard to learn and improve his English, going beyond the opportunities the team provided, and they saw this as indicative of his personality. Luis Victoria, the education and culture coordinator, commented:

> Let's use Bobby Puason, for example. He knows that he has a lot of money. He knows he signed for a big amount. And on top of that, that the organization expects a lot from him. . . . He understands that there's pressure, but he also enjoys the process, too. He enjoys English, he enjoys being able to learn new things and he embraces it.

Luis's description of Bobby was consistent with how other baseball people talked about language socialization; beyond the instrumental utility of learning English (or Spanish or Mandarin Chinese), players, coaches, and team personnel saw successful language learning as evidence of desirable personality traits—for example, "He enjoys being able to learn new things," that the pressure from his signing bonus had not affected him—that would benefit players on and off the field. Similarly, Yosmi Fernández's self-directed English-learning efforts appeared to support the Royals' staffers' belief that he had "all the makeup."

I asked Kevin Goldstein if language ability ever factored into evaluations of a prospect's "makeup," a hard-to-define word that refers to intrinsic, intangible qualities like work ethic, leadership ability, and love of the game. "It should not, but it does for some, and [to] my mind, people who do it are just flat out wrong," Kevin commented, saying that makeup was "a totally separate thing" in his definition. I understood Kevin's point to be that factors that were not *directly* related to someone's approach to playing baseball should be excluded from judgments about makeup. Even so, numerous people suggested (not in so many words) that elite makeup and rapid or eager language learning went hand in hand, at least for some prospects.

Perhaps the term *makeup* is misleading in the context of language socialization, but in baseball, as in other social domains, someone's stance toward language learning can be "read" in ways that presume a connection between language outcomes and moral qualities. For example, in accounting for Colombian-born pitcher Luis Patiño's dramatic uptick in velocity after signing, achieved through strength training, one might appeal to Patiño's "similarly proactive approach to learning a new language (he became fluent in English very quickly, totally of his own volition)" (Longenhagen, 2020). Or in discussing Venezuelan-born catcher Salvador Pérez's unapologetic use of his non-native English repertoire in postgame interviews, one might connect his linguistic risk-taking to his fearlessness on the field, as Jeff Diskin did:

Salvy's been great, and . . . his interviews have gotten a lot better, but he never worries— that's how he plays. His catching, his hitting, is all that way. He doesn't worry about making a mistake.

Thus, whether Bobby Puason's English learning was seen as relevant to his makeup, it certainly shaped the team's view of his personality and *potencia*. Bobby's path to English proficiency was a unique one. As a highly touted, advanced prospect, he came to the United States at sixteen, when most international signees are still attending classes at Dominican academies. (Jeff Diskin remarked that this was a challenging situation for any prospect because players who had the opportunity to spend time at the Dominican academies were "so much more ready for the adjustment to the States" than those who made the transition soon after signing.) This presented the A's with the dilemma of how to meet his educational needs. The team considered enrolling him in a local public high school but ultimately decided on intensive English classes at Arizona State University, located fairly close to the A's spring training facility. Bobby was the only student from the A's organization in the class, which Zak Basch described to me as a short-term English immersion program designed for international students from largely affluent backgrounds (e.g., Saudi Arabia) who hoped to pursue higher education in the United States. It's safe to say that the class wasn't packed with 6'3" teenaged Dominican infield prospects.

When I asked Bobby about the English immersion class, he vividly recalled his initial disorientation in the United States and his sense of triumph at having attained conversational proficiency in a relatively short time. Though we had been chatting in both languages, he insisted on recounting his language-learning experience in English. This puts me in the tricky situation of deciding how to represent his words on the page. Linguistic anthropologists have noted that written representations of so-called nonstandard speech can evoke stigmatized racial and class-based identities, and baseball journalists have criticized the practice of quoting non-native English speakers—for example, Minnie Miñoso, the "Cuban Comet" and the first Afro-Latino in MLB—in "broken English," such that their speech comes across as parody (A. Jaffe, 2000; J. Jaffe, 2021). As Alexandra Jaffe commented, transcribing nonstandard speech always "involve[s] the management of sameness and difference." Making Bobby Puason sound like an L1 English speaker would be inauthentic and would devalue his efforts to learn the language; yet overemphasizing the "differences" in his way of speaking might make him sound like a social stereotype (A. Jaffe, 2000, pp. 502, 504). I've tried to manage sameness and difference carefully in my transcriptions of learners' English, using learners' original words but smoothing out disfluencies and adding context in brackets where needed.

Bobby's version of his English immersion experience fit into the classic narrative of "foreign" language acquisition—a "silent period" of input, in which he was surrounded by English but "didn't understand," followed by incremental progress in his ability to speak and make sense of the language, with the support of a bilingual instructor who pushed Bobby into the zone of discomfort where learning was unavoidable (Ellis, 1994; see also Iddings & Jang, 2008; Ohta, 2005):

> I come here and I say, "Oh my God." I'm scared because I don't understand *nothing*, because all the people [are] talking English. . . . I think I'm stupid because I don't understand. . . . I talked to one of the guys who works here, [and he said], "The Oakland A's say you need to go to school." I say, "Yeah, perfect," because I [needed] it. . . . My first three or four weeks at [Arizona State], I didn't understand nothing. I said to the teacher, "Please help me because I don't understand."
>
> [The teacher said], "Don't worry." . . . The teacher [spoke] Spanish but said, "I don't talk Spanish with you because you need to learn English. . . . If I [speak] Spanish with you, you'll never learn English." . . . Six weeks, I'm better. Seven weeks, I'm better. Nine weeks, he said, "The class is done next week. You're done. You're very good. You learned a lot."

Learning English, Bobby said, had made him feel more connected with his teammates and coaches, since he "[understood] a little more" as time went on, "talk[ing] a lot with [his] partners, with his coach[es]." He noted that English was especially relevant to his team's performance because as a shortstop, he was positioned between other infielders and needed to be able to communicate with them throughout the game—for example, to remind them to move in case of a shift.[11] As we will see later on, certain positions have greater communicative demands and seem to favor language learning for that reason (e.g., pitchers and catchers need to talk over signs and approaches for different batters; middle infielders need to be in contact with teammates on either side).

Bobby used a number of strategies to improve his English proficiency following the immersion class. For one, he started what he called a linguistic "exchange" with L1 English-speaking teammates, using the whole-team morning gatherings as an opportunity for conversation practice:

> I'm [ex]chang[ing] a little with about five people here, American guys. I say, "You [teach] me English; in [ex]change, I'll talk to you in Spanish." . . . They say,

"Good, perfect!" In the meeting—in the morning—the Latin guys [are] speaking English and the American guys [are] speaking Spanish.

He also said that he had asked his agent to find him an English tutor in the DR so that he could keep up with what he called his "job" of "learn[ing] a lot of English" in the off-season:

> I have my agent. I say, "I need to take a class in [the] Dominican." . . . I pay for school. I have [a] personal teacher who [goes] to my home. Because . . . I need English. That's my job. I need to try to learn a lot of English. That's it.

As with the prospects I met at the Royals' Dominican academy, both Bobby and the A's personnel described English learning as a continuous process of self-improvement through which Latin American players were encouraged to develop professional selves. Notwithstanding the educational opportunities that teams provided, it was generally agreed that "becoming professional" hinged on "how much initiative [players] take," to quote Dan, the A's assistant general manager, and the extent to which prospects "embrace" learning new things, as Luis put it. Because of this, as we see with Bobby (and as we will see with other English and Spanish learners in subsequent chapters), teammates' and coaches' perceptions of Latino players' language-learning efforts and English proficiency figure in positive and negative evaluations of players' *moral* development in the context of becoming professional (Martin-Beltrán, 2010). Making strides in English can be taken as evidence of someone's intelligence, work ethic, and adaptability.

The flip side, of course, is that linguistic difficulties—a low level of proficiency or a simple miscommunication—can be taken up in ways that presuppose moral deficiency: a poor work ethic, a lack of respect for the game, or an unwillingness to adapt. In the next chapter, we will see how, in the words of Cuban-born pitcher Richard Guasch, "*Me tocaba ser* bad boy"—he ended up as a "bad boy" in his coaches' eyes upon coming to the United States because he struggled to communicate in English (and, lest we forget, because people often jump to moral conclusions based on linguistic evidence).

English Socialization in Difficult Transitions

During the transition from Latin America to the United States, players' language development is often entangled with their on-field experiences and struggles. "They're baseball players first," after all, and players' unpredictable trajectories upon arriving in the United States—being traded to a different organization, traveling to short-season affiliates in different parts of the country, and so on—meant that educators and player-development personnel thought deeply about how on-field and off-field contexts were mutually reinforcing. At times, this took the form of using English learning as an example of what prospects could achieve (off the field) when they were struggling to live up to their *potencia* on the field.

For example, at the A's facility, after the mental skills meeting for the Latino group that included Robert Puason, the facilitator asked Junior Pérez—who, he joked, was in the *silla caliente* (hot seat)—to hang around for a one-on-one pep talk. I later remarked to Luis Victoria that I had noticed something about his interactions with Junior in this meeting. Instead of immediately interpreting the facilitator's English utterances for Junior, Luis had waited to gauge how much Junior understood, verbally checking in, and interpreting or expanding as necessary. I had also noticed that Luis kept up a stream of positive reinforcement with his metacommentary (i.e., his comments *about* language in use) on Junior's progress in English. For example, when Junior responded without hesitation to the question of how many times he had struck out at the minor league affiliate in the past season ("133"), Luis could not conceal his delight: "He says he does not know English but he understands English. I'm proud of you!" he exclaimed, fist-bumping Junior for good measure.

The staffers present, especially Luis, were highlighting Junior's success in learning English to build him up as they also sought to get to the bottom of his struggles at the plate, which, according to the facilitator, had to do with his inability to recognize different types of *picheos rompientes*, or breaking balls. However, the facilitator was struggling to understand Junior's apparent confusion about his motivational message, a fine-tuned version of the message from the group meeting: Don't be so hard on yourself and focus on process over results. Language was not the source of the confusion; rather, the facilitator seemed frustrated that he couldn't get through to Junior. "We want you to enjoy this experience," the facilitator said, "rather than it being a battle every day," which it had been to that point—hence the 133 strikeouts. Junior described his time at the rookie league affiliate in Stockton, California, as, "*Ya no era disfrutar, era aprender, aprender, aprender.*" (It wasn't enjoyable anymore, it was learning, learning, learning.)

It eventually dawned on the staffers and coaches that Junior had come to the A's as the "player to be named later" in a trade and had not, therefore, gone through the same onboarding process as the other prospects.[12] The unpleasant learning curve Junior mentioned—"*aprender, aprender, aprender*"—was related not just to baseball but to his experience of being adrift in Stockton, adapting to a new cultural and linguistic context with a new group of teammates. The facilitator had been talking himself hoarse trying to express the team's concern for Junior's well-being—"We need to understand where you're coming from" so that we can help you—but finally paused and asked, in Spanish, "*¿Lo que nosotros sentimos sobre ti—alguien te explicó algo en eso?*" (The way we feel about you—has anyone ever explained that to you?). Junior said no, and the facilitator said, "That's our fault—*culpa de eso*," turning to his fellow staffers and commenting, "We failed to provide an opportunity for him to relax and have fun."

The uneven nature of prospects' socialization into organizational cultures, as in Junior's case, is also reflected in their uneven opportunities to learn and use English. After all, young players join the organization at different times and may be shuffled from one location to another—or even one organization to another—numerous times during a season or a career, and the team's minor league affiliates or Dominican academy may have different types of resources and support for language learning than the MLB club's instructional league or spring training facility. Luis explained his exuberant reaction to Junior's English development by way of the fact that he hadn't interacted with Junior in five months and wasn't sure if, or to what extent, Junior had been able to continue with English. Luis, like others, observed that prospects often lacked confidence to take risks in speaking English, even once they had attained a decent level of proficiency:

> Junior is a person that I know has been working hard in English. But because I haven't seen him for five months because he was in Stockton, I didn't know where his English skill level was at that point yet. But it was amazing. And I was able to see that he was understanding. . . . The problem . . . is that he could not express himself in English. So they sometimes lack the confidence. Not because they're not *understanding*, but because they don't feel that they can actually speak.

Symbolic Competence in Professional Development

While the one-on-one meeting gave Junior an opportunity to showcase his newfound competence in English, at least in a receptive (listening) sense, the other attendees' use of their bilingual repertoires was also significant. The facilitator had been speaking mostly in English once he realized that Junior could understand without Luis's interpretation, but he switched to Spanish to express his concern for Junior's well-being, asking if anyone had explained that the A's wanted him to relax and enjoy himself. The facilitator, as mentioned, was a native English speaker who appeared to have developed a high level of communicative competence in Spanish, switching codes to align himself emotionally with Junior (Ladegaard, 2018). Another coach in the meeting spoke less Spanish than the facilitator (from what I could tell) but still jumped in with Spanish utterances at moments of heightened emotion, especially when the staff were trying to emphasize a point. He used "*¡Coño!*" (damn it) to echo Junior's words to himself—Junior had been reporting his reaction after striking out—and dismissed with "*No chance*" (colloquially, not a chance) Junior's insistence that being hard on himself would improve his play.

The English-speaking coach's revoicing of Junior's *¡Coño!*, in particular, struck me as an outstanding example of "symbolic competence" in professional baseball. Symbolic competence may include "the ability to express, interpret, and negotiate meanings in dialogue with others," like communicative competence, but it also entails "the ability to produce and exchange symbolic goods in the complex global context in which we live today" (Kramsch, 2006). The coach in question did not need conversational proficiency in Spanish to participate in the mental skills session. He appeared to understand a good deal of what he heard, judging by the way he tracked the conversation, and he had a sense of when a Spanish word or utterance might carry more symbolic weight than its English equivalent. *Coño*—arguably the signature profanity of Caribbean Spanish (see also the concluding chapter)—indicated that the coach had been listening to Junior and indexed the coach's familiarity with that variety of Spanish. More importantly, it allowed the coach to align himself emotionally with Junior as the staff urged him to imagine a future where he could "trust the process" and stop swearing at himself in the dugout.

"You Don't Understand My Situation": Bridging Communicative Divides in Transnational Baseball

It would be hard to imagine a more outspoken and optimistic cheerleader for diversity in professional baseball than Luis Victoria, the 29-year-old education and culture coordinator for the A's at the time of our conversation, and now the club's coordinator of minor league operations. Luis credited the A's organization for doing "a tremendous job at embracing diversity" from the top down:

> We already know baseball is . . . probably [one of] the most diverse sports that there is in the world. Embrace it . . . and be happy with it because, I don't know, [if] you only hire or sign American players, how would this sport be?

To build relationships with young Latino prospects in the A's system, Luis drew on his own experience as a third baseman and catcher born and raised in Santo Domingo who left the Dominican Republic to pursue his baseball dreams at Mesabi Range Community College in northern Minnesota. However, he acknowledged that others had not always embraced diversity on his transnational baseball journey. In Luis's words, the "cultural shock" following this move—for him *and* his white American teammates, who "had never seen a Dominican like that before"—prepared him for his future role as a mentor for other young Latinos in MLB organizations, first at the Royals' DR academy and then with the A's prospects in Arizona. As with Johan's comments about the importance of being a "Dominican leader" for Dominican prospects, encountering racism and cultural misunderstanding allowed Luis to anticipate that younger players might face similar challenges in the United States.

In Minnesota, Luis said, he initially felt so alienated from his teammates that he ended up hanging out mostly with Black basketball players, the only sizeable group of people of color at the college; some of the basketball players hailed from Florida and "knew what [his] culture was about." Even Luis's "very formal" English, which he had studied from a young age in the Dominican, proved inadequate to the task of connecting with his teammates, since he was not a proficient user of American slang. After a while, Luis's teammates adjusted to what he called his "different flair" and came to accept him as a valued member of the team.[13] Still, the experience he repeatedly called "rough" set him on the road to guiding other young Latinos through the process of linguistic and cultural adaptation to US baseball:

> Without knowing it, I was already learning about culture, the development and adjustment to the United States. . . . I was [like], "Okay, I get it now. And I get how difficult it might be to adjust to that."

Based on Luis's rough adjustment to college baseball in Minnesota and his interactions with other Latino players, he developed a "five tools" curriculum for incoming prospects, a play on the traditional "five tools" of baseball (hit, hit for power, run, throw, field) that included essential cultural knowledge related to financial literacy, technology, the English language, life skills such as airport travel and cooking, and so on. Nevertheless, neither Luis's personal history nor his enthusiastic attitude toward linguistic and cultural diversity prepared him for all the situations he would encounter as coordinator of educational and cultural programs. For one, some players' multilingual repertoires exceeded the limits of his own; he mentioned a recent signee from Curaçao who spoke five languages, including Papiamentu and Dutch, as well as prospects from places like the Bahamas where different English varieties or English-based creoles are spoken.

Luis also discovered that he had much to learn about what was *behind* the communicative behaviors of teenaged players from lower-income backgrounds in the Dominican Republic and Venezuela, whose trajectories in professional baseball bore little resemblance to the path Luis followed as a college recruit. When he started in his current position, other A's staffers asked him to investigate what they saw as confusing or problematic behaviors that inhibited their ability to communicate effectively with Latino players. For example:

> When I got here, everybody was like, . . . we have an issue with Latino players always changing their WhatsApp numbers or their [phone] numbers. I was just like, "Okay. I'll see what's going on." I mean, hopefully I can . . . dive into the root of the problem. I said, "Give [me] an example of a player," and then they gave it to me.

Rather than jumping to conclusions about the players' behavior or assuming it reflected some unknowable "cultural" preference, Luis listened and asked questions—in this case, approaching the player whose name had come up and asking him why he had just changed his WhatsApp number for the third time. Like Johan, Luis was careful to differentiate "judging" from "understanding" when confronted with an unfamiliar cultural practice. According to Luis, the player said, "'Luis, you don't understand my situation in Venezuela.' I was like, 'Okay, explain it to me.'" It turned out that the player had to keep changing his number to evade extortionists in Venezuela who were threatening his mother and sister—a situation that seemed outrageous to Luis, but one that was not uncommon, according to other Venezuelan prospects. After all, it's hard to keep a signing bonus secret, and even the smallest bonus by MLB standards is a windfall in poorer areas of Latin America:

> [The first player said], "As soon as I signed"—it was not even for a lot—"I already had an email, text messages from people saying like, "I'm gonna kidnap your sister. I'm gonna kill your mom if you don't give me the money, like you need to give me this amount of money. Or remember when you owed me this much." . . . I ask[ed] another [Venezuelan] player. Just the same thing. "Like, we have issues at home that . . . It doesn't matter if you sign for ten grand or two hundred grand, to them, it's just money that . . . needs to be taken from that person." So obviously we just signed this player thinking, like, we made their life. . . . But we don't know of everything that happens as soon as they sign the contract.

This anecdote caused Luis to reflect on the importance of his job. Even if he couldn't change the situation in the players' home countries, he could at least help new signees get a US SIM card to avoid the constant barrage of harassing and threatening messages and provide a "safe environment" where players saw him as an empathetic listener whom they could trust with personal information. That was just one side of it, though. Luis launched his inquiry into changing WhatsApp numbers in his capacity as a linguistic and cultural broker for the A's staff; thus, he closed the loop with the staff in a way that built the staff's intercultural competence:

> And then you have to explain it to the staff. . . . Now you understand why these players are changing their numbers on a constant basis. It's not because they want to; it's because, you know, they're getting so many people at them that it's like, "Oh, you owe me money. No, you gotta do this. And you gotta do that." . . . That was key for me to understand myself. 'Cause I was like, "Okay, like now I get it." You know, I didn't have that issue in the Dominican with the Royals, because I never heard of it.

It's worth taking a step back to analyze this speech situation more closely. As with the interaction between the Korean umpire and Mike Montgomery discussed in Chapter 4, a misunderstanding arose between the A's staffers and young Venezuelan prospects not because of *linguistic* difference per se, if we take "linguistic difference" to mean a contrast between named codes like English and Spanish. Nor was the "unevenness" of people's communicative repertoires primarily to blame—that is, the fact that some people in this situation knew more or less Spanish or English, relative to others. The source of the misunderstanding, rather, had to do with how A's staffers were framing or interpreting a particular communicative behavior—changing phone numbers frequently—as "an issue with Latino players." Staffers had observed this behavior often enough or talked about it often enough that over time, it had begun to "accrue" as a characteristic of the social persona, or type, "Latino player." It was part of a stereotype, in other words. That isn't to say that it had no basis in reality, simply that it had become recognizable, within the speech community of the A's minor league organization, as part of how "Latino players" communicate (Agha, 2007).

What Luis came to understand, and what he had to communicate to the (US-based, English-speaking) staff, were the social and cultural circumstances underlying this apparently meaningless behavior. The key insight, as he put it, was that players were not changing their phone numbers because they wanted to—out of flakiness, or irresponsibility, or technological ignorance, or whatever "cultural" characteristic staff might have been tempted to attribute to them—but because of the socioeconomic circumstances surrounding professional baseball in Latin America. These circumstances lurked in the margins of bilingual baseball contexts, sometimes becoming more central. On the A's backfields, a group of team personnel strategized with a young Venezuelan player about travel plans following the instructional league, helping the player contact a driver who could take him from Colombia to Venezuela, since the security situation would make it impossible for him to fly directly home.

The case of the changing WhatsApp numbers underscores just how different the process of "becoming professional" can be for Spanish speakers coming from different countries and communities within Latin America. Even Luis's experience growing up and working in player development in the Dominican Republic did not allow him to guess why Venezuelan prospects kept changing their numbers. He had to prod at that cultural "rich point"—the point of incomprehension or misunderstanding that on inspection yields rich insights into cultural behavior—in order to serve as a mediator between staff and players. Being able to broker this interaction effectively meant that Luis had to understand how the *cultural* meaning of a signing bonus depended on the context (Keane, 2010). From the team's perspective, it meant, "We made their life"—and indeed, the bonus represented life-changing money for some players and families. Nevertheless, to paraphrase a staffer's musings on Robert Puason and his bonus, "I mean, I don't feel *bad* for him. Five million dollars is more than I'll ever see. But that doesn't mean it's easy."

2

English, Spanish, and the Afterlives of Latin American Prospects

"The True Development of a Person and a Professional": From the Dominican Academy to the Big Stage of MLB

Jill Long de Mercado of Higher Standards Academy, the education and ESL contractor for several MLB teams, mentioned that her company was "very conscientious about who we work with." She brought up a persistent area of awkwardness in talk about young international signees: in the most basic terms, "they're investments" for the MLB organization, yet teachers and player-development staff strive not to treat them that way. "They're still a person, they're still a world citizen," Jill said, emphasizing the humanity and worldliness of Latino adolescents who are expected to "become professional" as they are still becoming adult human beings.

Because of this, she emphasized, HSA would work only with organizations that were dedicated to "the true development of a person and a professional" as opposed to those that treated players and their English education strictly as "investments." She offered Dan Feinstein, the A's assistant general manager (see Chapter 1), as an example of the former approach:

> He is busy, but you know, on the drop of a dime, they'll investigate on any player at any time, and not just a prospect. And that's when you know you're working with a team that is actually involved in the true development of a person and a professional.

"Not just a prospect" gets to the heart of the issue: a front-office executive who will "investigate any player at any time," regardless of how promising he is as an "investment"—that is, irrespective of prospect status—implied, for Jill, that the team was "totally into education across the board."

Not all MLB organizations were alike in this respect, in Jill's experience. She shared that HSA had previously been working with another team but decided not to renew their contract because "the dedication wasn't there; the commitment wasn't there." By "dedication and commitment," Jill meant the organization's willingness to provide an educational program that was "wrapped around" operations in the DR and the United States rather than one that would fade into the background as players adapted to life in a new country. She marveled at

> the amount of work that [the A's] do up front at the academy level [in the DR] to help the transition, to Stateside, what they do for the players in Arizona and at the affiliates. They really keep education at the forefront across the board, whether it's making sure that the players are participating in an engaging way and an active way for the required MLB education seminars, the seminars that they put on themselves as an organization, English, Spanish[-speaking] coaches. I mean, it's wrapped around.

For Jill and other teachers, as you might imagine, it was thrilling to see their efforts to "keep education at the forefront" bear fruit when a player achieved a degree of success and visibility in the major leagues. At the time of our conversation, one of Jill's former students was playing in the 2021 World Series, the pinnacle of the sport:

> As a matter of fact, there is a player who's in the World Series right now, who I started with online classes . . . and they knew that they were going to move him up to the forty-man roster,[1] so we did just an intense month of classes . . . . That was years ago, before he even made his [MLB] debut. [And now he's] in the World Series, so that's awesome. It's incredible for them, because, you know, it's not life changing just for that person; it's their family and their extended family, their friends, their country.

Seeing a former student fulfill his dream at the highest level, against long odds, with "life-changing" consequences for him and his community, was a dream fulfilled (if rarely) for Jill and other educators who worked with *peloteros*. In the DR, I asked Johan Febrillet, the Royals' lead educator at the time, if he ever stayed in touch with players who had moved on to the States, and he brought up Angel Zerpa, a left-handed pitching prospect from Venezuela who had recently been called up to Kansas City:

> One of our players, Angel Zerpa, we just got his [MLB] debut a couple of weeks ago. And when that happened, I reached out to him to say, "Hey, man, congratulations on that! I feel really, really proud of how much you have progressed."

> Because it's really cool and amazing to realize that that guy who just made it to the big leagues, a couple of months or possibly years ago [was] here sitting down in front of you, taking classes, having fun with you, talking about important things for him, you know, asking you for pieces of advice, and all of a sudden, you see 'em, they're on a big stage, that is really rewarding. I would say incredible. You feel as if you're part of that success, you know, like . . . you did your part in there, whenever you see them using the English in front of a camera. That's amazing. I think that's one of the most rewarding feelings you can have as an educator.

For Johan and Jill, there were two sides to this experience. For one, there was the "amazing, rewarding, incredible" feeling of witnessing a former student's debut "on a big stage," and beyond that, watching him use English in front of a camera. On the other hand, teachers experienced a degree of cognitive dissonance when contrasting the students they knew personally—"that guy was here sitting down in front of you, taking classes, having fun with you"—with the consummate "professionals" they had become. Somewhat wistfully, Johan showed me a video of a scrambled sentence activity from 2018 in which a teenaged Zerpa and his academy teammates held signs with English words as another player moved them around to form a grammatical sentence. On our visit to the Royals-sponsored orphanage later that day, a staffer remarked that Zerpa used to love going there and playing ball with the kids.

Jill, likewise, commented on the strangeness of watching her former student in the World Series, considering the circumstances in which they got to know each other and the role she played in his success:

> I think, my gosh, I had a conversation with you two weeks ago about, "Yes, you are an athlete. Yes, we want a somewhat relaxed scene so that you're comfortable, and we can get through the language process, but it's still part of your job. Put a shirt on."
>
> Because these guys are athletes, right? They're athletes, they're in and out of the gym all the time. And so learning how to flip between registers and ambiences, obviously, it's a big deal for them. And once they get those small pieces, those small nuances, it's magic. The language just is magical. So, yeah, it's hilarious. I thought, my God, two weeks ago I'm telling you to put a shirt on [laughing].

As we saw in the previous chapter, English learning was just one dimension of a broader process of professionalization for young Latino prospects. Jill's humorous account of having to reinforce "professional" norms—"It's still part of your job. Put a shirt on"—with her former student is another reminder that *peloteros*' language socialization has to be understood in the context of their identities as athletes who, in this case, are "in and out of the gym all the time." But Jill's reference to "learning how to flip between registers and ambiences" underscores the complexity of becoming professional for Latin American players who make it to the major leagues. Linguistic codeswitching (from Spanish to English "in front of the camera," say) is one part of the picture, but "flipping between registers and ambiences" suggests that "professional" behavior involves a more varied, situational form of communicative competence—one that includes "small pieces [and] nuances" of linguistic registers but also how to present one's body in different "ambiences" (e.g., when to put a shirt on).

This chapter begins with Jill's and Johan's stories because they preview the hoped-for outcome of language learning for Latin American ballplayers: a bilingual professional who can adapt readily to a variety of settings and whose language ability and communicative repertoire support his on-field success. Teachers like Jill and Johan are rightfully proud when their former students excel as bilinguals on "the big stage" of MLB. Nevertheless, to take those stories as representative would obscure the fact that English learning in Dominican academies and the US minor leagues happens against the backdrop of almost certain failure. Most language learners in professional baseball will never make it to the major leagues; many will not even make it to the United States. Players and staff, while reluctant to entertain the possibility of life after baseball, must confront it eventually, and that reckoning shapes educators' decisions about curriculum and pedagogy as well as *peloteros*' approach to language learning and acculturation.

In this chapter, I explore what happens as former Latin American prospects strive to carve out careers in the game they love and the role of language in this long-term process. Chapter 2 continues the story that began in Chapter 1—it picks up at the end of players' initial experiences of "becoming professional," in and through language, and examines their continued development as bilinguals and professionals during their time in the minor leagues and, for some, beyond the end of their careers. In the next section, as a counterpoint to the feel-good stories of Jill's and Johan's students, I discuss the experience of a pitching prospect whose journey to the United States and linguistic and cultural transition to MLB were profoundly different.

"*Me Tocaba Ser* Bad Boy": Getting Off on the Wrong Foot Professionally

Right-handed pitcher Richard Guasch's path to signing with an MLB club was markedly unlike those of the Latin American prospects we've encountered so far in the book. "I don't know how much you understand about the situation in Cuba, but it's a little bit different than the rest of the world," he began. The understatement hinted that he had met quite a few people who did not fully appreciate the challenges Cuban players face. Richard defected—as he put it, "I abandoned my team"—on a trip to Mexico with the Cuban national youth team in September 2016, taking off running from the team hotel. This was his second escape attempt of the trip; he had previously been stymied by a locked gate at the stadium. And so began an ordeal he described as *"un proceso bastante incómodo y largo también"*—a really uncomfortable and long process.

Richard finally attained his dream, signing with the Oakland A's in July 2018, but the two intervening years were an ongoing nightmare. After escaping from the hotel, he spent five months between Mexico and Guatemala, crossing a river to enter Guatemala by clandestine means. From Guatemala, he reached El Salvador, where he was arrested and imprisoned with tattooed members of the notoriously violent gang Mara Salvatrucha for three days: "I was only eighteen years old and seeing that was something really tough." Eventually, he made it to the Dominican Republic, where he planned to work out with trainers while establishing residency in order to be able to sign with an MLB team.

Even then, life did not get much easier. During training, Richard sustained a shoulder injury that would require surgery to repair, according to doctors. He was unable to afford the surgery, but after several months, thanks to *"la mano de Dios para mi vida"*—the hand of God in my life—he made a miraculous recovery and returned to throwing at full strength, attracting the notice of major league clubs. He first agreed to sign with the Philadelphia Phillies, but the deal fell through because of dirty dealing on the part of *inversionistas* and *agentes*—investors or agents, go-betweens who take advantage of vulnerable young players in the free-for-all of Dominican amateur free agency and *"hacen muchas cosas malas para sacarte dinero"*—do lots of bad things to get money out of you.

In the end, Richard signed with Oakland for much less money than he'd agreed to with the Phillies. Upon arriving in the United States, Richard found it difficult to adjust to "living" the English language, as opposed to speaking it in classroom settings. In this, his situation resembled that of the prospects profiled in Chapter 1 and the Spanish learners in Chapter 3, all of whom were unprepared for the language variation they encountered among coaches and teammates:

> I went to the United States, and that's where the story begins, with the language and those things that were really uncomfortable. They were giving us English classes here [in the DR], but taking a class isn't the same as living it. You can talk in class, but when you're going to talk with whatever coach or something, it's

very difficult because many of them don't have the same accent. Others talk this way or that way, or they talk fast. So that's really uncomfortable.

In contrast with someone like Robert Puason, who was deemed advanced enough to move from the Dominican academy to the United States at sixteen, Richard Guasch was relatively "old" for a prospect—twenty—during his first spring training with the A's. Along with his poor preparation in English, Richard felt the effects of a lack of cultural socialization in a Dominican professional academy, where other prospects "become professional," and struggled to understand and communicate the professionalism that was expected of an A's player. A former executive told me that for Cubans coming to the United States, more so than other Latin American players, "it's like landing on Mars, [compared to] where they were from."

In Richard's case, early in spring training, he garnered a reputation as a "bad boy" among the A's coaches because of what he characterized as a miscommunication:

> I had a little bit of a bad experience precisely because of the language ... or like, it was the fault of the language and because I wasn't understanding [the coach] and he wasn't understanding me either.

Until that point, things hadn't been going badly. Richard had even been named captain of a group of pitchers. The trouble stemmed from an incident near the end of a spring training game. The A's were up 7–4 in the top of the ninth inning. Richard and the other pitchers, who had been sitting in the dugout for the whole game without pitching, after a long day of training, were watching for the third out so that they could get back to the clubhouse as quickly as possible. Thinking the game was already decided, they didn't realize that the other team had tied the score in the ninth—thus, with the third out, the group took off for the clubhouse, until they recognized their mistake and returned. No matter. As the captain, Richard was held responsible for this unprofessional lapse. One of the coaches started to berate him in English: "Why are you here? What are you doing up here [i.e., out of the dugout]?" Richard remembered:

> But I didn't understand, and I didn't know how to tell him, how to explain it to him. I told him, "The game's over. *No más juegos* [no more games]." And he didn't understand. So he was really annoyed with me. And that was my first impression on the team. It was bad. ... And it was just a little bit of confusion because of the language issue.

In Richard's case, the beliefs and discourses that associate language development and acculturation with moral qualities valued in baseball—hard work, selflessness, taking initiative, being a good teammate—worked against him. Unlike Robert Puason, Yosmi Fernández, or Salvador Pérez (to name a few examples from Chapter 1), whose eager English acquisition and risk-taking underscored their *potencia* on the field, Richard's inability to function in the language led his coaches, indirectly, to view him negatively as a baseball player. Once Richard had been designated a "bad boy," it wasn't easy to shed the label: "They thought I was undisciplined, that I wasn't on time, that I didn't follow rules, all of it." The coach in question continued harassing Richard about the incident for months afterward, making an example of him in front of his teammates. Richard joked that his lack of English proficiency at the time was a blessing in disguise:

> In the training room, he told me a lot of nasty things in English, for many hours in front of everybody, in front of dozens[2] of people. And I didn't understand that either. If I had understood, probably it would have bothered me.

Richard "kept being who I was," in his words, and the coaching staff eventually realized "that I was different than they'd thought." In fact, Richard became particularly close with the coach who had called him out. He said that the coach had apologized for his harsh treatment of Richard and even cried when he was traded to the Washington Nationals in 2021. Still, Richard had learned a painful lesson. He blamed "language issues" for his initial difficulties and said that learning conversational English had been *liberador* (liberating) in that he no longer felt as excluded in group settings.

On reflection, however, it didn't seem that language itself was the whole issue. The issue was also that English proficiency, or a lack thereof, could be taken up by English speakers as evidence of professionalism, on the one hand, or moral deficiency (in baseball terms) on the other. Richard, who had just "landed on Mars," figuratively speaking, and had not spent time at a professional academy in the DR, did not have the same degree of exposure to the ideology of "becoming professional," much less the linguistic resources to navigate that process successfully.

"They Didn't Know How My English Was This Good": Making a Professional Impression

The Covid-19 pandemic, which interrupted the 2020 baseball season along with teams' training and educational programs, was disastrous for many prospects' development on and off the field. Not so for Michel Gelabert, the Arizona

Diamondbacks' Cuban-born lefty we met napping with his daughter in Chapter 1. Because Michel spent only a month at the Diamondbacks' Dominican academy after signing, he had limited exposure to English classes there. In 2018, the Diamondbacks dispatched Michel to their rookie league affiliate in Missoula, Montana, where he took English classes but "didn't learn much."

Things changed in 2019 when he met his future wife—a Montana native, coincidentally—who was visiting Arizona during spring training. Being in a relationship with an English speaker sharpened Michel's desire to learn the language, which he expected would also benefit him with the team: "I wanted to be able to speak with my wife *well*, without using a translator or something like that." Besides increasing his motivation, Michel's future wife provided appropriate English input and support for his classroom learning: "She kinda helped me a lot in the classes I was taking and all that, kinda like everything combined, and I was getting better."[3]

When the pandemic struck, Michel and his family decamped to Billings, Montana, where he had an English immersion—if not submersion—experience that was dramatically different from Bobby Puason's experience with international students at Arizona State University (see Chapter 1) (see, e.g., Fazio & Lyster, 1998). Still, Michel described the initial feeling of disorientation in similar terms to Bobby:

> At first, I was like, "I don't get anything [that] they say," but eventually, you get it. By the actions they do and all the stuff, you're kinda like, "Oh, she went to the bathroom and she said 'bathroom.'" So I kinda like knew what she was talking about.

In Billings, Michel used familiar strategies to improve his English—for example, watching movies with English subtitles, switching his phone's interface to English—and was surrounded by speakers of the target language and isolated from Spanish speakers to a degree that was rare among *peloteros* (Valdés, 2001). As he put it, "It's hard to find a lot of Latin people" in Montana. Yellowstone County, where Billings is located, is about 83 percent white/non-Hispanic and 6 percent Hispanic, and Michel was no longer sharing a clubhouse with a cohort of Spanish-speaking minor leaguers, unlike in Missoula.[4] He spent a good deal of time learning to communicate with his in-laws and also extended himself into the community, looking for opportunities to continue honing his English and keep up his conditioning during the pandemic:

> So actually, 2020 helped me a lot because I spent more time with my wife speaking English, with my brothers-in-law, my mother-in-law. I made some friends, and this academy [where] I went to practice, everyone there speaks English.

The "academy" Michel mentioned was a training facility for the Billings Scarlets, an American Legion team of high-school-aged ballplayers, whom Michel volunteered to mentor as an unofficial pitching coach.[5] In a local news story from early 2020, Scarlets players and coaches gushed about Michel's generosity and positive impact on the team, calling him "the best guy," "such a good person," and praising his "work ethic"—a perception that Michel's rapidly developing English may have reinforced, in contrast to Richard's case (as discussed previously) (Letasky, 2020) (Figure 15).

Once pandemic restrictions eased, Michel returned to the Diamondbacks, where his apparently sudden leap in English proficiency dumbfounded the staff. The key moment came at a one-on-one meeting with Michel's coaches and coordinators:

> So I came to spring training and they didn't know how my English was this good. Every year, we do a meeting, one-on-one. So it's one player and all the coaches. So we did that meeting, and I went there. One of my coaches is from [the] Dominican. They started speaking in English, and I'm understanding everything. And so Barfield—that's the coordinator of the minor leagues—[said] to the coach, "Can you translate [for] him?" And I said, "No, no, no. I got it." I start speaking. Everyone was like, "What?" Everyone was like, "What just happened?" It felt good, for sure. They were surprised.[6]

As we will see later, learning English transformed Michel's relationships with his coaches, helping him to "maximize his experience" in professional baseball by enabling in-depth communication in off-the-cuff interactions. However, it also allowed him to move quickly into the role of language broker on behalf

Figure 15 Diamondbacks minor league pitcher Michel Gelabert in the Billings (MT) Scarlets' dugout, June 2020 (John Letasky/Billings Gazette/Lee Enterprises). Reproduced with permission of Billings Gazette.

of Spanish-speaking teammates. Soon after arriving for Covid-delayed spring training, Michel got injured and then spent most of the season doing rehab alongside "rookies that just came from the Dominican [that] year" for extended spring training. He ended up becoming the primary interpreter between the newly arrived Latino players and the trainers, which "felt good." Michel saw it as a matter of "paying it forward," as it were, or providing the language support that bilingual teammates had provided for him in the past while inspiring younger players to take English seriously:

> Because when I was [at] that point, [there] was always someone to help me. And now I look back and I'm like, now I'm the one that's helping them. So I hope they see that and they're like, "Okay, I need to learn [the] language. So if I do, in three years, if someone needs my help, I can help."

Michel imagined passing the torch to his younger teammates, just as he had assumed the mantle of language broker once he was able to do so. As with other language learners in this book, and as in some immigrant communities, Michel's English socialization first equipped him to survive in an unfamiliar context—through workplace and interpersonal communication—and later positioned him to advocate for fellow *peloteros*.

An Atypical Case of Naturalistic Language Learning

Among Latin American ballplayers in the United States, Michel was an atypical case in having learned English in primarily "naturalistic" settings or relatively unstructured everyday interactions, as opposed to a more structured classroom environment. He was also atypical in terms of his success; as his coaches' flabbergasted reaction would suggest, his language development proceeded more rapidly—not to mention under different circumstances—than anyone in the Diamondbacks organization expected. Atypical cases are useful for forcing us to rethink our assumptions and disrupting "common sense" understandings of language and culture. As such, it's instructive to consider what Michel's experience might teach us about approaches to language learning in professional baseball.

Jill Long de Mercado mentioned that some educational researchers had collaborated with Jill's company, Higher Standards Academy, to investigate best practices in "language-supportive coaching" for athletes who are learning English, or ALEs (Ettl Rodríguez & Kandel-Cisco, 2021). The resulting article is admirably accessible and concise, clearly intended for coaches and educational staff, and highlights several well-known, sensible strategies for scaffolding L2 input, some of which I observed or heard about from players and teachers—complementing verbal input with visual aids, using total physical response (TPR—i.e., physical demonstrations), checking for understanding, and so forth (Donato, 1994).

While I was heartened to see others pushing for better language support for athletes and found much of the authors' guidance useful (if unsurprising), I was struck by the difference between Michel's experience and some of the received wisdom about L2 learning and teaching in the article. For example, the authors exhort coaches to "speak clearly" and "enunciate," singling out a certain class of English verbal auxiliaries as problematic in this regard: "English speakers often say 'gonna,' 'wanna,' 'shoulda,' and/or 'I need ya' ta,' when many beginning and intermediate language learners need to hear 'going to,' 'want to,' 'should have,' and 'I need you to' in order to fully comprehend the words" (Ettl Rodríguez & Kandel-Cisco, 2021, p. 5). They also advise caution in the use of "slang" or "lingo" with ALEs.

Michel's speech, however, which he developed in a naturalistic context, argues against this "teacherly" view of what is necessary for language acquisition. Take, for example, his repeated use of *kinda* as a pragmatic particle—that is, a cue for the hearer to interpret what is said in a certain way. At times, he seems to use *kinda* as an approximator or an indication that "the phrase should not be interpreted literally"—as in, "You're *kinda* like, 'Oh, she went to the bathroom'" (Margerie, 2010). (We're not meant to imagine that Michel actually uttered that phrase out loud in the past.) *Kinda* is not a form that Michel is likely to have learned in English class. It's an expression that he probably learned in conversation with English speakers, apparently without "fully comprehend[ing] the words" involved, since *kind of* didn't occur in his speech.

Another example is Michel's consistent use of quotative *be like* for reported speech, as in, "And *they're like*, 'Okay, I need to learn [the] language.'" Using *be like* to quote someone is not necessarily how you're taught to speak English, but it has become the most prevalent quotative form—supplanting *said*, *told*, and so on—across the English-speaking world and is also being diffused among L2 speakers (Labov, 2018; Davydova, 2021). (Compare Michel's categorical use of *be like* with Bobby Puason's use of *say/said* as quotatives in Chapter 1, recalling that much of Bobby's English input came from the university classroom.)

Does any of this matter? I think it does, because it suggests that Michel was (and is) participating in diachronic, or historical, changes to the English language *along with* the L1 English speakers who surrounded him during the pandemic. That is, rather than hewing to someone's idealized version of "standard" English, he learned a variety of English that closely resembled the input he received in Montana, at least in some ways. The first historical change is that forms like *kinda, sorta, type-a*, which originated as content words—that is, those that "describe things, actions, and qualities"—are gradually becoming function words, or words that don't have a descriptive meaning but that play a role in helping language cohere or perform a grammatical function.[7] This is called grammaticalization: the process by which content words turn into function words. For example, modern English *while* (a "temporal connective" function word) began life as an Old English construction meaning "that time that" (Hopper & Traugott 2003, p. 4). Just so, the expression "(a) kind of" has taken on a range of grammatical functions, becoming *kinda* over centuries of language change (Margerie, 2010; see also Dehé & Stathi, 2016). The second historical change is much more recent: the rapid, nearly universal adoption of *be like* as the dominant quotative form (i.e., what you use to quote another speaker or yourself) over the span of just a few decades (1980s–present) (Tagliamonte & D'arcy, 2007). Like *kind of/kinda*, *be like* originally had a more restricted range of uses and has gradually expanded to cover nearly every context for reported speech.

Of course, Michel didn't need to know any of this to pick up *kinda* as a useful function word or *be like* as the appropriate way to report what someone said. He simply needed to be around people who were speaking that way. Perhaps just as importantly, he needed to be in a setting where ideas about "right" and "wrong" usage were largely irrelevant to intercultural communication. It matters that Michel learned language differently compared with other *peloteros* (like Bobby) because he's using it differently. That is, he's using it in ways that mirror historical processes of language change that are ongoing among L1 English speakers, which aligns him more closely with those speakers. Not every ALE can count on having an English-speaking life partner and an extended period of immersion in the vernacular language. But Michel's example is an interesting rejoinder to ideologies of language learning that predominate in ESL classrooms, including those discussed in the next section.

"Their Time Is Pretty Limited": Time-on-Task Ideologies and the "Ticking Clock" for MLB Success

The scarcity of time came up again and again in my conversations with language educators in baseball. Talk about time limitations was related to two different temporalities, or cultural ways of understanding time (Irvine, 2004). The first was the "ticking clock" temporality of professional baseball, according to which a young prospect has to keep pace with a strict developmental schedule, constantly improving his skills in order to "level up" from the Dominican academy (for international prospects) to short-season/rookie league ball, and on to full-season affiliates at low-A, high-A, AA, and so forth, at fairly regular intervals. A prospect's value to his team as an investment diminishes as time goes on; thus, in baseball, time is first of all scarce in terms of *time to succeed*, or time to "make it."

The second way of talking about time had to do with the lack of time *for* learning language. Educators' beliefs that there wasn't enough time for language education were related to the "ticking clock" temporality, since the imperative to improve oneself constantly as a baseball player left little time for activities that weren't directly related to on-field performance, like learning English. However, this second temporality was also connected to "time-on-task" ideologies of language learning, which stipulate that (a) more linguistic input will lead to greater proficiency in a second language—that is, more is better—and (b) second-language learners require a minimum level of input (measured in hours or years) to attain a certain degree of proficiency (Tollefson, 2007).[8] Language educators in baseball drew on these ideologies, which are prevalent in the field of second-language acquisition and teaching, to make sense of their teaching practice and their students' language outcomes.

According to time-on-task ideologies, the teachers were in an impossible position. There would never be enough time for their students to become as proficient as the teachers and team wanted them to be. This was frustrating for educators, whose beliefs about language development were at odds with the amount of time available to teach students English (or Spanish, as in Chapter 3). Some, like Jill, spoke of the scarcity of time in a "big picture" way, or over what we might call longer timescales—the scale of a player's entire career in the minor leagues, or the scale of L2 development over several years (Lemke, 2000; see also O'Connor, 2020):

> So we know it takes about 720-ish hours on a traditional academic path to gain an intermediate high speaking level in a second language. And we don't have that amount of time. We have anywhere between two-and-a-half to three-and-a-half years to work with a player, in regard to being able to have a sufficient amount of time to work with them on the language, [and] they have anywhere between four to six years to make it [to the major leagues].
>
> So, you know, their time is pretty limited. So we define success by getting them up to an intermediate high speaking level because that's what they need to be able to communicate in a stressful game situation. So we use the ACTFL

speaking guidelines, because they're working for a US organization and that's the language that we have to build around.⁹

As Jill framed it, language education in Minor League Baseball requires teachers always to keep the "ticking clock" of prospect development in mind, gauging how much time they have left with a given player—how long he has to "make it or break it"—versus how much time would be needed to close the gap between his current level of proficiency and an intermediate-high level per the ACTFL guidelines. Emily Glass, the former education coordinator for the Miami Marlins, said that the situation was compounded by teams' unrealistic expectations that players would attain a certain level of proficiency in a short time:

> I don't think [the team] understands what it means to gain even intermediate level, let alone fluency in another language. It takes like eight years of education or immersion, you know. And the average baseball career is like four years.

Emily and Jill had differing beliefs about exactly how much time was necessary, but both viewed players' language learning against the backdrop of what Emily called "the average baseball career." Even then, language educators did not have access to players for all four to six years of the "ticking clock" for MLB success. As Jill mentioned, players were usually in English classes for half that time at most. Higher-ups like Dan Feinstein and Jeff Diskin told me that once players made it to the upper levels of the minor leagues (AA, AAA), they were expected to be able to function independently in English and were no longer taking regular classes. From Johan's perspective, this process began sooner, as soon as players left the Dominican academy for facilities in the United States, where their days were less structured:

> Once they get to Arizona, they become a little bit more independent because once they're done with their practices or baseball games and they get back to the hotel or wherever they're staying in the [minor league] affiliates, they're free. They just step out, walk around. And if you have that freedom, we gotta make sure that you are prepared for it, that you have received the education.

In addition to the shortness of players' careers in the lower minors, another difficulty was the lack of time during the baseball season for English and other classes. Deron Dolphus, who was originally from North Carolina and taught English at the Marlins' Dominican academy, explained that he couldn't teach "a full English curriculum" because players were not consistently available throughout the year and English classes had to compete with other priorities— for example, opportunities to play elsewhere and injury rehabilitation:

We don't have the time to do a full English curriculum 'cause, for example, a traditional school starts in August and it ends in June and you have all those months to go through the lessons and see the improve[ment] and the progress. But in baseball, it's a little bit different because they have fall leagues, they have winter leagues, and then they have spring when they're all in the United States, the minor league baseball season.

They may spend maybe two months straight in the classroom and then they go out to do something and then they might come back, you know, or a player might get injured and he needs to go to the United States for a month to have surgery. . . . So they don't spend ten straight months taking English classes, maybe a couple months here and there. It changed fast because they're constantly moving players around the country or around abroad.

Johan stressed that players' schedules could also be unpredictable on a day-to-day basis—for example, if a game went into extra innings or there was a doubleheader—meaning that flexibility was paramount for the educational staff. This was why the Royals were adamant about not contracting out for their educational programming, instead choosing to have a lead educator and support staff on site. In Johan's eyes, a contracted employee would be unlikely to demonstrate the flexibility necessary to make the most of the very limited time for English, high school completion, and technology classes.

Maximizing Your Experience: How Much English Is Enough?

As documented in Chapter 1, with so little time for players' education, teachers sought to equip their English learners with "transitional skills" for life in the United States and "workplace English," or "what they need to be able to communicate in a stressful game situation." Per Jill, players' status as professionals employed by MLB teams dictated the curriculum they received to a large extent: "They're working for a US organization and . . . [that's what] we have to build around, so we focused a curriculum on baseball phrases, baseball vocabulary." At the Royals' academy, too, the sequence of English topics included terms for baseball equipment, describing the strike zone, and using key baseball verbs correctly in different tenses. Jeff made the point that educators had to "do what the team feels is important"—establishing their value added to the player-development process—before "enlighten[ing]" the front office about other educational goals:

> To have success in this industry and to get the organization to believe in you and what you are attempting to do, teachers have to view their jobs as professional development in nature. Once that is established, then teachers have the freedom to expand their programs to do what they feel is necessary.

Despite this, as Deron pointed out, educators' goals for *peloteros* were not always aligned with the organization's goals for their development. The players' education was the priority for teachers and education coordinators, as you'd expect, but learning English (or completing high school, or gaining technical skills) was not the *reason* players had signed with MLB teams. Because of that, language learning was not the most important form of preparation for prospects. Deron said:

> There's so many kinds of training and preparation they go through, and you know, English is not the main one. It's important, but baseball is the most important thing and the job. They're basically employees. And you try to, you know, push education on them and try to get them to see the importance of education. . . . This is the first time [some] players had an opportunity to learn English. Also the first opportunity for them to work on the computer.

Like the scarcity of time, the realities of player development placed ESL teachers in a difficult position, since language outcomes, on their own, would not be a decisive factor in players' success or failure in the major leagues. Jeff Diskin acknowledged, "I mean, you can make the big leagues without speaking English. You can be a Hall of Famer without speaking English." The Royals' Jorge Guzmán agreed: "There's no denying that there's been plenty of players who have made the major leagues without [strong] English. I think *on* the field—I mean, you see a ball hit, you can throw the ball. It doesn't matter what language you're talking." Because of this, there was a contradiction at the heart of ESL teachers' practice: as a teacher, "you try to push education on them and try to get them to see the importance of education," as Deron put it, knowing that this might be some players' best chance at formal schooling. All the same, the players know perfectly well that their English proficiency will not determine whether they stick in MLB.

Nevertheless, baseball people distinguished between needing English proficiency to make the big leagues—which was not the case—and needing English to "maximize your experience" as a professional ballplayer. As Jorge implied, it's one thing not to need English *on* the field—though many players attested that bilingualism benefited them on the field—but what happens *off* the field is also crucial to players' lives and careers. One answer to "How much

English is enough?" is "None"; another is "More than players are likely to learn by attending required English classes."

In young Latino prospects' initial exposure to English (in Chapter 1), investing in language learning was treated as a dimension of "becoming professional," beyond the practical utility of knowing the language. Subsequently, becoming a *proficient* bilingual was seen as necessary for reaching one's ceiling as a player and person, as opposed to "strictly getting by on your talent." Jeff evoked the examples of Pedro Martínez and David Ortiz, Dominican Hall of Famers who were beloved by American fans and parlayed their iconic standing into second careers as English-language broadcasters:

> I think if you wanna reach your ceiling, it's critically important. . . . I'm not saying you can't make the big leagues. But you're not gonna be Pedro Martínez and David Ortiz sitting on the TV. . . . You're not gonna have any of those opportunities. So if you want to get the most out of the professional baseball playing experience, . . . it's needed. I mean, to help you reach that level.

Jeff contrasted "making the big leagues" with "getting the most out of the professional baseball playing experience," suggesting that while being bilingual wasn't a precondition for the former, it was essential for the latter. At least some players agreed and were proactive in seeking out English. These efforts went beyond "becoming professional"; they involved players' actively beginning to fashion selves, or craft public identities, that might vault them to the legendary status of a Martínez or an Ortiz (Greenblatt, 1980). Kevin Goldstein, formerly of the Astros, singled out star shortstop Carlos Correa, whom the Astros drafted first overall in 2012, as "the most extreme example" of this:

> There are players who are all over it and all in [with learning English]. Like, the most extreme example is probably Carlos Correa. I don't know if you've seen him interviewed but his English is perfect. Correa grew up in Puerto Rico. So when he was in high school, he told his parents, "I'm gonna be a baseball star in America and I need to learn English." And then he got English classes, right?

This seems fundamentally different than learning to align one's verbal behavior with a club's professional expectations through a process of cultural socialization at the academy and in the minor leagues. Correa is indeed an extreme example, though—not just for having the foresight to learn English in high school but because he's an exceptional ballplayer and wasn't deluding himself by thinking he would be a star in MLB. He was also able to gain access to effective English classes while in high school, which isn't the case for all prospects.

"Maximizing one's experience," in Jeff's words, by becoming bilingual, was not just about personal branding or securing one's legacy with an English-speaking fan base. Jeff, Jorge, Michel, and others saw English proficiency as a gateway to stronger relationships with teammates, coaches, and the public. (In Chapter 3, we'll hear from Spanish learners—i.e., L1 English speakers—who talked about Spanish proficiency in remarkably similar terms.) Jorge argued that the team as a whole would not play up to its potential if language barriers kept players from "crossing over" between ethnic and linguistic groups:

> You start to see cliques within the clubhouse. And if there's no crossover, if there's no relationship between those two parties, then I think the team itself doesn't reach its full ceiling. And that's something that probably brings me the most joy is being able to see players connect with each other, relate to each other a little bit.

Michel Gelabert professed that his relationships with coaches had improved considerably since he became comfortable speaking English. This was not, as in Richard Guasch's case, because Michel needed to correct mistaken perceptions of his work ethic but because Michel and his English-speaking coaches were able to communicate in greater depth and about a wider range of topics. While language brokers (interpreters or translators, whether professional or situational) are present in some baseball interactions, a player's day is filled with brief conversational exchanges with coaches and teammates—during a bullpen session, while taking batting practice, on the field, and so on—and there isn't always someone available to interpret. Jeff Diskin framed this as a missed opportunity for both players and coaches: "teachable moments, all those are lost. . . . If you struggle with a bullpen session or a side session, and every answer to the coach is just 'Yes,' that doesn't sit well."

In Michel's experience, learning English opened up new possibilities for short conversations throughout the day, which meant more immediate and detailed feedback on his development as a pitcher:

> I think I [got] to know better my coaches and stuff, because they were talking to me more than just like, "Hey, what's up, man?" or something like that. They're helping me, like, "Oh, what if you do this with your mechanic[s]? Or do this with your arm?" When before, when I was only speaking Spanish, they couldn't tell me that, because I obviously wouldn't understand what they're saying. So now I feel more comfortable and at the same time they feel more comfortable to talk to me about those [things] because they know I will understand what they're saying.

As we have seen, moments of successful bilingual, intercultural communication are not just about getting the referential meaning of an utterance across; they also serve a "phatic" function in that they demonstrate social attentiveness and solidarity (Jakobson, 1960). As Michel attested, they have the potential to transform relationships over time, allowing people to feel more "comfortable" talking to each other and providing a basis to grow and deepen relationships. There were two sides to this dynamic, Richard pointed out: if you can speak English, "they're going to understand you better and feel what you really want to express." Also, he said, speaking English "looks a lot better"—*se ve mucho mejor*—than having to rely on an interpreter.

Nevertheless, Michel's and Richard's cases also bring up a problematic dimension of intercultural communication in the United States: the onus is almost always on Spanish speakers to make English speakers comfortable and not the other way around.[10] (The situation is a bit different with Korean and Japanese speakers in MLB, who are fewer in number and generally come later in their careers, rather than signing with a US team as teenagers.) The next chapter discusses this issue at greater length and features the exceptions to the rule: namely, L1 English speakers in MLB organizations who have become proficient in Spanish.

The Ritual of the Postgame Interview

As Bobby Puason and I wrapped up the conversation recounted in Chapter 1, Luis Victoria interjected to confirm that Bobby had recently done his first postgame interview in English at the A's Stockton (California) affiliate. It was evident that Bobby took pride in what must have been a giant step toward "becoming professional": demonstrating symbolic competence in a "platform event," one in which an individual addresses a large audience (Goffman, 1983). Conducting postgame interviews in English emerged as a benchmark of Spanish-speaking players' acculturation and language socialization in the eyes of team personnel. Again, it wasn't so much about the meaning of the words; postgame interviews tend to be light on content, in any case. Rather, a Spanish-speaking player who took the risk of speaking English publicly "in front of the camera" was making a visible effort to be "endearing" (Jorge's term) to fans and showing his commitment to building a relationship with the community.

The Royals sought to drill the value of English interviews into their Dominican academy prospects. "What type of relationship are you gonna have with the fans at the big-league level if you're always using an interpreter?" Jeff asked rhetorically.

Even so, the team recognized that they couldn't expect a second-language speaker to embrace the postgame spotlight right away. Jeff remarked, "There's a lot of native English speakers who don't like giving interviews to the public" (in English). To assist in this process, the Royals had started interviewing their academy players after games in the DR in Spanish and posting the interviews on the team's social media channels. This had the advantage of "giv[ing] them as many interview opportunities as possible" to address "the public speaking part," if not the English part, as well as allowing family members in Venezuela and farther afield in the DR to stay in touch with the players.

Still, the Royals felt strongly as an organization that their Latin American players should be able to use English to connect with English-speaking audiences. At the academy, I reviewed electronic books that the Royals' educational staff had created with a variety of English resources and information about life in the United States. One of the books had links to videos of Spanish-speaking major leaguers (e.g., Venezuela's Miguel Cabrera) giving interviews in English as a model and a form of encouragement for the prospects. The ritual of the postgame interview was another area in which educational staff brought up the tension between providing *enough* linguistic support, so that players could develop and thrive, and providing *too much* support, which was perceived to stunt players' development by making them less apt to take initiative. (Recall Luis Victoria's comment about not wanting to be a "safety net" and Zak Basch's contention that "the biggest cultural challenge" of his job was knowing how much to support players, both in Chapter 1.)

Similarly, Jeff expressed that interpretation could become a "crutch" for Spanish-speaking players who, though capable, were reluctant to use the English training they'd received, especially in highly visible and public situations, and sometimes needed additional prodding from the organization to do so. He brought up the examples of Carlos Hernández and Emmanuel Rivera, from Venezuela and Puerto Rico, respectively, who had made their major league debuts with the Royals in 2021:

> Their initial postgame interviews were all in Spanish, all being translated. And the Royals weren't happy with that. So if you watch their succeeding interviews, you'll see the more effort they did for English, like maybe the translator might translate the question, but the answer comes back in all English. Instead of just doing everything through the translator.
>
> So both players grew in that area just based on the expectations that were placed on 'em by the organization. . . . Put faith in the training that you've had. Put faith in the process. . . . And sometimes, they didn't need even need the translator to,

to translate the question once they were in tune to the interview. Sometimes they did, if they needed help with a word, but they took ownership of the interview.

Language socialization, however, is a winding road, not a one-way street. With Jeff's comments in mind, I noticed Hernández relying on an interpreter in postgame interviews in 2022. It may have been significant that English-speaking journalists were often asking the young pitcher to account for his early-season struggles with control and run suppression, which might have raised his "affective filter"—put differently, his frustration and embarrassment could have interfered with his verbal performance.

It was not the case that players attempted postgame interviews in their second language only because of pressure or encouragement from the team. As Richard's and Michel's examples suggest, many players aspired to be able to function in conversational situations and platform events without the support of an interpreter. Especially as they contemplated long-term futures abroad, players who had initially relied on bilingual teammates or professional interpreters to mediate their interactions with coaches, teammates, or journalists began to chafe at their linguistic limitations. During Michel's time with the Diamondbacks' low-A affiliate in Hillsboro, Oregon—prior to his pandemic-driven English submersion—the manager was Venezuelan, but the pitching coach was an English monolingual from the United States. "Another Latin guy who knew English" translated for Michel and the other Spanish-speaking pitchers, but, Michel said:

> At some point, I was like, "I don't wanna [have] somebody translat[ing] me all the time." For example, if I got an interview, I don't want someone tell[ing] me like, "Oh, they say this, this, and this." I was like, "I wanna do it myself."

In the English classroom at the Royals' spring training facility in Surprise, Arizona, I saw a bulletin board with written testimonials from program graduates, including Dominican shortstop Adalberto Mondesi, who marveled, "Nobody has to translate for me. That is an advantage in baseball. And I am now giving interviews on my own, in front of the camera and everything."[11]

As we will see in Chapter 4, L1 English speakers in Taiwan and South Korea spoke in similar terms about interpreter-mediated interactions, balancing their respect for interpreters' essential role with the desire to interact directly with others in their L2. In "Conclusion," I'll examine Japanese speakers' subversive efforts to poke fun at the conventions of the postgame interview and, in so doing, to call attention to the absurdity of holding bilingual players to a monolingual standard. The remainder of this chapter, however, focuses on the role of bilingualism in the "afterlives" of Latin American prospects—that is, the majority who will not go on to long, lucrative careers in the United States.

"I Have Friends Who Call Me a Fake Cuban": Contact-Induced Change in Baseball Spanish

As Spanish-speaking ballplayers began learning English, they were simultaneously being socialized into a new *Spanish* ecology, which concentrated Spanish varieties from North, Central, and South America, as well as the Caribbean, in MLB settings. Like Spanish-speaking residents of other diverse communities in the United States, Latin American players in MLB had to deal with two interrelated forms of "contact-induced language change"—that is, change over time because of contact between speakers of different languages or varieties (Erker & Otheguy, 2016). Some changes to individuals' Spanish came about because of contact between English and Spanish, while others stemmed from contact between different regional varieties of Spanish.

English-Spanish contact was visible in the large number of English loanwords and borrowings in *peloteros'* Spanish—*dagaut* (dugout), *picheo rompiente* (breaking ball), *eswingeando* (swinging), and *bateador* (batter), to give just a few examples attested in my notes.[12] This is a common feature of "baseball talk" in other languages—Japanese, for example—where early promulgation of the game by US educators led to widespread borrowing of English terms.

More interesting, in my view, were individual players' perceptions that contact between different Spanish dialects was changing the way they spoke. This was especially true of players like Michel and Richard, who, as Cubans, were outnumbered by Dominicans and Venezuelans and therefore interacted mostly with non-Cuban Spanish speakers. The outcome, Michel said, laughing, was that he "didn't speak Cuban" anymore. His two-year stay in the Dominican Republic prior to signing with the Diamondbacks and his encounters with speakers of Mexican and Venezuelan Spanish (as well as Dominicans) in the United States had led him to "combine everything" into a mishmash of dialects:

> Because I've been a long time in [the] Dominican and I've been knowing a lot of [guys] from Venezuela, Mexico. And I've been getting all the stuff they say, like *todas las palabras de ellos y cosas así, todo se me ha apegado* [All of their words and stuff like that, it's all stuck to me], it [sticks] in my head. So I combine everything.

Broadly speaking, Michel's account squares with what sociolinguists have discovered about Spanish dialect contact in the United States: that sustained contact has resulted in "diminished regional differentiation," such that speakers of smaller or less "prestigious" dialects will tend to share more features, over time, with speakers of locally dominant or prestigious dialects (Erker & Otheguy, 2016). As with just about everything related to language, it's not that simple. For one, appealing to community-wide trends of "dialect leveling"—the process by which regional differences get "ironed out"—does not imply that individual speakers will behave in a uniform manner (Erker, 2018). It's also challenging to separate the effects of English contact from the effects of contact between different Spanish varieties.

I asked Michel what his mother, still in Cuba, said when they talked on the phone:

> *Que ya no me reconoce,* that she doesn't recognize me [anymore]. She tells me, everything's changed—your voice, or like, your accent, is completely changing. If I were in Florida, it would be different. Here [in Arizona], you don't see Cubans. In Florida, you see Cubans all over the place, so the accent sticks with you.[13]

On a personal note, I've gotten similar reactions from family members in the Northeast United States, where I grew up, about unfamiliar regional features in my English, no doubt because I've spent most of my adult life in Texas and Arizona. However, in the context of semipermanent exile from Cuba and his growing linguistic distance from his mother, I wondered if the attrition of Michel's Cuban Spanish bothered him. He responded without hesitation: "No, on the contrary. I feel good because I'm learning. I like to learn. I'm learning from the other accents, the other countries. It makes me special." Michel added that if he went to Mexico or returned to the Dominican Republic in the future, he would be able to fit in seamlessly due to his familiarity with those Spanish varieties. I had thought that Cubans and other speakers of less common varieties in MLB might experience linguistic homesickness as they converged with the Dominican majority. Michel and Richard Guasch, however, both saw their ease with different Spanish dialects, like their English proficiency, as a cosmopolitan tool for pursuing opportunities across borders.

For Richard, changing the way he spoke Spanish, like learning English, was "*un proceso de adaptarte a la vida*" (a process of adapting yourself to life). One might speculate that Cuban *peloteros'* need for exceptional "adaptability," in order to chase professional success in other countries, had contributed to their appreciation of linguistic flexibility at the expense of "authentic" speech. Like Michel, Richard affirmed that his time in the DR and with Dominican teammates in the United States had shaped his Spanish—so much, in fact, that he was often mistaken for a Dominican:

> I speak more like a Dominican. In a lot of settings, they think I'm Dominican. . . . I even have friends who call me a fake Cuban because they say that I don't talk like a Cuban, that I'm Dominican. So that does make you change a little, and besides, Cubans spend a lot of time here in the Dominican before signing. If we spend it together with Dominicans, well, the dialect that sticks to us the most is the Dominican one.[14]

Being called a fake Cuban sounded hurtful, but Richard strenuously denied that the change in his Spanish bothered him: "*No, no, no, para nada*" (in no way). He saw language change over the life span as a natural process, rather than something that discredited him as a Cuban, whatever his friends might say. From Richard's perspective, "if we spend [a lot of time] together with Dominicans," it stood to reason that Dominican features would "stick to" speakers of Cuban Spanish.

Even so, dialect differences were a popular topic of conversation among Latin American ballplayers. Some of this took the predictable form of metacommentary—talk about talk—on salient dialect features like "accent" or phonological differences, and differences in vocabulary or the lexicon (Rymes, 2014). As Michel put it, "We don't fight, but we argue about . . . which [word] is right." In Chapter 3, we'll hear similar stories from L2 Spanish speakers (i.e., native English speakers) about encountering new Spanish varieties in MLB and, like non-Dominican L1 Spanish speakers, adjusting their own speech in response.

Richard contended that speaking more like a Dominican and less like a Cuban did not bother him, but he also said that the superficial linguistic resemblance among Latin American players—that is, they all spoke Spanish—concealed weightier social and cultural differences, which could surface in tense moments:

> In spite of the fact that we're part of the same language, there's different personalities and different perspectives. Many times, the Dominican tells the Venezuelan, "No, like, that's bad, in Venezuela they're hungry," that kind of thing, and the same thing with Cubans. "No, they make it all easy for you Cubans. And all you Cubans do this and we don't—why?" And the same thing with the Mexicans, the Colombians.

In Richard's account, Dominican teammates were not bringing up cultural difference in a nonjudgmental way. Rather, the Dominicans were appealing to conditions in players' home countries (e.g., the economic abyss of Venezuela) or differential treatment of players in the US immigration system (such as the special rules that apply to Cubans) to confront non-Dominicans about their "perspectives." Encounters with different Spanish varieties evoked the uneven political and economic landscape of the Americas, within which Dominicans, Cubans, Venezuelans, and others were positioned differently and did not have access to the same opportunities. Players' awareness of this uneven landscape, then, led them to connect dialect differences to different social personae, or "types" of people, allowing Richard's imaginary Dominican to make the leap from "[The US government] make[s] it easy for *all you Cubans*" to "*All you Cubans* do this"—linguistically, I took him to mean—"and we don't" (Agha, 2005). Connections between language learning, language use, and socioeconomic factors surface in slightly different form in Chapter 3, in English-speaking players' and coaches' discourse about the high stakes of professional success for Latino *peloteros*.

Tellingly, when Richard voiced the Dominican player in the previous excerpt, he did so in a stylized Dominican accent that was audibly distinct from the rest of his utterances (Coupland, 2001). (You can hear me chuckling breathily on the recording as he slips into his Dominican voice.) Richard's Spanish might indeed have changed, but his use of Dominican Spanish to narrate negative talk about non-Dominicans implied, to me, that linguistic differences remained relevant to persistent social divisions among Latin American players in MLB.

"What Happens When You Go Home?": Confronting the Economics of Transnational Baseball in English Education

The apparently trivial example of changing WhatsApp numbers among Venezuelans and widespread talk about the educational deficits of Dominican players (both in Chapter 1) are examples of how the economics of transnational professional baseball make their presence felt in discussions of language diversity. The deeper I dug into the dynamics of English learning and bilingualism among minor league players, the harder it became to ignore the socioeconomic dimensions of Latino players' English learning and the ways that language was, and was not, treated as a form of social capital (Bourdieu, 1991). The perspectives of English educators from the low minors and players who have been through the system provide a sober contrast to the triumphant stories that opened this chapter.

In 2015, Eric Johnson's second year moonlighting as an ESL teacher for the short-season A level Tri-City Dust Devils of Pasco, Washington, the team's affiliation switched from the Colorado Rockies to the San Diego Padres, bringing a new group of players and staffers and a larger ESL class—fifteen or twenty students, compared to the six from the previous year. The class, to Eric's relief, was moved to an air-conditioned lounge adjoining the locker room and was no longer held in the claustrophobic, stinky, "hundred and five degrees and sweating" press box.

Eric described the personality of the class as "rugged." It included players from Venezuela, Mexico, and Panama, in addition to the Dominican Republic, and their professional competitiveness carried over to the ESL class in ways that were not always helpful from the teacher's perspective. Players would sometimes ridicule each other for not knowing answers—Eric paraphrased: "How do you not know? *Pendejo, cabrón!* [fucking idiot]"—leading, on one occasion, to Eric's having to break up a physical fight. Staffers also contributed to the atmosphere of merciless competition. Eric recalled a Spanish-speaking coach who was shadowing a player deemed to need supervision, for some reason, and was "chastising the guy"—"*Ay, pendejo! ¿Por qué pusiste eso?*" (Oh, you idiot! Why'd you put that?)—because the player had written something in Spanish instead of English, a scaffolding strategy Eric had encouraged the class to use.

Johan Febrillet also commented that it took a good deal of work to teach players to support each other's learning in class, rather than making fun of others' mistakes. I observed a "competitive" lesson at the Royals' Dominican academy where two prospects were quizzing each other on English food vocabulary. When a player missed a word, Johan repeatedly prodded the pair to help each other by reteaching new vocabulary during the quiz game as necessary—a simple but seemingly effective way of ensuring that competition wouldn't lead to hard feelings.

To Eric, the rigidity of schedules and expectations, including expectations for English learning, seemed "militaristic" in a way that evoked *Learning to Labor*, Paul Willis's classic account of working-class youth's socialization in UK schools (Willis, 2017; Klein, 2014):

> It reminded me of that, where they're just being channeled into this system where that's just how it is. Like, "I'm an idiot. I have to pass this test to get out of this so I can go be the next Robinson Canó."[15]

Eric's comment about the players' needing to "pass this test to get out of this" suggests that the "rugged" character of the class wasn't just because of the individual players and coaches who were involved. A deeper issue, and one that Eric was never able to resolve to his satisfaction, was that the participants had profoundly different understandings of what the point of the class was. This was not so much indicative of the circumstances surrounding the class itself as it was of a broader disjuncture, verging on incomprehensibility, of the purpose and place of English learning in Latin American ballplayers' professional socialization. Eric described the second year's class:

> Guys that were being *made* to [be] in this class who didn't want to be there [laughs]. They would rather be sleeping or eating.... They weren't disrespectful. I'm just saying, the notion that it was a service and that [the organization was] trying to help them—that wasn't communicated to them. It was like, "No, there's a test you gotta pass and take this class to pass that test."

Eric, an expert bilingual educator, quickly abandoned the teaching materials he was provided by the Rockies in the first year, likening them to "an elementary ESL curriculum from the eighties—like, 'This is a grape, this is an apple.'" Instead, he searched for ways to make English relevant to his students and began attending games and snapping photos of the players in action, which he then used as in-class conversation prompts. For example, a photo might be used to elicit talk about injuries, leading into vocabulary and sentence frames related to body parts and the medical professions.

In confronting disparate beliefs about the purpose of English learning, Eric found himself increasingly troubled by what he called the "manufacturing mentality" of international scouting and player development, or the "global commodity chain" of baseball, as Alan Klein called it (Klein, 2014). Knowing that very few of the young Latino players were likely to make it to the major leagues, he started to incorporate discussions about their life chances into the ESL class, using media commentaries and face-to-face encounters to prompt critical reflection on their futures in light of the economics of transnational baseball. Eric spoke of "the allure of money" for Latino ballplayers who leave home and dedicate themselves to baseball at a young age. The allure of money is also connected to transnational athletes' masculinity—namely, their "ability to provide for others" in its extreme form: "the fantasy of redistributing untold wealth," recirculated in the stories about Dominican superstars, like Pedro Martínez, whose prosperity transformed their hometowns (Besnier, 2015, pp. 851–2; Klein, 2014). Eric didn't necessarily disapprove of his students' choices, but he worried about what awaited those who wouldn't make it and didn't have a backup plan.

In the ESL class, then, he encouraged the minor leaguers to think carefully about their "social location" within professional baseball—that is, how their and others' lives had been shaped by power and privilege and what those dynamics might entail for their outcomes down the road. For example, Eric's students did not believe him when he told them that most American families wouldn't allow their children to leave school, even for a $1 million signing bonus:

> I said, "Here, parents wouldn't let their kids leave high school to go pursue a career in sports. Like, you wait till you're *done* graduating and even more, like, you go to college." And they were like, "No way! If you offered a kid a million dollars, they would do it." And I said, "Okay, your homework is to go home and talk to your host families[16] and ask them: Would they let their son or daughter leave home at fifteen years old for a million dollars to go train to potentially be a pro athlete?"
>
> The next day, I asked, "Okay, *qué dijeron?* What'd you find out?" And they're all just like, "We have no idea. They all said no." And I was like, "Well, why do you think?" They didn't really understand. And I was like, "Yeah. A million dollars when you're fifteen is gone by the time you're twenty."

While Eric had previously taken the *peloteros* to local elementary schools, he started looking for ways to make higher education beyond baseball seem realer and possibly more attainable to his students. Near the end of the 2015 season, Eric decided to take his Dust Devils ESL students to Washington State University-Tri Cities in Richland, where he also taught, to give them a chance to interact with bilingual/ESL education students at WSU. The team's manager was resistant to the idea, since the timing of the campus visit would interfere with the minor leaguers' schedule for the day, but Eric "worked [his] relationships" with the Dust Devils staff, including the third base coach, to secure the manager's permission.

The players were excited, to put it mildly, to spend time on a university campus: "The guys were like, *duded up*, man. Popped collars, bright white shoes, smelling like a perfume factory. It was just awesome." They stuck out among the female preservice teachers in the Intro to ESL class—in the photo of the event, "it's very easy to tell who is a baseball player"—but the result was "one of the coolest moments I've ever had as a teacher, K[indergarten] through doctorate," Eric said. The WSU students and Dust Devils went through five-minute conversational rotations, so that all the ballplayers and college students got to meet each other. Eric and the *peloteros* then dropped by an advanced Spanish grammar class for heritage speakers, where the ballplayers and Spanish-speaking students connected on a personal level: "The [WSU students'] questions were like, 'How do you contact your family?' or 'Do you miss your family?' And the guys were almost in *tears* up there"[17] (Figure 16).

Figure 16 Elvin Liriano and a Tri-City Dust Devils teammate converse with Washington State University students on a campus visit during the 2015 season (Eric Johnson). Reproduced with permission of Eric Johnson.

As they were preparing to head back to the stadium, the players spotted the campus recreation center and asked Eric if they could stop in to buy soda. A quick soda stop turned into an extended session of pool playing, "rapping," and flirting with WSU students. Eric knew they would be late getting back for batting practice and that there was a game later in the evening, but he didn't have the heart to cut their visit short. Watching the players hang out with college students in the rec center, he thought:

> This is the first time that these guys have gotten to be kids, like twenty-year-old guys, you know? They're not baseball players, they're just young adults, in with this mix of [students]—I don't even know if they *told* them they were baseball players.

For a little while, as Eric saw it, the *peloteros* had a break from "the pressure of all of this"—that is, the pressure of having to succeed at all costs—and could imagine themselves in the college students' shoes: "At least those guys [had] the chance to experience for one day what it was like." Upon arriving at the Dust Devils' stadium, Eric had to deal with the manager, who was "super furious" that the players had stayed at WSU for longer than planned. Despite the success of the campus visit, the manager's reaction "left a sour taste in [Eric's] mouth" and from his perspective was emblematic of the "exploitation" of young Dominicans in professional baseball. The team gave the impression they were only valued as ballplayers, not the "twenty-year-old guys" they were allowed to be on campus.

On another occasion, during class, Eric directed the ESL students' attention to their US-born teammates in the nearby locker room:

> I was like, "What do you see your *compañero gringos* (American buddies) over there wearing?" One dude had a University of Arizona sweatshirt; another guy had a Tennessee baseball cap on. I go, "Those are universities . . . . Those guys went to university. On a scholarship. They got a degree, and so when their career's over here, they have a pathway for success and getting a job and having a normal life." And I go, "For you guys, what happens when you go home?"

But "going home" under those circumstances was unthinkable for young athletes whose *potencia* and determination had already taken them far beyond where most of their peers had ended up. This was, in part, a function of mental skills and toughness, without which professional success would be impossible. There may also have been some magical thinking involved. Baseball players can be a deeply superstitious bunch, owing to the inherent "risk and uncertainty in pitching and hitting," and mentioning the elephant in the room—that not everyone would make it—may have been seen as tantamount to inviting catastrophe (Gmelch, 1992).

> I played an excerpt from . . . the [National Public Radio] show that gave a statistic of like one out of a hundred Dominicans actually makes it to the major leagues, and . . . we worked on the math of all that, and I said, "Okay, of all of you here—there's twenty of you—let's say, you know, one only one of you makes it, like, who's gonna be the one to make it?" And . . . of course, they all raise their hands . . . [laughs]. Okay. I go, "What are you going to do if you *don't* make it"?

While the players were reluctant even to entertain the possibility that they might not make it, they all acknowledged that they had friends who "had come and gone through the system and didn't make it," leading Eric to push further: "So what happened, what are they doing now?" A "very religious" and disciplined student named Elvin who "never swore" and acted as a peacemaker in the classroom spoke up: "*¡Mira, maestro, solo hay dos opciones!*"—Look, teacher, there are only two options. "*Calchar*"—drive a motorcycle taxi—"*y la otra*"—and the other option? He looked at Eric and mimed a handgun. Eric remembered: "Dude, it was a grave moment in that room. And they're all like [silently nodding]."

It was, of course, a moment of gross hyperbole, notwithstanding Elvin's teammates' somber reaction. Still, during my admittedly brief time in the Dominican Republic, it was hard to ignore the myriad ways in which baseball intersected with the economic life of the country—not just the "magicians," as the educators called the groundskeepers, kitchen crew, and cleaning staff at the Royals' academy (since they provided the often-invisible labor that allowed the players to focus on training), but, for example, a large crowd of laborers in yellow hard hats waiting for the *guagua* (bus) outside the Miami Marlins' new academy, under construction at the time of my visit. Many of the coaches at the Royals' academy were former players with dashed professional hopes. I heard stories of Dominicans who ended up elsewhere, like a group of coaches recruited to work at a new baseball training facility in Kuwait—skilled guest workers pulled into someone's passion project, half a world away.

As I was writing this chapter, MLB owners and the players association were debating the merits of an international draft as part of a new collective bargaining agreement, with many Dominican players arguing that a draft would "kill baseball" in the DR by taking away prospects' rights to negotiate with teams, despite the well-documented issues with the current system (see Chapter 1). Legendary Dominican slugger David Ortiz framed the issue in terms that recalled Elvin's words to Eric above, as well as Jill's comment about the potentially "life-changing" consequences of baseball success for Latin Americans: "Baseball is one of the secret weapons of the Dominican economy. If you talk about a draft here in the States, you have choices . . . . [The] Dominican has baseball to make your way out. That's it. You have to be careful."[18]

Linguists often talk about people's investment in language learning in terms of "imagined futures": in other words, what kind of future are people imagining for themselves when they decide to invest time and resources in learning a language? What communities do they envision being a part of in this imagined future? (Kanno & Norton, 2003; Pennycook, 2001). For Eric's students and other minor leaguers who are "good enough to dream," to borrow Roger Kahn's phrase, imagining a future that did not involve a successful career in professional baseball was taboo (Kahn, 1986). It was incompatible with the "failure-is-not-an-option" mindset that Eric so admired in them. There was simply too much at stake.

Not everyone endorsed Eric's approach. Jill, for example, who worked with many players in several MLB organizations and coordinated education programs and staff, found it counterproductive to focus on the possibility of failure in her English classes. She admitted that she and other teachers were aware of the statistics Eric cited. However, she emphasized the transferable skills that *peloteros* were learning in English class, which she hoped they would be able to use in their personal and professional lives after baseball:

> Speaking to them directly and saying, "So, you know, only seven or eight percent of you are going to make it". . . . You know, we don't have those conversations, and I tried to remind instructors not to do that. We know that on the back end, but it's not something that we want to bring up. What we want to bring up is their ability to use technology, on a personal and professional level. What we want to bring up is how they've learned all of these new skills through English that they can apply in their daily life.

Nevertheless, as Elvin's intervention suggested, players understood that many, if not all of them, would have to confront such a future, whether or not they were eager to contemplate it in the present. In the globalized labor market, professional sports are unique in that "workers, and more specifically their bodies, can be bought and sold—and, as soon as the body's performance begins to decline, unceremoniously let go of" (Besnier, 2015). That looming eventuality came up repeatedly—not just in conversations with players, but with the development staff and teachers who wanted to make sure players could make the best of whatever future awaited them.

"Ninety Percent of Latinos Don't Think about a Plan B": The Reality of Release

Elvin Liriano, now twenty-nine and back in the Dominican Republic, a world away from Pasco, Washington, remembers the day in 2017 he was released by the San Diego Padres in vivid detail. The possibility of release shadowed Elvin's career, even as he drew closer to the big-league success he'd worked so hard to achieve. For Elvin, as for many other young *peloteros*, release was an existential issue, not just an economic one. When you've dedicated your life to a single goal from the age of eleven or twelve and you're released, who are you?

> I put a lot of pressure on myself because I would say, "What am I going to do if they release me? What am I going to do?" Because for the Latino, normally . . . plan number one is baseball. That's how the majority of us think. Ninety percent of Latinos don't think about a plan B. "Well, if they let me go and I can't play

baseball anymore, I'm going to dedicate myself to my studies. I'm gonna become a good lawyer or a good doctor, a good engineer." Ninety percent of Latinos don't think like that. Hey, you're already a professional. The goal is to play in the major leagues. So . . . when I saw the situation, that it was possible that they would release me, then I'm living with that fear. What am I gonna do if they let me go?

I was surprised to hear Elvin speak in such absolute terms about not being able to imagine a future beyond baseball. He told me that his late mother had valued education highly, insisting that Elvin finish high school before signing with the Padres—an unusual expectation, based on what I heard from teachers like Eric and Johan.

Still, Elvin understood that the worst-case scenario might come to pass, based on an earlier conversation with the Padres' minor league director during spring training, in which Elvin had asked about the team's plans for him and was told, "Honestly, we don't know where we're going to put you this year." On hearing this discouraging news, Elvin realized, "there's a good possibility that they're going to let me go. . . . But I didn't hang my head, I didn't give up. I stayed strong." Soon after, the unimaginable happened:

> I remember that one Sunday. . . . I arrived very early; I always arrived early at the stadium. I remember that [when] I arrived, they called me to the office. Nobody else was there. Just a friend and me . . . . And they released me. I remember that I went back to the clubhouse. I took all my gear. And I said, wow. I went to the training room, said goodbye to the trainers . . . . I really didn't understand the magnitude of their appreciation for me, because I was always very disciplined. . . . I felt like they felt, the sadness I felt seeing the decision they had made to let me go. I said goodbye, hugged everybody, and when I'd packed everything, I grabbed my gear and headed out the door. Wow. What a moment.
>
> I remember that when I was heading out the door, I remembered everything, back to the first day when they signed me. I lasted almost seven years with the organization. . . . I gave it seven years of my life. And then I remember that my eyes filled with tears and I just said, wow. . . . I went home and I didn't delay. I said, "Ok, they released me. I know that I can. I know that I have the ability. I'm going to keep playing."

When we spoke, Elvin had just finished throwing a live batting practice session, hitting ninety-five miles per hour with his fastball. "*Como yo tengo mi brazo ahora, si yo tuviera cuando estaba en San Diego*"—"If I had my arm like it is now when I was with San Diego," he told me, grinning, "I'd be in the major leagues. . . . *Pero todo pasa por una razón.*" Everything happens for a reason.

I sought out Elvin because I wanted to hear directly from players about what it was like to be released, what awaited them post-MLB, and whether their English education had benefited them after baseball. Speaking of Dominican *compañeros* who, like him, had been released, Elvin sketched out several post-baseball trajectories: the majority of released players, he said, tried to stay in the United States, establishing themselves where family members were living and looking for work. He did not bring up the fact that without employment in an MLB organization, Dominicans become undocumented and must deal with the many challenges of being an unauthorized immigrant in the United States, including the perennial threat of deportation (Brotherton & Barrios, 2011; Golash-Boza, 2017).

Others, said Elvin, "know that they have talent," and with sufficient "*motivación y fe*"—motivation and faith—return to the DR to continue training and, in time, "get another opportunity with an independent league or return to organized baseball."[19] Finally, Elvin admitted, other *peloteros* found themselves in the position of "crawling back to the Dominican" (*vuelven gateando a la Dominicana*) and, feeling they'd been taking advantage of, were too discouraged to make progress, with or without baseball:

> Sadly, I have a friend, and I've tried on a number of occasions to call him, motivate him, tell him, "Hey, you've got a lot of tools, lots of possibilities to keep playing. Don't give up!" .... I tell him, "Let's keep moving forward!" And sometimes there are many [players] who feel like they've been deceived.

Elvin was in the second group; he believed in his talent, and baseball dreams die hard. The Padres had asked if he was interested in becoming a pitching coach, but, at present, he was maintaining "*el enfoque en el béisbol cien por ciento*"—100 percent focus on playing baseball. He was training with a group of younger players who were hoping to be signed, staying in shape and staying alert for professional opportunities, and patching together resources from various short-term baseball contracts to support himself and his family: "What I do is—intelligently—when I get a contract to play in an independent league or play winter ball, I try to save up a bunch so that when I'm here at home, I can support myself." Like many baseball lifers who never truly "make it," a look at Elvin's player page since his release tells the story of an itinerant career—stints with the Southern Illinois Miners, the Napa (California) Silverados, and the San Rafael (California) Pacifics, all US independent league teams, as well as a brief appearance with Panama in the 2021–22 Caribbean Series. It can't have been easy, especially with a young son, six years old at the time of our conversation.

I recounted Elvin's story to a friend who played college and Minor League Baseball and understands the "ticking clock" for professional success all too well. My friend remarked that at twenty-nine, Elvin was getting "long in the tooth" for an aspiring player. In talking with Elvin, I couldn't tell how long he thought he could keep the dream alive. I asked him if he thought that his English competence—"I focused a lot in [English] class," he told me—would benefit him in the future, and he mused about the possibility that, as a bilingual pitching coach, he might be able to work abroad:

> [English] will be able to help me, among other things- maybe in the future I decide to become a pitching coach. They give me the opportunity and maybe because of the level of English I have, I can develop myself more. They can send me to the United States.

For the time being, though, he was sticking with plan A—training, staying in shape, maintaining his newfound arm strength and velocity, reading the Bible, taking care of his son, and waiting for another opportunity to take the mound.

Language and Life after Baseball

Some staffers, like Juan Mosquera, the A's international scout for Latin America, were optimistic that teams' educational efforts, including English learning, might benefit players in the long term, even those returning to their home countries, and might also have a ripple effect on what Juan called the "educational base" in poorer countries:

> The truth is that at the end of the day, it's an impact, because for [all] the potential [that exists] in Latin America—as in the case of the Dominican [Republic] . . . a country that's lacking that . . . educational base. Today they're studying a little more, and I think that for the Dominican ballplayer, it's going to have a much greater impact five years in the future because . . . I'm seeing a phenomenon, for two years now, that they're already helping talented players a little more. [Our] people are grabbing them and getting them to study—"Look, this is A and B, this is one, two, three."

Juan expected that MLB teams' investments in players' education would bear fruit in a higher standard of education for the Dominican Republic, and it's possible that increased attention to English classes and high school completion could prepare young Dominicans (and others) to have a broader impact on local education systems.

However, not everyone I spoke with had such a sanguine view of players' educational development. Teachers who had been in the classroom with Latino prospects were often concerned about how the players' long-term commitment to baseball could ultimately have negative effects on them and their communities. This did not come across as cynicism about players' chances of "making it"—or the entire process of player development, for that matter—so much as cold-eyed awareness of the long odds facing players and the existential question that Elvin raised previously. Deron Dolphus, who went from teaching English for the Marlins to teaching in a non-baseball-affiliated Dominican school, commented:

> It hurts the community because these kids, they spent their entire life trying to get into MLB and then you tell them, okay, you're not a baseball player anymore . . . and they work their entire lives for this. So when they come back to the [DR], they don't have any skill sets. 'Cause all they know is baseball.

DR-based educational staff took umbrage at this characterization of prospects' education, which they described as a misconception or an outdated view of pro academies as obsessed with youth's athletic development at the expense of everything else. This, in the view of many MLB personnel, was a stereotype about academy life that they had worked to change. They had a point; I saw ample evidence of staff's tireless efforts to carve out time for English education from the prospects' packed daily schedules and to steer players into high school completion and technology courses, which they hoped would pay dividends down the road, within or beyond baseball.

Even educational personnel from supportive MLB organizations acknowledged that their efforts to secure different routes to social and economic success for players went against the grain of what was valued in player development. Jeff Diskin commented that while the Royals had not discouraged his efforts, neither were they overly concerned with them: "They're not coming to me like, 'Hey, the Mets had twenty-five high school graduates!'" The organization's success did not hinge on Latino prospects' educational outcomes but their on-field performance. Thus, anything that did not contribute directly to their development as baseball players was not a primary concern for the front office. Put more colorfully, the educational team was "never gonna win a pissing match" with the player-development staff, if it came to that.

Many of the Spanish-speaking players I talked to had only a vague sense of how English would benefit them if they didn't make it in MLB. Yosmi Fernández (see Chapter 1) voiced the common belief that English would be helpful simply because "it's everywhere." Michel, who was married to an American citizen and could stay in the United States if he wished, mentioned the possibility of becoming a bilingual coach (like Elvin) and assumed that he would have more job opportunities because of English. Richard thought he might pursue a career as a bilingual broadcaster, and as a devout Christian, he dreamed of being able to share his faith in English as well as Spanish. Others envisioned using English to travel; a prospect at the Royals' academy whose father had played in the major leagues excitedly told me about the cities he'd visited as a child and said he wanted to return to the United States to see "the big TV," as he put it, in Times Square.

Deron spoke of what he termed a "needed change" in MLB teams' approach to player development, which went beyond players' education at Dominican academies to "provid[ing] job training for the players who don't make it."

> Ninety percent or more of these players are not going to make it . . . and they need to have a fallback plan and use that English in order to get jobs . . . whether it's in the United States or in the Dominican Republic. I think that's something that's missing, that we've been trying to fight for, to get teams to invest into education for players, as far as college education or job training, to use those English skills to prepare them for a job.

While he was with the Marlins, Deron said, he had participated in a conference with multiple teams about how to prepare players better for life after baseball. As he saw it, however, the Dominican government ought to apply pressure to MLB organizations to devote more resources to *peloteros'* education and skill development so that players like Elvin's friends wouldn't feel that they'd been "deceived" through the process. Not every team took their educational responsibilities as seriously as the Royals seemed to do, in Deron's experience:

> I think it's something that the Dominican Republic, as a country, needs to push the MLB teams to do more because the MLB teams are in the country. They basically have businesses in the country. If the country says, "Okay, if you wanna have your schools here to recruit our baseball players, we need you to provide a high school program for the players."

Following the virtual high school completion program, Jeff and his staff had steered a select handful of released but academically promising players to small colleges in the United States, where they were able to play baseball while working toward their degrees. During my time at the academy, the staff was thrilled to receive news that one such player, who had recently graduated from Mid-America Christian University in Oklahoma City on a baseball scholarship, had been hired as another MLB team's education coordinator.[20] But Jeff realized that this was not a realistic goal for many of the team's academy prospects, and he was troubled by the absence of a structured program for released players in the DR.[21]

In our first conversation, Jeff identified "career transitions" as one of the educational staff's top priorities for the coming year, acknowledging that the team's efforts had been limited but affirming that they were committed to making progress in this area. He thought that the players' English proficiency, even if limited, and the computer skills they acquired in academy classes would give them an advantage in the Dominican labor market. Furthermore, he was convinced that ex-*peloteros* would be attractive to Dominican employers because of what they had learned on the field: "Even in the States, a lot of companies like to hire athletes because of the competitiveness, the accountability, the discipline."

In the past, the team had experimented with training players for jobs in tourism and the service industry. Recently, however, Jeff had turned his focus to Dominican *zona francas*, or special economic zones where multinational companies can import raw materials and export finished goods tax free. Part of the appeal of jobs in *zona francas* was that they existed in almost every province of the country, meaning that if the team developed a network of relationships in different zones, released players who returned to their hometowns would have access to opportunities there.

During my visit, Jeff and another staffer drove to Santiago, several hours north of the Royals' academy, to meet with representatives of the Swisher Sweets cigar manufacturing plant at a *zona franca*. The purpose of the trip was to sell the cigar makers on the idea that ex-*peloteros* were candidates not for entry-level positions (which paid so poorly, according to Jeff, that players had little interest in them) but for supervisory or management roles because of what they had learned in baseball. The meeting went well, but team staff knew that building an economic support system for released players, along with strengthening educational offerings and getting players into higher education, would be a long term, largely thankless undertaking. Staff's role was to educate prospects for careers in baseball, even though most of them would not make it. Efforts on behalf of players who were no longer with the team could be a seen as a distraction from this primary duty.

While in the DR, I heard about an initiative to create academic standards for *peloteros*' education in amateur and professional academies, which involved amateur academy owners alongside representatives from MLB teams. The person who spearheaded the effort, it turned out, was the operator of one of the leading amateur academies and also an industrialist who owned a *zona franca*—where, in this imagined future, failed MLB prospects with some English proficiency, computer skills, and leadership potential might go to work. As with so much of what I encountered in the world of Latin American baseball, it was hard to know what to make of this. Per Juan Mosquera, could this be seen as a promising, cross-sector effort to strengthen the DR's "educational base" and ensure that teenaged ballplayers' schooling was not neglected (as Deron Dolphus urged)? Or, per Eric Johnson, was this a classic case of "learning to labor," in which the global commodity chain of professional baseball would produce reliable workers who, barring fame and fortune in MLB, could be neatly slotted into manufacturing jobs back home?

It's tremendously complicated. As Alan Klein wrote in his pioneering research on the Dominican baseball industry, the "self-driven and coveted" nature of being a professional athlete requires us to maintain respect for *peloteros'* agency and intelligence. That doesn't mean that we can't criticize a system that plainly reinforces inequalities between the United States and "an impoverished neocolonial world that is nevertheless endowed with a seemingly inexhaustible supply of sporting talent to be offered to the sports industries of the industrial world" (Besnier, 2015, p. 853). All the same, "Albert Pujols is no sluggish and unmotivated drone; nor are the yet unproven Dominican rookies at the academies."[22] A Latin American baseball player may indeed be a commodity from the team's point of view, but he is also a "cognizant human" (Klein's phrase) who takes an active role in the "true development of a person and professional," as Jill Long de Mercado put it.

Many of the cognizant humans on the MLB side, for their part, were not content just to teach the *peloteros* English and American culture but made concerted efforts to provide for the players' future well-being. The players themselves took diverse paths through the process of language learning and cultural adaptation in the United States, seeking to "maximize their professional experience" through bilingualism and, eventually, beginning to contemplate life after baseball.

3

Non-Native Spanish Speakers Challenging Linguistic and Racial Divides in Major League Baseball

In 2021, when Oakland A's prospect Parker Dunshee was playing for the Las Vegas Aviators, the team's Triple-A affiliate, his batterymate (catcher) was Dominican journeyman Francisco Peña. Despite their different backgrounds, the two quickly figured out how to use their bilingual repertoires to communicate sensitive information during games—for example, whether to change the signs with a runner on second base—while having some fun at the expense of an unsuspecting umpire:[1]

> Funny story: So Francisco Peña, we were in Reno, and I was pitching, he was catching, and he just yelled out to me in Spanish, . . . "You wanna change the signs? Or . . . are you good with the signs right now?" There's a guy on second. And I just yelled back at him in Spanish, . . . "I'm good." Like, "We're good here."
>
> Then the umpire, who was—I can't remember where he was from, maybe Venezuela—he couldn't believe it. He was like, "What? That guy speaks Spanish?" . . . And Peña told him like a joke, like a lie . . . , "Oh yeah. His parents were missionaries in the Dominican. He grew up there." I was like, "Why did you tell him that?" . . . And then he told [the umpire] the next inning, "Nah, that wasn't true. I just wanted to see your face when I said that."

I found this story interesting for several reasons, but it is especially revealing with regard to language ideologies about native English speakers in multilingual baseball. As documented in the previous two chapters, Spanish-speaking prospects are expected to learn and use English as part of their professional development within MLB organizations, a process that includes but transcends language socialization. On the other hand, an English-speaking pitcher like Dunshee, who knows enough Spanish to participate in a brief back-and-forth with his catcher, is seen as so exceptional that his bilingualism demands some explanation *beyond* the fact that he must have spent years in clubhouses surrounded by Spanish-speaking teammates—hence the Spanish-speaking umpire's willingness to believe that Dunshee had been raised in the Dominican Republic. A white American guy who speaks functional Spanish, even one who has been around Dominicans and Venezuelans for his entire professional career, beggars belief. As Parker put it, "No one ever believes me initially when I tell them I speak Spanish.... They'll just come up and start testing me. Or like, they won't really believe it for a while until they see me in action."

Triple-A is often the last rung on the professional ladder before the major leagues or the first rung on the way back down. Such was the case for Dunshee and Peña, respectively, who had taken wildly different routes to Las Vegas. Dunshee, born and raised as a monolingual English speaker near Indianapolis, Indiana, graduated from Wake Forest University in 2017 and was drafted by the A's as a senior sign—a low-cost flier on a player who has proven himself in college but no longer has the option of returning to school as leverage in draft negotiations. Dunshee had worked his way up through the minor league system, weathering the Covid-19 pandemic—and, like many players, post-pandemic injury issues—before arriving in Las Vegas, waiting for the call to Oakland. Peña, on the other hand, hailed from a famous baseball family in the Dominican Republic—his father, brother, and uncle all played in the big leagues—and, like the prospects profiled in the preceding chapters, had started playing professionally as a teenager after signing with the New York Mets.

By the time he and Parker became teammates in Las Vegas, Francisco had had several "cups of coffee," or brief stints in the major leagues, with Kansas City, Baltimore, and St. Louis, spread over five seasons. The last of those was in 2018; since then, Francisco had played Triple-A ball for the Cardinals and Giants and, in the off-season, had picked up gigs with the Águilas Cibaeñas of the Dominican Winter League. Before the A's signed Francisco as a minor league free agent in 2021, he and Parker had never played on the same team, but Parker was tickled to discover that his reputation preceded him:

> I'd played against [Francisco] in years past, and I'd always chirp at him or just ... say stuff to him in Spanish, and he'd look at me, because I'd be sitting in the dugout with Jesús Luzardo, who obviously speaks English and Spanish.... When [Jesús and I] were playing together, he would be ... talking to some of the Latin guys, and I'd be sitting next to him, and I'd jump in talking to him. And the guy on the field would just look at me with the weirdest look, and Francisco Peña was one of those guys. And he ended up playing with us this year, and he's

like, "Oh, you're the *gringo* with the *bigotes* [mustache] who speaks Spanish!" . . . And I was like, "Yup, that's me."²

Unexpected uses of language are worth talking about because they expose assumptions about how language is connected to other aspects of identity like race and nationality. If it's unexpected that someone speaks a certain way, it's unexpected according to whom, in what situation, and why? When people react to someone's use of Spanish as unexpected, that reaction speaks volumes about the language ideologies *associated* with Spanish—and English—in that context. Here, "language ideologies" are the beliefs that people hold about languages, their speakers, "appropriate" or "standard" uses of language, or any other dimension of language as a social practice.³ The fact that Parker was singled out as *the* mustachioed white guy who speaks Spanish—and Francisco, pointedly, was *not* singled out as the one Dominican guy who learned English—tells us something about multilingual baseball that is much bigger than the two individuals involved. For a Spanish speaker to have learned English is unremarkable; for an English speaker to be able to function in Spanish is surprising.

I caught wind of Parker's Spanish prowess from his former teammate Richard Guasch, the Cuban pitcher whose harrowing defection story and early experiences with English are covered in Chapter 2. I had asked Richard if his English-speaking teammates ever made an effort to learn more Spanish, and he first brought up Reid Birlingmair, another A's minor leaguer with whom Richard would trade language lessons as the two hung out in the dugout on non-pitching days: "And during the week, we're in the dugout together, talking. And he always wants to learn. And he's taught me some English, too. I've taught him Spanish, and he's taught me English. But there are others like him." I was curious, though: Did English speakers usually just learn a few words—*palabrones* (swear words) or baseball terms, maybe?—or did some develop enough Spanish competence to hold conversations? Richard replied that yes, some could hold a conversation in Spanish—for example, Parker Dunshee: "He speaks Spanish perfectly." I was intrigued. How did he learn it? "He says that in school and talking like this with us, in baseball, he learned it."

Parker's story made me think of Nate McLouth, another white ballplayer raised in the United States as an English monolingual who has garnered admiration—more than that, *amazement*—for his supposedly near-native command of Spanish.⁴ "It's amazing when you see an American guy speaking perfect Spanish," said Alexi Casilla, his teammate on the Baltimore Orioles, during a 2013 television interview with Fox Sports.⁵ "I think he's Dominican. I think his real name is Manuel Peralta," Casilla quipped. As with Parker

Dunshee's fictional upbringing in the Dominican Republic, Alexi Casilla had to invent a Dominican alter ego, "Manuel Peralta," to account for McLouth's performance.

Stories about L1 English-speaking ballplayers who are unexpectedly competent in Spanish testify to what the late scholar Richard Ruiz called the "paradox of bilingualism" in the United States. Immigrants and non-native speakers of English are expected to discard other languages in favor of English as an integral part of the "conversion experience" of becoming fully American (Ruiz, 2016c). When native English speakers pursue other languages, however, they are seen as impressive, sophisticated, and intelligent. Sociolinguist Guadalupe Valdés observed that the same tendency distorts the equity focus of many bilingual education programs in favor of "elite bilingualism" (Valdés, 1997).

There's nothing dramatic or inherently impressive about the way Parker learned Spanish. He started studying the language in middle school in Indiana, found that he had an affinity for it, continued taking Spanish coursework in college, and developed his conversational skills by talking with teammates in the clubhouse and on the field. When I asked Parker why he thought his Spanish was so surprising to other players, he brought up widespread beliefs about Americans' English monolingualism and "pompous" resistance to accommodating other languages. He speculated that Spanish speakers might think:

> "Americans, they don't know other languages. They know they only have to speak English".... Maybe they just have [a] little bias, like.... "Americans are a little pompous. There's no way that a guy that looks that white would ever know Spanish." Maybe it's some of that. I really don't know.

Parker enjoyed confounding his Latin American teammates' expectations and stereotypes about ignorant Americans by surprising them with his Spanish proficiency—or, as he described it, looking for the "shock value" in going public as a Spanish speaker and humorously stoking language paranoia among his Latino teammates:[6]

> I got drafted in 2017 and went to short season and . . . I didn't just walk in the clubhouse on the first day being, like, "Hey guys, I also speak Spanish." . . . I was just like, yeah, it'll happen organically. People'll figure it out eventually. And so I would just be like . . . sitting there minding my own business, but, you know, guys would be playing cards or whatever, and it'd be all Spanish-speaking guys. . . . And I'd just like laugh or like turn my head and look at 'em when someone said something like controversial, or, like, . . . I would always laugh at the right

times at their jokes. . . . And they're like, "Oh, what's this guy's problem? . . . This guy's weird."

And then one day, I was just like, all right, I'm gonna jump in. So I just jumped into one of their conversations, speaking Spanish, and they were like, "Whoa, what have we been saying these past couple weeks that this guy has been telling everyone that we've been talking about? And we had no clue he knew what we were saying!". . . . I didn't try to make 'em feel bad about it or whatever. . . . It was the shock value that I was looking for- like, "Whoa, you gotta be careful."

As in the opening anecdote about chirping at Francisco Peña and fooling the umpire, Parker was not above exploiting his status as an unexpected Spanish speaker to tease Latino teammates or rivals. In his telling, though, what happened *afterward* was more significant than his teammates' initial shock at discovering that he spoke Spanish. Parker let them know that he wanted to use his bilingualism as a resource for helping them adjust to life in the United States. Not only that, but he told them in a way that clearly communicated his empathy for his teammates, in view of the difficult process of socialization that Latin American prospects undergo, and his respect for their adaptability and willingness to learn:

Talking to guys in the dugout or in the locker room and during batting practice, talking to guys out on the field . . . as your teammate, trying to be a leader or whatever, I want to be here for you. I can't imagine how nerve wracking it is if your English isn't very good, as a Spanish-speaking player, being in a completely different country, playing baseball, going places you've never been before, living in a place where you don't speak the language very well. So I just tried to let guys know, "Hey, seriously, if there's anything I can ever help you with, if you need me to go somewhere with you, just to make you feel more comfortable, to help you translate, if you ever are reading something on your phone or somebody texts or calls you, . . . I'm more than willing to do that for you." And I think a lot of guys felt a sense of comfort with that. Once I gained their trust a little better, they got to know me a little bit better.

As with many of the US-based staffers in the preceding chapters who worked with young Latino players, Parker expressed profound appreciation for the way his Latin American teammates dealt with challenges on the way to becoming US baseball professionals. As we will see, he deepened this appreciation through meaningful encounters with friends like Francisco Peña, who pushed him to improve his Spanish proficiency to be a more effective advocate for his teammates.

Bringing the Clubhouse Together: Convivial Uses of Spanish in Segregated Settings

The broad outline of Parker's story is a useful illustration of the sociolinguistic dynamics at work in professional baseball clubhouses in the United States. When Parker appeared on the scene, his Latino teammates assumed that he was not a Spanish speaker; his self-disclosure of his Spanish proficiency took them by surprise and caused shock, laughter, and semiserious paranoia; he made himself available as a language broker for his teammates, and once they got to know and trust him, they started to seek him out for his bilingual expertise.

The video clip about Nate McLouth's Spanish (mentioned previously) was titled "McLouth's Spanish Brings the Clubhouse Together." Language-ideological statements like this often raise interesting questions. For one, why was "bringing the clubhouse together" credited to a single L2 Spanish speaker but not his many L2 English-speaking teammates? Alexi Casilla's fluid bilingualism is rendered invisible in this framing. Another question, one that gets closer to my point, has to do with the presupposition in the video clip's title: if McLouth's Spanish (or Casilla's English, for that matter) brings the clubhouse together, doesn't that mean that the clubhouse must have been divided in the first place? In that case, to understand *why* unexpected uses of Spanish are thought to have a powerful unifying effect, we need to understand where these social divisions come from.

Professional baseball clubhouses are an example of what sociolinguists sometimes call a "superdiverse" setting, where people from a wide range of language backgrounds are concentrated in a way that seems "new," or at least unprecedented in the experience of the speakers themselves. As Michael Silverstein pointed out, such settings often involve linguistic or discursive "phenomena relocated from . . . global peripheries to current global metropoles, where they are perhaps not welcomed" (Silverstein, 2015, p. 8). Things have always been "superdiverse" on the "margins"—but, again, who gets to say what is marginal? Often, it is only when certain forms of diversity make their way toward the center that they attract notice and provoke reactions. If we take the United States as the "global metropole" of professional baseball—the center of economic power that draws the best talent to itself—this means that so-called peripheral ways of speaking (from the perspective of US "monoglot standard" language ideology, anyway) are "relocated" to MLB clubhouses (Silverstein, 1998). There, they meet with a variety of responses—some welcoming, like Parker Dunshee's and Nate McLouth's, others less so. In such settings, whatever people might think of this diversity, they are forced to figure out how to deal with their "thrown-togetherness," and over time, they work out social norms for communicating across difference in an emergent speech community (Massey, 2005). But, Silverstein also argued, there is a difference between a speech community and a *language* community, and the speech communities in MLB clubhouses are embedded in a national language community that has historically been invested in English as the *sine qua non* of American identity.

Players coming from places as different as Wake Forest (Parker Dunshee) and a Dominican amateur academy (Francisco Peña) end up in the same clubhouse. Zak Basch, a former minor leaguer and Oakland's director of minor league operations at the time, reflected on the evolution of his linguistic and cultural awareness within clubhouses. After being drafted, Zak was assigned to a short-season team with "maybe five or six Latin guys" but "a lot of college guys," which gave it a familiar feel. Extended spring training, though, was another story:

> That's hard, when you go in to extended spring training, when you get drafted, you know, as a white college-educated player. . . . And then you get to extended spring training, and that's really where I felt that . . . I am *definitely* a minority. . . . And for me, it was cool. Like, I'm not trying to like pat myself on the back. . . . You're like, "Whoa, this is frankly kind of anthropological."

Beyond language, Zak found himself having to adjust to different cultural expectations and practices among his Latino teammates, some of which had to do with "proxemics," or ways of using space—"like personal space didn't exactly exist," Zak put it, laughing and being clear that he was not criticizing (Hall, 1966). Juan Mosquera, the A's area scout for Latin America, who grew up in Panama and pitched for the Cardinals organization, brought up the image of the "professional" American ballplayer—the role to which young Latino prospects were meant to aspire in Chapter 1—in describing clubhouse conflicts stemming from what he saw as cultural differences:

> We Latinos are used to a lot of noise. . . . For the majority of Americans, maybe they don't like so much noise, and they're very professional in what they do. So . . . maybe if you're dealing with a very professional person who's dealt with a Latino before, it doesn't bother him. But what are you gonna do with a person who doesn't understand anything about Latin America? It creates conflict. They get upset by the noise or one thing or another.

"Professional," in Juan's telling—as at the Royals' Dominican complex—went beyond a player's work ethic and dedication to the game to encompass comportment and "appropriate" behavior, like how loudly you take up space in the clubhouse and how you wear your uniform. Juan saw this as unproblematic, a simple matter of adapting to a different cultural context: "We're well received, but truthfully, this isn't our house. So we come back to the theme of culture. You have to understand that you can't make so much noise in the neighbor's house." Still, Juan hinted that US players and teams might also have to adapt, given the increased visibility of foreign-born players in MLB: "The foreign player is bringing a lot of value to an American business or organization, and I think you have to understand that point of view [too]."

In his administrative role, Zak had watched the A's recent draftees encountering stark cultural and linguistic differences on their first trips to the Arizona complex, just as he had in his playing days: "I do notice the draft guys, they're coming from Vanderbilt or Stanford or wherever, and like, you walk in the clubhouse, you're *in* it. You're in a Latin clubhouse. Immediately." Emily Glass, the former education coordinator for the Miami Marlins, affirmed that draftees from the United States were often taken aback when entering the clubhouse:

> You think about baseball players that are coming from like Ohio and Texas and, you know, all these different places. . . . I think one of the most shocking things for those guys, whether they're out of college or high school, when you walk into a pro clubhouse, it sounds and looks really different than what they're used to.

I asked Zak if most other native English-speaking players, in his experience, had a similarly enthusiastic reaction to "being a minority," as he put it, in majority-Latino clubhouses. "No chance. And I'm not saying I'm special," he continued, but offered the hypothetical example of a high school draftee from a rural town in the American South who might not have had contact with very many people of color beyond what he had seen on television. Zak added that "it takes a while" for players from different backgrounds to get comfortable with each other but that friendships and trust develop once "they've gone through battles together."

Zak brought up an issue that I heard about from others: the tendency for players to group themselves together by language or nationality in clubhouses and other common areas like cafeterias. This tendency is certainly not limited to baseball teams. As the title of Beverly Tatum's classic book *Why Are All the Black Kids Sitting Together in the Cafeteria?* suggests, it is a question that educational researchers have wrestled with for years (Tatum, 2017). Asking why the Black kids are sitting together begs—or sidesteps—the question of why the white kids (or Asian kids or Dominican kids) are sitting together.

People sometimes regard such homogeneous groupings as "self-segregation," or an innate predisposition to gravitate to people who, you perceive, are "like" you in certain respects. For young Spanish speakers (and others) who end up far from home, negotiating an unfamiliar language and cultural context and subjected to the rigors of becoming professional in MLB, there is a comfort level in hanging out with peers who are similar culturally and linguistically. Kevin Goldstein, the former Astros' executive, now with the Minnesota Twins, described the scene this way:

> If during spring training you go to the lunchroom where it's not like twenty-five players, it's your whole minor league system, it's 180 kids, right? It is very, very culturally demarcat[ed], if you will. By the tables. The white kids sit with the white kids, the Black kids sit with the Black kids, the Dominican kids sit with the Dominican kids, the Venezuelan kids sit with the Venezuelan kids, you know, and there's nothing wrong with that. They have a commonality, they can communicate better, you know. But it is what you get.

However, as Kevin's hedge implied—"there's nothing *wrong* with that . . . *but*"—team personnel and players also recognized that a roster divided by language, race, or nationality was not ideal in terms of getting players to pull together toward common goals. Kevin brought up the image of the lunchroom in response to a question about Alex Bregman, the Astros' star third baseman and another member of the Parker Dunshee/Nate McLouth Spanish-speaking white unicorn club. Bregman, like McLouth, has been feted for his Spanish proficiency; like Dunshee, he appears to enjoy using his unicorn status to humorous effect. An internet search turns up numerous videos of Bregman interviewing and joking around with Spanish-speaking teammates, along with "Alex Bregman's White Boy Spanish Lessons!," a tongue-in-cheek video—posted by Bregman himself—in which Bregman teaches simple Spanish phrases to non-Spanish-speaking Latinos.[7] The video is an offshoot of a popular genre of performances by "YouTube polyglots"—for example, someone who looks phenotypically white/Northern European and (supposedly) shocks the locals by speaking Cantonese at a market (Knafo, 2022).

The very existence of such videos is evidence, if more were needed, of the paradox of bilingualism that surfaces in accounts of English ballplayers' bilingual exploits. Bregman is another of the exceptions that proves the rule. This is not to say that his embrace of Spanish was inauthentic ("White Boy Spanish Lessons" notwithstanding) or that it stemmed only from a desire for positive media attention. Kevin attributed Bregman's Spanish learning to a combination of individual-level characteristics—the player's intensely determined personality—and his immediate social context, namely, the speech community of the Astros' infield. The result was an L2 Spanish speaker who was highly motivated to learn and use the language for specific purposes and had access to a community of speakers (teammates) who provided consistent, appropriate input (Wong Fillmore & Snow, 2000):

> I mean, Bregman's a psychotic person. I say that in a good way. He's a very intense person, and, like, if he just says to you in an aside, "I should learn Spanish so I can talk to my infield better," you know in a month he's probably gonna be speaking Spanish.
>
> But I think a good chunk of that was really what was around him. He needed to communicate with his infield, which was—you know, to his left was [Carlos] Correa, [José] Altuve, and Yuli [Gurriel]. Correa obviously speaks beautiful English, but he speaks Spanish to Altuve, who is a very good English speaker, and Yuli, who doesn't do English. . . . Bregman was the minority. The infield other than Bregman communicated all in Spanish and also hung with each other, right? In *Spanish*. And he wanted to be a part of *that*.

In Kevin's view, Alex Bregman worked to improve his Spanish not just because it was useful for communicating with teammates but because "he wanted to be part of that," meaning that as a recent arrival to the Astros' infield, he wanted to fit in and participate fully in an established peer group whose everyday language was Spanish. Kevin said that Bregman "needed to communicate with his infield," but he could have done so in English. Correa and Altuve, from Puerto Rico and Venezuela, respectively, are both bilingual; first baseman Yuli Gurriel, a Cuban legend who started playing in the United States in his thirties, speaks less English, but the others could have relayed messages (Figure 17).

Bregman was a linguistic minority in the infield, but as we have seen, there is no *expectation* in US professional baseball that English speakers will accommodate to Spanish speakers to a meaningful extent. His choice to invest in Spanish learning, then, is a reminder that language use in multilingual communities is never just about enabling communication. Alex Bregman's Spanish signals to his teammates that he wants to belong, that he understands and respects the place of Spanish in the local language ecology, and that even as a white, native English speaker, he is willing to shoulder the burden of communicating in his L2—not always, but at particular moments. Still, Kevin saw Bregman as exceptional—"I think the Bregman case is very, very rare"—both because of the player's "psychotic" determination to succeed and because of his unique situation as a newcomer to an infield packed with Latin American stars who would become the core of the 2017 World Series–winning team.

Figure 17 Alex Bregman sitting between Spanish-speaking teammates José Altuve and Carlos Correa in the dugout, June 14, 2018 (Michael Zagaris/Oakland Athletics/Getty Images).

Exceptional or not, it is important to consider the social implications of native English speakers' efforts to use Spanish—not at the expense of Spanish speakers' work to "bring the clubhouse together" by speaking English but as the other side of the coin. Social scientists have used the notion of *conviviality* to capture the way that people "negotiat[e] shared meanings," or manage to understand each other well enough to coexist across differences of language, race, and culture (Bauman, 1996).

Conviviality—or "living together" in "moderate solidarity," which I take to mean "getting along and understanding where your interests are and aren't aligned"—requires people to "constructively create modes of togetherness" through language (Blommaert, 2014; Nowicka & Vertovec, 2014). That is, in a superdiverse speech community, there is no way around the fact that your communicative repertoire, or your toolkit for communication, differs significantly from others' (Rymes, 2014). Because of this, you and everyone else in the community must seek ways of being together ("modes of togetherness") *despite* the unevenness in people's repertoires. This is not to say that English and Spanish speakers in a baseball clubhouse are on equal footing in convivial encounters. They are not, and nothing in the foregoing discussion should be taken to suggest that they are. It is only meant to suggest that it is possible to heed dynamics of linguistic power and privilege in such encounters without treating culture or race as an "unbridgeable division" (Gilroy, 2002).

As Tatum and others have asserted, so-called self-segregation is not merely a matter of individual preference, because institutional decisions and policies also shape which individuals spend time together and come to trust and understand each other. Staffers understood this very well but struggled with the question of what changes in team policy or practice would motivate players to bridge divisions of race and language. Zak spoke openly of the difficulty, from the team's perspective, of wanting to encourage players from different backgrounds to socialize without forcing the issue and bringing US-born and Latin American players together "artificially"—that is, in ways that might be ineffective or even counterproductive:

> I'm not gonna lie to you and say all the white players and the Latin players are going to dinner every night. . . . It's weird; it really is a slow process. And I don't want to *force* it. We've toyed with the idea . . . 'cause they live in the hotel with two players to a room, and I've had thoughts of, like . . . every room is one white player and one [Latin player]. And . . . is that really for me to force?
>
> So we don't do that. So we mostly room guys that're good buddies. . . . And that's more like, listen . . . you're sleeping two feet away from somebody, you want to have some shared experiences and comfort level, especially the Dominican kids that are here for the first time.

The Royals' Jeff Diskin seconded Zak's point about not assigning roommates but framed it as a matter of respecting the players' autonomy in light of the Royals' commitment to treat even very young players as the "professionals" the organization wanted them to be. He asked me if my university would force me to room with someone on a business trip; when I replied that they would not, Jeff went on:

> In any company, [when] you travel, you don't tell people who they gotta live with. . . . So even though the kids are younger, that's the professional part of it. As opposed to the amateur part of it, they treat 'em like professionals in that sense.

Many of the players and staff I spoke with believed that this divided situation was changing, albeit slowly. There is probably some selection bias at work, since I sought out people who were either involved with language education, working with international players on a regular basis, or recommended to me as bilingual and interculturally competent. That being said, across these conversations, a somewhat consistent picture did emerge: Spanish-English bilinguals from Latin

America affirmed that many of their L1 English-speaking teammates showed some level of interest in Spanish; players and staffers singled out exceptional cases, like Parker Dunshee and Alex Bregman, implying that *conversational* Spanish proficiency among L1 English speakers in baseball, while rare, was not unheard of; and player development and education staff acknowledged that divisions persisted in clubhouses but argued that they were becoming less stark. When I raised the issue of language and clubhouse divisions, Jorge Guzmán, the Royals' former assistant for Dominican operations, commented:

> It is getting better. There's no doubt that over the last X amount of years, it has improved. . . . In clubhouses, I do see a little more interaction, but I still think that it has a ways to go.

Luis Victoria, like the others quoted here, had an optimistic take on the issue, saying that he had seen progress even in the year he had been with Oakland, while acknowledging that social barriers persisted. And like Parker Dunshee, Luis was reluctant to entertain the possibility that prejudice reinforced these barriers, placing greater emphasis on individual personality differences:

> You can see the division, but this year, I've seen more embracing diversity. . . . You have guys that don't speak to Latinos or Latinos that don't speak to Americans. They're shy. They're not comfortable. They don't know each other very well, but they're all teammates at the end of the day. . . . You don't see discrimination or racism here.

I pushed Luis a bit on that final point, suggesting that it was certainly *possible*, even if uncommon, for prejudicial attitudes to play a role in hardening racial and linguistic boundaries in MLB clubhouses, and he grudgingly agreed with me. "We know the world we live in today," he said, laughing. He then brought the conversation back to the "tremendous job of embracing diversity" that the A's organization was doing, crediting their leadership with creating a multicultural community that was "beautiful to see," especially considering "the world we live in today."

Jeff generally agreed with Luis's, Jorge's, and Zak's assessments of the situation but added that the Royals had work to do, noting that divisions existed even within the community of Latin American players, based on nationality, as some of the minor leaguers in Chapter 2 suggested:

> To be honest with you . . . there are even cliques [within the] Latin community itself, between Dominicans and Venezuelans. I mean, our Venezuelans at our DR academy, they don't get offsite. Dominicans are going home for a weekend, and

you think that they would take a Venezuelan home with them, [but] that does not happen very often. So, I mean, we can even do better with just internally within our own [Latin players].

Individual Agency and Sociolinguistic Change in MLB Organizations

In settings where racial and linguistic "demarcation," to use Kevin Goldstein's words, was taken for granted, bilingual speakers' efforts took on added significance both for facilitating communication and for building community among players and staff with different repertoires. Richard Guasch, Parker Dunshee's former teammate, affirmed that language was key not just for getting referential meaning across but so as not to feel excluded in bilingual settings like the clubhouse. He described gaining L2 proficiency as *liberador*—"freeing"— and reflected on his gradual process of getting comfortable communicating in English, distinguishing between what he called "real" and "basic" conversations. Richard was talking about learning English, not Spanish, but his remarks are germane to the broader point about building community through efforts to use language even in limited ways:

> As time went on, I was learning more English, I was communicating a little more. Generally, it's more freeing, you understand more, you don't feel like you're excluded from the group, you don't feel like you're apart, because at least you can converse a little. And I think there's something that a lot of times, for players and coaches, limits what we can say, [our ability] to have real conversations, conversations about what you think and not just talking about the basics.

In addition to helping individual players feel better integrated into clubhouses and lunchrooms, players and staffers agreed that strategic, convivial uses of bilingualism could have a positive effect on team cohesion, regardless of individual speakers' levels of proficiency. Parker Dunshee observed, "The most fun teams I've been on [are] when everyone just communicates with everybody, no matter what level of whatever language they have. They're the most fun teams." Parker's phrasing was apt: using "what[ever] level of whatever language you have" to communicate with teammates is an excellent description of how members of superdiverse speech communities use their competence strategically to "make do" or get the job done in specific interactions (Dörnyei & Thurrell, 1991; see: de Certeau, 1984).

I saw many such examples of strategic competence, where even limited uses of the L2 went a long way. Jeff Diskin was not very complimentary about his own Spanish (which sounded just fine to me) because he worried that he would miss "teachable moments" with Spanish-speaking players and would not be able to "peel the onion" with them—to go deeper, as opposed to sticking with "functional" but surface-level interactions. All the same, he said, he thought that his efforts to use Spanish "functionally" were a good example for the players, since he was not afraid to use "whatever level of Spanish he had," to borrow Parker's phrasing:

> I do a pretty good job, but I miss a lot of teachable moments. And that's always bothered me a lot, where I can peel the onion a little further. . . . I'm not afraid to make mistakes. I'm not afraid to speak in Spanish in front of them. I'm not afraid to use the Spanish that I have. . . . And they don't make fun of me, or they seem to understand what I'm saying. And I think in some ways, it's a good example for them.

As the opening example with the umpire showed, what comes across in a speech situation has as much to do with who the speaker is, how he's positioned relative to others, and how he's using language as it does with the speaker's intended meaning. Recall the discussion of the "total linguistic fact" in "Introduction." Understanding the weight of Richard's, Parker's, or Jeff's words in a bilingual interaction, beyond their grammatical structure and literal sense, means examining the intersection of *use* (what the form of language indicates about the context) with *ideology* (ideas or models that people use to make sense of language behavior) among everyone involved (Silverstein, 1985).

Luis Victoria of the A's offered shortstop Max Muncy, the team's recent first-round draft pick, who was signed out of high school in Thousand Oaks, California, as evidence that linguistic norms were changing in the organization.[8] Pointedly, Muncy's status as a first rounder who had received a nearly $3 million bonus and his use of Dominican Spanish were relevant to Luis's assessment of his impact on the clubhouse:

> I talked to Max yesterday and said, "I am very—not only grateful, but proud of you for *coming* to the organization, and the *first* thing that you do is you to talk to everybody, doesn't matter *who* they are. Doesn't matter *where* they come from". . . . A seventeen-, eighteen-year-old kid. . . . First round guy, and it's amazing how he just sits down on the tables with the Latino players, and then first thing, he goes, "¿*Qué lo qué, papi*?" [What's up, bro?], and he talks and then says hi and bye to everybody. He's like, "All good, *papi*?" And I'm like, "That's *great*. That's

amazing." That's what [the team wants] because they want the American players and English-speaking players to be inclusive as well and include the Latino players into their tables. . . . But with the players, when you see a player [of] his caliber and [with] what the organization is expecting of him, to do that with the other players, that is a big impact.

Luis saw Muncy's behavior as aligned with "what the team wants." As Zak and Kevin suggested, teams want a more integrated community but one that comes about through players' own efforts and not as a matter of official policy. Luis implied that Max Muncy's efforts at being inclusive were especially impactful coming from a "first round guy"—"a player of his caliber," from whom the A's organization is expecting great things—in that they set the tone for others to reach across ethnic and linguistic boundaries. Juan Mosquera also singled out Muncy for praise as a cultural broker, extending his "house" metaphor to say that the young first-rounder was "opening the door" to welcome his Latin American teammates to the United States:

> I'm really happy that we had such a person, like our first [draft] pick, Max Muncy, trying to speak Spanish with the Latinos, trying to communicate with them, trying to sit to eat with them. He's understanding the importance of foreign players, in this case, for the future of the sport that we all love so much.

It is significant that Luis quoted Max as greeting Latin American teammates with "*¿Qué lo qué, papi?*," a noticeably slangy, youthful, and Dominican phrase, as opposed to "*¿Cómo estás?*" or another expression that L2 Spanish speakers might have learned in high school. Whatever Spanish competence Muncy had prior to entering professional ball, he likely had to make adjustments on the fly, as ballplayers are accustomed to doing, to learn what forms and varieties of Spanish "belonged" in the context of the A's training facility.

Similarly, teammates' and journalists' reactions to Nate McLouth had less to do with his speaking Spanish than they did with his speaking *Dominican* Spanish. Alexi Casilla may have remarked that McLouth spoke "perfect Spanish," but McLouth's Spanish was not "perfect" because it was "proper" or standard. Rather, it was perfectly fitted to the speech community of the clubhouse. McLouth might be seen as exceptional, but his "elite bilingualism" did not set him apart linguistically from his teammates. It made him resemble them more closely. During the TV interview mentioned earlier, McLouth's Dominican-sounding speech, honed through years of contact with Caribbean teammates, painted a marked contrast with the Dominican interviewer's more "standard" Spanish, which did not sound all that Dominican. Viewers roared with laughter, according to the comments, when McLouth paused to tease the interviewer, "*Ah, tú ere(s) dominicano también?*" (Oh, so you're Dominican too?), aspirating the /s/ sound in *eres* in vernacular Caribbean fashion (Guitart, 1997). (As Zak Basch put it, "The letter *s* might as well not exist" for Dominicans.)

As with Dunshee and the umpire, however, framings of language use as unexpected or remarkable generally point to other issues beneath the surface of interaction. Of McLouth, "*Ese es un niño que fue robado en un hospital en Santo Domingo jajaja*" (That's a kid who was stolen from a hospital in Santo Domingo), joked a fan on YouTube, evoking Francisco Peña's apocryphal story that Dunshee was the child of missionaries. White, native-English-speaking Americans are not "expected" to sound Dominican because Dominican Spanish is not a sought-after form of linguistic capital for elite bilinguals in the United States—outside of baseball clubhouses, anyway (Bourdieu, 1991). You would be hard pressed to find a high school Spanish class where Caribbean Spanish was the preferred variety, unless the students were heritage speakers, and even then, there is a good chance that they would be told that they were speaking "improperly."

The deficit discourses about Dominicans' linguistic practices and educational potential (in Chapters 1 and 2) are evidence that language varieties like Dominican or Caribbean Spanish, as well as specific forms ("*¿Qué lo qué, papi?*") and features (/s/ aspiration or deletion) associated with those varieties, are not just treated as "different" in a value-neutral sense. The long-term social processes that caused Dominican Spanish to diverge from other Spanish varieties are not essentially separate from the social processes that have generated recognizable stereotypes *about* Dominicans. As such, Dominican Spanish indexes understandings of what makes Dominicans different *in terms of* race, ethnicity, and social class, as well as geography. This helps to explain the need for astonished onlookers to resort to humorous explanations (switched at birth, child of missionaries) for why a white American L2 Spanish speaker would be speaking in a way that points to a very different set of identities.

Encountering Spanish Variation

The foregoing discussion brings up another paradox of bilingualism in professional baseball: the ways of speaking that carry social cachet in clubhouses are generally *not* the ways L2 Spanish speakers have been taught to use the language. In addition to having new opportunities to use Spanish for a variety of functions, L2 Spanish speakers in MLB organizations encounter an unprecedented amount of variation in Spanish and realize quickly that they need to adapt to function successfully in bilingual settings.

Parker Dunshee, who excelled in advanced placement (AP) Spanish in high school and went on to major in Spanish at college, commented, "I've learned, I would say, more in four years playing professional baseball, just conversationally, than I did in middle school and high school."[9] In college, unlike high school, Parker's teachers were L1 Spanish speakers and helped him make progress in understanding "how . . . people actually talk versus what you've heard in school. Just phrases, idioms, stuff like that. That's really helpful conversationally." Parker certainly seemed to be well prepared for life in professional clubhouses. All the same, he affirmed, the learning curve was steeper than anticipated:

> Like I said, pro ball. There's nothing like talking to people who only speak Spanish, and . . . you gotta just figure it out, sit down there. [In some cases,] I'm the one guy that they can talk to that speaks English in the clubhouse and Spanish.

When Zak Basch—who, like Parker, had a background in school Spanish—first found himself in majority-Latino settings in professional baseball, he said, "I was feeling pretty confident that [with] my four years [of] AP Spanish, I could do it. And I certainly couldn't." For one, some of the Spanish forms that had been valued in AP classrooms were useless in pro ball, such as the distinction between *tú* and *usted*, the informal and formal second person singular pronouns ("you"). "No one uses" *usted*, the formal pronoun, in baseball, "but that's like all you learn for *years*—not even weeks, *years* on learning that shit" in Spanish class.

Some of Zak's existing Spanish knowledge was useless; he also discovered that he was missing crucial pieces of the language as it was spoken in baseball settings. This posed logistical difficulties in addition to making it harder to build relationships with teammates:

> A big part of the daily schedule, every day, is when you get picked up. . . . Let's say at the airport, like, when's the bus com[ing], right? Or the van or whatever. So it's like, I know the word *autobús*, like it's an easy one, like "auto-bus," like day one [of Spanish class]: *autobús*. "What time is *autobús*?" And these guys are looking at me like, "Fucking *gringo*, I don't even know this word." They do not know the word.

I chuckled, remembering similar gaps in my vocabulary from when I started working with Cuban refugees: *"La guagua!"*

Always *guagua*. I'm like, fucking *guagua*? Like, what are these guys *talking* about, are they calling me a crybaby? Like, I have no idea. And it was not just a word of conversation; it's a word I need to know. Frankly, it's the *only* part of the day you need to know. You just need to know what time to be outside the hotel. That was the first Dominican word to learn.

Even with a considerable degree of Spanish proficiency—or so he thought—Zak was missing the word he needed to unlock "the only part of the day" he needed to know: What time does the bus leave for the ballpark? Having an academic formation in a language does not mean that someone has the right words or the right *kind* of language to function competently in a speech community, which can have practical consequences, like missing the bus. Similarly, Luis mentioned the difficulty of making the transition from "very formal" classroom English to his teammates' "different slang" in Minnesota, along with learning regional dialect features of American English (such as whether to say "soda," "pop," or "coke" for a carbonated soft drink).

Beyond the practical consequences, speakers who are unprepared to encounter language variation are also painfully aware of the social implications of being unable to participate more actively in communities, as Zak implied in his self-deprecating account of the *guagua* incident. Zak imagined his Spanish-speaking teammates' seeing him as a "fucking *gringo*," a word that connotes white, English-speaking identity but can also indicate a stance of prideful ignorance toward Spanish, Spanish speakers, and Latin American cultures (Schwartz, 2008). Likewise, when Zak first heard *guagua*, he feared that his teammates were calling him a crybaby, a reaction that smacks of run-of-the-mill language paranoia but underscores the way L2 speakers can be infantilized or made to feel incompetent, just as Jeff Diskin said sometimes happened with Latino players in English-dominant settings.

In a sense, this was the flip side of Max Muncy's and Nate McLouth's experiences. Those two players were able to align themselves with Latin American teammates by using forms and features that were recognizably Dominican or Caribbean, while Zak stumbled over unfamiliar Dominican features, embarrassing himself in the process. Zak's discomfort calls to mind Richard Guasch's humiliation (in Chapter 2) shortly after arriving at the A's facility in the United States, when a miscommunication led him to be branded temporarily as a "bad boy" within the organization.

Both Zak and Parker found teammates who played key gatekeeping roles, coaching them to improve their Spanish. In Zak's case, this happened in the bullpen at extended spring training for the Red Sox, where the recent college graduate threw sessions alongside Anibal Sánchez, a young Venezuelan pitcher. At the time, Sánchez was recuperating from Tommy John surgery, a common though dreaded procedure to reconstruct the ulnar collateral ligament in the elbow. Otherwise, Zak said, the two probably would not have ended up throwing together, since Sánchez was clearly more talented and would go on to a distinguished career in the major leagues.

> Anibal was only probably eighteen or nineteen, and he was coming off [Tommy John surgery]. That's why he was there in extended [spring training] with me. I was just there 'cause I was bad. I think I probably helped him quite a bit with his English and he helped me certainly a lot with my Spanish.

Zak found Anibal's Venezuelan Spanish easier to understand than the Spanish of his Dominican teammates, so his early interactions with Anibal helped him bridge the gap between US classroom Spanish and Caribbean Spanish. At present, while he would not call himself a proficient speaker, Zak has gotten comfortable enough with the language to advise other *gringos*, as he put it, on how to improve their pronunciation and function successfully in baseball Spanish settings.

Prior to pro ball, Parker said, he had never had to communicate in Spanish without "the crutch of just being able to flip back into English." Francisco Peña noticed and took it upon himself to push Parker out of his comfort zone, urging him to rely on his Spanish proficiency without first-language support:

> He really challenged me, like, "Dude, some days I just won't talk to you in English and I'm gonna force you to talk to me in Spanish." 'Cause he was another guy that I would talk to, but I'd have the crutch of, he knows English just as well as I do.
>
> He's like, "Why are you scared? Are you scared to mess up? Like, are you scared that you're gonna say something wrong or you're not gonna pronounce something right?" And I was like, yeah. I mean, I usually try to talk in short spurts where I can think of what I wanna say, have time to kind of prepare my thoughts and stuff. He's like, "No, dude, you can't be scared."

Thanks in part to Francisco's intervention, Parker thought his Spanish had improved in several ways. In terms of listening, he had gotten more adept at "locking in" and understanding the gist of interactions with Caribbean Spanish speakers, even if he did not understand every word:

> [If] he's talking really fast, or his accent's really thick or, you know, he has a Dominican accent where he doesn't pronounce any *d*'s or any *s*'s ever, I'll just be like, "All right, I gotta listen really close here." And so that has really helped

me conversationally, obviously being able to understand sentences or just being able to put things together in context when you don't understand all the words.

As Parker already mentioned, he also started to adjust his own discourse patterns in conversations with Spanish-speaking teammates. Where previously he spoke in "short spurts" to maintain expressive control ("have time to prepare my thoughts"), he began to take more risks and to worry less about verbal infelicities or transgressions.

"Language across the Board": Spanish Education for English Speakers in MLB

Parker marveled at what he called "completely broken conversations" in both English and Spanish where the players involved nonetheless "know exactly what they're talking about." All the same, given others' reactions to non-Latino, American Spanish-speaking "unicorns," it is fair to assume that most L1 English speakers in MLB clubhouses, if they use Spanish at all, do so in fairly limited ways and for a restricted set of functions—for example, playing cards, playing FIFA on PlayStation 4, trash talking, and "busting each other's chops" during games.[10] Such uses of Spanish scan as "convivial" in a facile sense. That is, they could be dismissed as mere "gestures of responsibility" or forms of "niceness"— the bare minimum for coexistence, with relatively little effort required from speakers of the dominant language (Laurier & Philo, 2006).

Despite this—*because* of this—it is important to acknowledge the progress that some individuals and teams have made toward creating a more bilingual culture in MLB clubhouses. Parker, for example, did not see Francisco Peña's Spanish tutelage only as useful for his personal language development but as a "great resource . . . [to] constantly [make] my Spanish better and my ability to be a resource for teammates better." Parker spoke of giving his Latin American teammates "a sense of comfort in a foreign environment" by serving as a de facto interpreter in everyday interactions and higher-stakes moments, such as when he had to translate a teammate's MRI results at a medical appointment. His belief that Spanish equipped him to be a better resource for his teammates led him to remark that he wished MLB teams would require their English speakers to take Spanish classes, just as Spanish-speaking players take English classes:

> I think that would be a great organizational thing to have. And I know it probably would ruffle a lot of feathers and people [would] be like, "I don't have to do this. We speak English here." That's part of the problem, probably. . . . But I think that

would be something really cool, a team being like, "We make these guys pass an English proficiency test or take English class to a certain point where they can do it. We're gonna do the same thing [in Spanish] for our English-speaking players."

In saying that mandatory Spanish classes "would ruffle a lot of feathers," Parker expressed his awareness of "monoglot standard" English-only ideologies in the national language community within which clubhouse speech communities are embedded, and in relation to which Latin American players' language learning takes place (Silverstein, 1998). However, in referring to these ideologies, Parker framed Spanish classes as a question of fairness: if Spanish-speaking players can be expected to learn English "to a certain point where they can do it," why can't English speakers be expected to gain a minimal amount of Spanish proficiency?

The desirability of Spanish classes for English speakers—and the importance of Spanish to communication and relationships among teammates—came up frequently in conversations with players and team personnel. While some were heartened to see individuals' efforts to bridge linguistic and cultural divides in the clubhouse, they also professed that a more systematic approach from organizations would have a greater effect. Jill Long de Mercado of Higher Standards Academy, the A's contracted education provider, said that "there are organizations that take language across the board . . . [and] do English and Spanish for players and coaches." Oakland was "planning to transition into" such an across-the-board approach, said Jill, though the Covid-19 pandemic derailed their plans. She speculated that the education team would "probably pick that up maybe halfway through the season." In any case, there was significant demand for Spanish classes, at least as Jill saw it: "Coaches are always asking about it, players are always asking about it."

Dave Bush, the Red Sox pitching coach at the time of writing, affirmed the need for English-speaking players to become bilingual professionals and pointed to the lack of support for doing so:

> I certainly think we could do a better job with immersion programs for American players. . . . The presence of Latino players is so strong and they're such a huge part of the game that I think [the] willingness on both sides, for Latin players to learn English and for American players to learn Spanish, is beneficial for both.

Dave was speaking as someone who had dealt with the limitations of his own linguistic repertoire while pitching in the Korea Baseball Organization (KBO) and coaching in international settings from China to South Africa to Australia (see Chapter 4). He was also speaking from his experience in the Red Sox organization, where he witnessed Puerto Rican–born manager Alex Cora's ability to connect with players in Spanish and English:

> I saw it with Alex Cora as our manager. Because he's bilingual, he can connect with so many people. He can sit down and talk with Latino players very comfortably and honestly, and he can do the same with the American players. And I think the ability to communicate one on one like that without having a third person in the room all the time goes a long way towards building the relationships that are so important.

Having been on the other side of the linguistic equation in Korea and elsewhere, Dave appreciated that efforts to communicate in a player's mother tongue, even with a "truncated repertoire" or a limited set of tools, could have a profound impact (Blommaert, 2010). This was especially true, he reminded me, in the heat of the moment or when things weren't going well. Dave painted a picture from his KBO days that evoked Mike Montgomery's difficulties in Korea (see Chapter 4):

> If I'm standing on the mound and the pitching coach comes out, it's probably not a good situation. They don't come out just to say, "Keep it up!" So I can remember those moments when my pitching coach in Korea tried to at least say a little bit of English. It's like, okay, I'm not totally lost here; at least I can pick up the word or two that you said. And there's some comfort there. So I have found with Spanish-speaking players that putting in the effort to try to learn Spanish— and I'm still trying to get better at, and I still have a ways to go, but I try to at least have a small conversation in Spanish with them every day.

Dave regretted that he had not understood the importance of learning more Korean or Chinese while playing and coaching abroad. He described his Spanish as "not great" and "certainly not fluent," but like Jeff Diskin, he saw his Spanish efforts as meaningful to the players, both in giving them a sense of comfort and in exemplifying a positive, proactive stance toward bilingualism. Spanish was useful for sense-making and "at-ease making," for simplifying in-game communication and welcoming Spanish speakers into the "house" of American baseball, to borrow Juan Mosquera's image (Richardson Bruna, 2009).

Jeff mentioned that L1 English speakers in the Royals organization had access to Rosetta Stone, the popular interactive digital language-learning program, and were encouraged to use the software to learn Spanish but were not required to take Spanish classes. "The Marlins do [require it]. Maybe we should," he mused, piquing my interest in the Miami Marlins' attempt to "become the first bilingual professional sports organization in the world," as a 2020 news article put it (Páez, 2020).

I reached out to Emily Glass, a scout and scout operations administrator for the Colorado Rockies, who, in her previous job as the Marlins' education coordinator, was tasked with creating a bilingual player education program. After college, Emily had interned with the MLB office in Santo Domingo, Dominican Republic, where she "got very interested in how different teams build out different programs in terms of baseball ops and player education and staff development," leading to her position with the Marlins. Emily led the education program for four years, and while she was hesitant to claim that the program had broken new ground—"I just want to clarify, there was definitely more than one team that has done it"—she was happy to talk about how the program got started and what made it possible.

According to Emily, two factors were crucial in the Marlins' development of a program that "[took] language across the board": the team's location in South Florida and ownership's belief in the importance of bilingualism. The Marlins were uniquely positioned to promote the benefits of becoming a bilingual organization, she said, both because of the demographics of Miami, a major destination for Latin American immigrants past and present, and because of the strongly Latino character of the organization (Carter & Lynch, 2015).[11] Nearly half of the Marlins' players in MLB and MiLB hailed from Latin American countries during Emily's time with the club. Because of this, she asserted, the team was conscious not only of having to prepare Latin American prospects for life in the United States but of ensuring that players from the United States were prepared to encounter the diversity of the Miami area:

> There was an emphasis on trying to make the program truly bilingual and prepare players [from] the US, as well, for the diversity of culture and life in South Florida. . . . The truth is that the program was created because to be successful in South Florida, you need to speak some Spanish. And it's not just about an emphasis on, you know, teaching the Latin players English and some of those skills. It was also about preparing our draft picks and the players from the US to understand the diversity that is South Florida.

The commitment to building a bilingual organization went beyond players' adaptation to South Florida. As other voices in this chapter have attested, many English speakers in MLB appreciate the potential of Spanish to break down social barriers in the clubhouse and on the field. In this case, Emily credited the Marlins' former chief executive officer, Hall of Fame shortstop Derek Jeter, with seeking to "instill a culture of communication and camaraderie" that embraced language learning across the board:

> The Marlins' CEO was a player, and he's very passionate about being a good teammate. And he was, I would say, integral in creating the program to try to instill in players a culture ... of communication and camaraderie.

Emily also mentioned that conversations with Gary Denbo, the Marlins' former vice president for player development and scouting, were pivotal in setting the stage for the bilingual program. However, she contrasted the team's grand designs for the program with what, in her view, would be required to create a "truly bilingual" organization in reality. While the front office was supportive, they may have underestimated the complexity and time-intensive nature of language learning, leading to what Emily termed "implementation issues." I asked how the organization had viewed the program—for example, what goals they had for their L1 English speakers and whether they saw it as a success. Emily quoted a Marlins executive who spoke in "big swaths," as she put it, but perhaps failed to recognize that the team's language goals were not aligned with prospects' career timelines and the demands on everyone's time in an MLB organization:

> "We're gonna be the first bilingual professional sports organization!" But, like, they're a baseball organization. So I don't think they understand what that truly looks like, but that's what the stated goal was, I guess. Or what it means to gain even [an] intermediate level, let alone fluency, in another language—it takes like eight years of education or immersion, you know. And the average baseball career is like four years, so ... I think that those were the stated goals, despite the implementation issues. I've come from public policy, so that's where I see that those weren't aligned.

An overly optimistic view of what can be accomplished in a relatively short period of language learning is not exclusive to baseball executives. It's a popular folk ideology—albeit one without research to support it—that has been used to pass laws stipulating that immigrant English learners only have access to one year of English instruction before transitioning to mainstream classes (Long & Adamson, 2012). Those who have worked directly with language learners, like Emily and Jill, tend to be more realistic about what players should be able to do with their L2 in view of the small amount of time set aside for instruction and practice. This accounts in part for the narrow focus on "baseball language" and transitional skills in most programs. As we have seen, individual players who are determined to learn the L2 well—Yosmi Fernández, Michel Gelabert, Parker Dunshee, Alex Bregman—recognize that they need to seek out their own resources (e.g., Rosetta Stone, Netflix subtitles, and Duolingo) and leverage interpersonal relationships with teammates and friends to get the input and practice they need.

The Marlins were keen to publicize their bilingual success stories on social media, posting video clips of L1 English speakers like JJ Bleday and Peyton Burdick and L1 Spanish speakers like Victor Mesa, Jr., conversing, or at least making an effort, in their second language. With Parker Dunshee's comments in mind, I was curious whether Marlins players had embraced the program or if its compulsory nature had "ruffled any feathers." Emily provided a few examples of players who had made the most of the program. As with Kevin Goldstein's comments about Alex Bregman, and as Derek Jeter's vision for the Marlins' program would imply, Emily tied players' investment in Spanish learning to their leadership ability and their pride in the "craft" of baseball (Peirce, 1995). They are baseball players first—as everyone reminded me—but Emily, like Parker, suggested that at least *some* English speakers saw bilingualism as a way to become a more complete player—the "Sixth Tool," as the Royals would have it:

> The players that have embraced it, like the JJ Bledays, and like Connor Scott, those guys really take pride [in] their craft and have leadership ability. So they embraced the program and wanted to do anything they could to get better and be poised to communicate to the community of South Florida [and] to their teammates.

It's hard not to be impressed with the Marlins' ambition and the dedication and progress of some of the players who participated in the bilingual program. Given the apparent need for such programs in MLB, it is also heartening to see what is possible in the right context with the right leadership—not to mention skilled educators like Emily and her team, who made the program a reality.

Viewed differently, however, Emily's story points out the fragility of such programs. The Marlins' program was susceptible to the "difficulty of gathering together" during the Covid-19 pandemic and the "scarcity of time," even before the pandemic, that led the program to be de-emphasized, in Emily's view, during her final year with the Marlins. Now that Emily, one of the architects of the program, has taken a different job, she was unsure how much of the program had survived her departure and the pandemic. Her pride in the program's successes, especially in strengthening the team's "culture of communication and camaraderie," was evident. So, too, was her regret at not knowing what future awaited the program she'd helped to create.

"Are You Gonna Be Willing to Fail like That?": Empathy in the Clubhouse and Beyond

L1 English speakers who found themselves at a linguistic disadvantage—speaking their L2 or immersed in a language they didn't speak—developed a profound appreciation for the trials that non-English speakers had to undergo on their way to the major leagues. Encountering and speaking different languages did not just affect English speakers' ability to communicate and their relationships with teammates. In small but consequential ways, it transformed their *subjectivities*, or the way they saw themselves in relation to others, as language learners and users (Vitanova, 2005). It inspired them to put themselves in the shoes of young Latin American players arriving in the United States, for example, while acknowledging the obvious differences between their situations. In reflecting on his experience playing and coaching in Korea, China, and elsewhere, Dave Bush commented:

> I have a huge appreciation for players that come to the US to play. Having been on the other side of that, where I was in a different country where I didn't speak the language and I was somewhat by myself, I know how they feel. I get it. I'm not in their shoes necessarily in that moment, but I have a good appreciation for what they're up against and how there can be a lot of comfort on the field, but there can be a lot of discomfort away from the field.

Dave was careful not to overstate the similarities between his experience and those of young *peloteros* in the United States, emphasizing that however difficult his time in Korea might have been, he could not imagine going through such a transition as a teenager "when you aren't as mature and you don't have the life skills to handle it": "In a lot of cases with Latin players, they're teenagers. I was thirty, thirty-one, thirty-two when I went to Korea. I was married with three kids. . . . Life was easier for me at that point." Still, he felt that he could empathize with young Latin American players and "appreciat[e] what they're trying to do and how hard it is." Dave commented on the ironic contrast between players' comfort on the field—baseball being baseball—and their discomfort off the field, where "you're not understanding what's wanted and [you] feel lost." Now, as an MLB coach who had "been on the player side of it" in the KBO, he saw the value in "being compassionate [and] understanding the challenges that [international players] are facing are more than just baseball."

When Parker Dunshee heard English speakers mocking or criticizing Spanish speakers' attempts to communicate in English, he pushed them to put themselves in their teammates' shoes, asking them to consider how they would feel if the situation were reversed. Parker's perspective as a Spanish learner equipped him to advocate for Latin American players who were "willing to fail," as he put it, by taking risks in English, just as Francisco Peña had urged Parker to do in Spanish. Without this perspective, said Parker, English speakers "don't necessarily understand" what their Spanish-speaking counterparts go through in the United States:

> I think that a lot of guys don't necessarily understand, when a Spanish[-speaking] guy's trying to say something in English and they're struggling [and] some of the English[-speaking] guys give him a hard time or whatever. I'm like, "Dude, you know how nerve wracking that probably is for that guy, just to put himself out there and be willing to fail?
>
> Try to put yourself in his shoes for a second. I'm just gonna drop you in Venezuela, and you're gonna play for one of their winter ball teams. And there are gonna be no other guys who speak English on the team and good luck. Like, are you gonna feel comfortable? Are you gonna be willing to fail like that?"

Thanks to his experience of learning Spanish, Parker was able to invite his teammates "to 'step out' of the flow of ongoing events and the world they constitute," to imagine how the world looked to someone else, and to modify their behavior accordingly (Duranti, 2009). In other words, he prodded them to experiment with the very process that underlies language socialization. For Parker, however, this process was not limited to empathizing with his Spanish-speaking teammates on linguistic grounds. He also brought a critical perspective to the clubhouse, encouraging English speakers to acknowledge how different their social and economic circumstances were from those of their Latino teammates. Dave Bush also hinted at this in contrasting young *peloteros*' transition to life in the United States with his own "easier" adaptation to South Korea in his thirties. At times, players and coaches who had lived abroad, like Dave, or learned an additional language, like Parker, echoed ESL educators, who understood how much higher the stakes were for Latin American players compared to players from the United States. As Parker addressed an imaginary English-speaking teammate:

> What poverty means to [Latin American players] is like nothing you've ever seen before. And some of those guys come from situations like that, and this is their chance. So give 'em a break every once in a while, if they're a little emotional or a little life or death on every pitch. They're playing with passion, like, that's just

what they have to do to make their dream a reality. They have the same dream as you, but their stakes, in some cases, are a lot higher.

Reading between the lines, it is evident that—in Parker's view, anyway—negative reactions to Spanish-speaking players are not only, or even primarily, about language but have to do with Latinos' supposedly "emotional," "passion[ate]," "life and death on every pitch" approach to the game. In one sense, this is unremarkable; anxieties about language diversity often veil concerns about demographic change and cultural transformation. Given young Latin Americans' dominance in MLB, their different understanding of "appropriate" baseball behavior has raised hackles among US players, ex-players, and coaches steeped in a different set of norms. These are the so-called unwritten rules of baseball comportment, which, like the unspoken rules of "appropriate" language use, are often applied unevenly to speakers and players from different ethnic and racial backgrounds (Flores & Rosa, 2015). To quote Parker's imaginary teammate, words like *passion* and *emotion* can function as coded language for *peloteros'* demonstrative on-field style, exemplified in bat flips and standing back to admire home runs (or "pimping" them), and seen by US baseball traditionalists as counter to the spirit of the game.

As I was revising this chapter, a related controversy was unfolding: the Atlanta Braves' Venezuelan phenom Ronald Acuña commented that he would not miss his former teammate, five-time All-Star Freddie Freeman (who had just signed with the Los Angeles Dodgers), because Acuña perceived that Freeman had treated him disrespectfully when the former debuted with Atlanta in 2018. Both players seemed eager to move on from a media frenzy that started with an off-the-cuff remark of Acuña's. Acuña said the situation had been "exaggerated and blown out of proportion" and Freeman called it "unfortunate," adding that he "love[d] Ronald" and would in fact miss him (Harvey, 2022).

What was interesting, from my perspective, was how differently the two players described what happened in 2018. Acuña saw Freeman's behavior as an attempt to enforce cultural expectations around "professionalism" (see Chapter 1) that might conflict with Latinos' "emotion" and "passion," but that were also tied to elements of how players *embody* the game. According to Acuña, "You come up from the minor leagues with the big eye black, the sunglasses, the hat low, and a lot of people see that as wrong."[12] I was reminded of the diagram that outlined the Royals' detailed expectations for how to wear the uniform "with pride" (also in Chapter 1). In Acuña's telling, Freeman and other "veterans" had intervened to wipe the offending eye black off Acuña's face. Freeman did not deny it but said that he was acting as one of the "older guys" trying to enforce "organizational rules"—the Braves, like the Royals and Yankees, have fairly stringent norms for players' uniforms, hairstyles, and so forth, which Freeman felt he was expected to communicate to younger players. (Acuña is also a notorious home run pimper, which apparently led Freeman to confront him on at least one other occasion.)

I do not mean to pass judgment on either player, only to point out that—as in Parker's comments about the high stakes underlying Latinos' "passion," college teammates' negative reactions to Luis Victoria's Dominican "flair" (in Chapter 1), and MLB staff's remarks about Spanish speakers' English learning (in Chapter 2)—Latin American players' verbal behavior and on-field comportment get yoked together with their hair and clothing, among other things, in a "discursive formation"[13] within which conflict between English and Spanish speakers becomes comprehensible, at least for media and fans. In other words, everything they do is understood in relation to the social persona of the brash, Spanish-speaking Latin American ballplayer.

This is the less "convivial" side of intercultural communication in baseball, which surfaces in remarks from English speakers who are unable or unwilling to put themselves in their Latino teammates' shoes. In a newspaper article from 2015 that sought to blame a "culture clash" within baseball for an increase in brawls and hostilities, then Padres pitcher Bud Norris, a California native, cited Latino players' "antics" as a contributing factor, adding, "If you're going to come into our country and make our American dollars, you need to respect a game that has been here for over 100 years" (Ortiz, 2016). It was impossible to miss the whiff of anti-immigrant discourse, which was ramping up as the 2016 US presidential election neared. The implication was that Latin American ballplayers are immigrants who are lucky to be making "American dollars," so they need to assimilate—behaviorally and linguistically—or get out. Recall Panamanian scout Juan Mosquera's comments about Latinos' needing to learn how to behave "professionally": "Truthfully, this isn't our house"—never mind the fact that Spanish-speaking Latinos have been playing baseball in the United States since at least 1869 (see "Introduction").

Rather than holding Spanish speakers accountable for violating baseball's unwritten rules, Parker Dunshee saw their passion and emotion as indicative of the high stakes of professional baseball for people coming from "poverty like nothing you've never seen before." The same emotion that other US-born players might dismiss as "antics" could just as easily be seen as "what they have to do to make their dream a reality"—and, as we have seen, such teenage dreams are fragile indeed.

Of course, not every Latin American ballplayer comes from the same socioeconomic background, and Latinos' on-field behavior varies as widely as their relationship with English learning. As Emily Glass said, the range of responses among Latinos is "vast." We don't need to accept Parker's premise—that Latinos' on-field passion stems from their constant awareness of the life-and-death stakes—to appreciate that his socialization into Spanish gave him the ability to empathize deeply with his Spanish-speaking teammates and approach everyday interactions with compassion and curiosity. Relatively few English speakers in MLB have attained a similar degree of Spanish proficiency. All the same, the voices of players, coaches, executives, and educators in this chapter suggest that as patterns of language use change in US baseball—however slowly—so, too, relationships like Parker Dunshee's and Francisco Peña's will become more common, as clubhouses move gingerly toward a less-segregated equilibrium.

4

Forging Transnational Connections through Language Brokering and Language Learning in Asian Baseball

The year was 2012, and right-hander Dave Bush was nearing the end of the road, as far as his major league playing career was concerned. The Toronto Blue Jays had drafted Bush in the second round in 2002, and he went on to play nine seasons with Toronto, Milwaukee, and Texas, pitching over a thousand innings and earning a reputation as a dependable and durable starter. Like Elvin Liriano (in Chapter 2), Dave was hanging on to his big-league dream. Still, after spending nine years in MLB, pitching for the Lehigh Valley IronPigs of Allentown, Pennsylvania—the Philadelphia Phillies' Triple-A affiliate—while waiting for a better opportunity was not Dave's ideal scenario: "I still had the desire to play and kind of push a little bit, but I didn't really want to be in Triple-A." This was especially the case since Dave's wife and three small children were at home in Maine.

Dave's fortunes took an unexpected turn on a road trip to Gwinnett, Georgia, where Lehigh Valley was playing the Braves' AAA team. He had noticed Korean scouts (he assumed) at a few of the IronPigs' games but had not given them much thought until he was accosted in spy movie fashion:

> I was walking back from breakfast one morning, this car pulls over to the side of the road, and these two Korean guys jumped out and started talking to me. One of 'em was the translator, spoke very good English. And so he jumps out and says who they are, and they're looking for a pitcher 'cause one of their foreign players had just gotten hurt. And he said, "Are you interested?" Just kind of a quick conversation. I said, "Yeah, I'm definitely interested. Like, tell me what's up, let's see what the options are." And the quick version is . . . within a week, I was on a plane to Korea.

Bringing the plan to fruition involved another "quick conversation" with Dave's wife as well as ironing out contract details with Incheon's SK Wyverns and the

Phillies.[1] Several quirks of US and Korean baseball were behind the apparently serendipitous match of player and team. As a major league veteran signed to a US minor league contract, Dave had an "Asian league out"—a provision that would allow him to pursue professional opportunities in Asia and opt out of his contract with the Phillies for a small buyout. At the time, Korean professional baseball (KBO) teams were limited to having two non-Korean players; one of the Wyverns' foreign players had just gotten injured, opening up a roster spot.[2] Dave was the right person at the right time: experienced, unsure if he would make it back to MLB, and open to a "cool opportunity . . . to do something different" and "get paid a little bit." After a fourteen-hour flight, Dave, his wife, and their kids—four and a half, two and a half, and five months old—found themselves in a hotel in Incheon, the adults' heads spinning:

> We're all jet lagged. And all five of us are awake at two o'clock in the morning, Korean time. And so we're sitting there, we're halfway around the world. We don't know what to do. There's no one to talk to. . . . We're kind of stuck. And so we find breakfast at the hotel, and my wife and I are sitting there, like, where are we right now? And what just happened in the last few days that we ended up here trying to find breakfast for ourselves and three little white kids . . . you know, in a country that's as homogeneous as they get?

As Dave acknowledged, his situation differed from that of the young Latin American players he would later encounter as a coach with the Red Sox (see Chapter 3). "Life was easier," in many ways, for a thirty-something father of three with a long track record in professional baseball compared to a teenager from Venezuela or the Dominican Republic living away from family and expected to "become professional" in short order. Unlike young Latin American players, however, Dave could not count on a community of teammates who shared his linguistic and cultural background. Restricting the number of non-Korean players ensures that KBO clubhouses reflect the ethnic homogeneity of Korean society (the same is true in Japanese baseball). In Dave's case, the Wyverns' other foreign player, Puerto Rican–born pitcher Mario Santiago, spoke English, but apart from one or two Korean players and the pitching coach, who spoke "a little bit," no one else did.

Even so, the challenges Dave faced in the clubhouse and on the field paled in comparison to his family's difficulties away from the field. Being responsible for three young children meant that Dave and his wife had no choice but to adapt quickly. Dave recalled their mindset: "Well, here we are. We're not going anywhere until the season ends. So let's figure it out." The family figured things out "slowly but surely," Dave remembered, beginning with the necessities—"We gotta find food that the kids'll eat. We gotta find baby formula"—and gradually branching out. The team provided them with a car, but since all the street signs were in Korean, Dave "had to learn [his] way around the city first before [he] was willing to drive at all." Even learning to give directions to taxi drivers took time.

Despite all this, Dave and his family discovered a sense of triumph in adapting successfully to life in Incheon, which Dave attributed in part to their "willingness to embrace the challenges": "Even though it's difficult, if you embrace them, then there's some satisfaction and enjoyment in getting through each day and finding something new." That attitude undoubtedly contributed to Dave's success—not only in Korea but in his subsequent work to promote baseball worldwide for MLB International.

Other American transplants to Asian baseball who, like Dave, "embraced the challenges" of thriving in an unfamiliar setting saw themselves as outliers, to a degree, and contrasted their experiences with those of foreign "imports" who were just looking to collect a paycheck. Nick Additon, the Florida-born pitching coach for the Chinatrust Brothers of the Chinese Professional Baseball League in Taiwan, put it this way:

> As a foreigner . . . you can go to Asia, you can go to the Dominican, Mexico, and be like, "Listen, I'm a hired gun. You guys are here paying me to help your baseball team win on the field. And I'm here to do a job and that's play on the field and I could care less what my teammates think." And that's honestly a lot of imports that come over.

As in the preceding chapters, some measure of what psychologists call "intercultural competence"—the ability to "function effectively across cultures," tied, among other things, to "social flexibility" and "adaptability to communication"—is crucial for ballplayers' successful transitions to new linguistic and cultural contexts, especially for building relationships with diverse teammates (Leung, Ang, & Tan, 2014). If you see yourself merely as a "hired gun," per Nick, regardless of on-field performance, your teammates and coaches might read your behavior as a lack of respect, leading to fewer opportunities in the future: "I've seen guys come over and pitch well [but] everybody hated 'em, and they weren't brought back. And I've seen guys pitch just okay, but man, everybody loved that guy and, 'Okay. We're gonna bring him back and give him a second chance.'"

All the same, it would be a mistake to see Dave's Korean encounters merely as the expression of a tolerant, curious disposition or evidence of "intercultural competence," understood as an inner psychological state. As in previous chapters, *enacting* intercultural competence, or being able to communicate effectively in cross-cultural interactions, required language brokers who acted as gatekeepers in supporting cultural novices (like Dave). Dave was quick to credit the skilled bilinguals who helped him and his family "figure out" everyday life in Incheon, through interpretation and translation, and "navigat[e] the differences culturally." His team-assigned interpreter played an important role. Even more important, however, was the family's relationship with a bilingual Korean American family who had recently moved to Incheon from California and were "a huge help in helping us get acclimated," said Dave, particularly since the other family also had young children.

Dave's story speaks to the central concern of this chapter: the unpredictable routes that people take to careers in Asian baseball and the place of language in making those journeys possible. In contrast to the one-way flow of young baseball talent from Latin America to the United States, migrant streams in Asian baseball are multidirectional. The best Japanese, Korean, and Taiwanese players often migrate from East to West—from East Asia to the United States—but many players and coaches from the United States and Latin America end up playing or working in NPB (Japan), the KBO (South Korea), or the CPBL (Taiwan). For some, this has as much to do with the allure of baseball as the "allure of money" (see Chapter 2). It didn't hurt that Dave would "get paid a little bit" in Korea—more than Lehigh Valley, anyway—but his decision probably had more to do with the desire to keep playing in the absence of MLB opportunities. Baseball dreams can die just as hard for MLB veterans like Dave Bush as they do for those who never make it to the highest level, like Elvin Liriano.

Asian professional leagues are sometimes the final stop for aging players whose skills no longer "play" in MLB. Sometimes, however, they provide opportunities for players to rebuild their careers and prove themselves in a high-level professional situation with the goal of securing major league contracts and returning to the United States (in recent years, Eric Thames, Miles Mikolas, and Nick Martinez, among others, have taken this path). Asian teams looking for a competitive advantage often employ ex-MLB players in coaching or player development. On the other hand, the transnational entanglements of US and Asian baseball can open up opportunities for speakers of Korean, Mandarin Chinese, and Japanese, who capitalize creatively on their bilingual and cultural capital to become the language brokers and gatekeepers for "imports" like Dave Bush and Nick Additon.

Brokering Transnational Careers in Korean Baseball

Hyunsung Kim, the Kansas City Royals' international scout for South Korea, was well aware that players and coaches moving from the United States to Asia and vice versa had to be prepared to navigate cultural differences, as Dave Bush put it. In his role as the Royals' only Korea-based scout, Hyunsung had to be a jack of all trades—scouting all levels of baseball, from high school through the KBO, shooting and compiling video, doing some analytics, hosting Royals staffers visiting Korea to cross-check (confirm) Hyunsung's scouting reports, and informally mentoring young Korean players who had signed with the Royals. The last two responsibilities, in particular, required extensive linguistic and cultural brokering. In Hyunsung's view, however, players and coaches tended to underestimate how much could be lost in translation from one baseball context to another. For Koreans as well as Americans, the folk ideology that "baseball language" was universal could hide what Hyunsung called "different cultural layers" that required behavioral "adjustments":

> I hear a lot of players say—especially Korean players going over to the States—and most of the time they'll say, "Baseball, it's just baseball," or . . . "We speak baseball" or something like that. To some point that's true, but you know, if you really dig deep in, there's these different cultural layers [so] that they'll have to make adjustments.

The story of Hyunsung's American baseball fandom and subsequent career in the game is a case study of linguistic and cultural cross-pollination in transnational baseball, where the presence of baseball is intertwined with colonial and military endeavors—as in the introduction of baseball to Japan (as a civilizing practice tied to military schooling), the forcible spreading of Japanese baseball to Taiwan and Korea, and the Cold War–era presence of the United States in South Korea. Hyunsung first encountered American baseball on a television network that was an artifact of the Korean and Cold Wars; he later spent time in the United States because of his father's job, which also depended on the close, asymmetrical relationship between the United States and South Korea; he learned English through schooling and everyday interactions in the United States and was able to use his bilingualism to carve out a space for Korean MLB fandom on the early internet. His story is idiosyncratic in that it depended on the circumstances of his young life, but it is also bound up with longer-simmering historical developments.

As a child growing up in Seoul, Hyunsung loved watching the World Wrestling Federation on the American Forces Korea Network (AFKN; now AFN), a television station for US military servicemembers posted in Korea. Wrestling was often preceded by Major League Baseball games, and over time, Hyunsung began to take an interest in baseball. He developed his fandom and his English during two childhood stints in the United States—owing to his father's work as a foreign correspondent for the *Korea Times*—most significantly during the second stay, in Hyunsung's middle school years. The family lived in New Jersey, but his father worked in New York City, where Hyunsung got to attend baseball games in person in addition to watching games on TV nearly every night during the season.

For Hyunsung, learning English and becoming an MLB fan went hand in hand. Back in South Korea, during his undergraduate years (1999–2000), he leveraged his English expertise from his time in the United States as a mediator for Korean speakers who wanted to follow American teams. He joined an online group that crowdsourced language work, assigning Korean-English bilinguals as "beat translators" for MLB teams.[3] (Google Translate could now do this work with a click.) Hyunsung was tasked with covering the Detroit Tigers. His affinity for the Tigers dated to childhood, because of their mascot—"I was more into the animals, what they represented"—and he found himself diving into written translation of game recaps from the *Detroit Free Press* and other English-language publications.

Multilingual, Intercultural Communication in an Umpiring Crew

The year 2013 brought the World Baseball Classic (WBC), an international tournament that was being held in Japan, and with it, an opportunity for a different sort of language brokering. A friend of Hyunsung's recruited him to provide real-time, simultaneous interpretation for a KBO umpire who had been dispatched to Japan for the event. In addition to Hyunsung's Korean-English bilingualism and background in baseball translation, his limited but functional Japanese made him an attractive candidate. He had learned the basics of Japanese in his Korean high school and developed conversational proficiency on a forty-day, two-thousand-mile bicycle trip across Japan in 2008, where, he said, he used the language "to survive—make orders at restaurants, buy stuff at the supermarket, look for a place to sleep, read road signs, ask directions . . . . Random people would ask me questions, and I wanted to at least have an idea what they were asking."

In all, Hyunsung spent twelve days in Japan during the WBC, interpreting for about sixteen games, and enjoyed the experience so much that he would hang around the video room with the umpires even when his language brokering services weren't required. Hyunsung's experience at the WBC testifies to the extreme diversity that characterizes the transnational game. As discussed earlier, this is sometimes called "superdiversity," meaning new and unexpected arrangements of people, and ensuing forms of communication, that arise as patterns of migration, settlement, and labor change, so that the "traditional" or "expected" forms of diversity are not the only or even the dominant ones. The idea is that diversity itself is becoming more diverse—in certain contexts, anyway—as social conditions change, so our analyses need to account for these "newer" dimensions of diversity in addition to the older, supposedly more predictable ones (see, e.g., Blommaert & Rampton, 2015).[4]

Umpires generally work in crews of four, at least in high-level professional leagues and international competitions, to cover as much of the field as possible. At the WBC, the Korean umpire to whom Hyunsung was attached was on a crew with a Japanese umpire (accompanied by a Japanese-English interpreter), a Puerto Rican umpire, and an umpire from the Dominican Republic. English was the lingua franca of the crew's pregame meetings, where the bulk of Hyunsung's interpretation took place, as the umpires discussed "how they're going to work together if there is an argument or . . . how they're going to solve the argument," along with technical aspects of the rulebook that might not be clear. During these meetings, the Japanese umpire would rely on his interpreter, while the Puerto Rican umpire, who spoke some English, interpreted informally for his Dominican counterpart. The reliance on informal language brokering in addition to compensated labor is not surprising. Children from immigrant families, for example, are often expected to interpret for free—at the doctor's office, in parent-teacher conferences, at the store, with first responders—despite the complexity of the task, the high stakes of many such interactions, and the fact that others would be relatively helpless without their language work (Orellana, 2009) (Figure 18).

While Hyunsung enjoyed interpreting during the crew's pregame meetings, he found it uniquely challenging because of the rapid-fire nature of the interaction and the need for discreet, simultaneous translation. He characterized those meetings as "tough situations," in contrast to non-baseball settings where he had worked and where there was generally more support for language work, in terms of technology and accommodations for interpreter-mediated interaction:

> It's a tough situation because during the meetings, it's more simultaneous translation that you have to do, or whispering and simultaneous translation, whereas, you know, when you go to a big conference . . . unless you have someone talking in the booth and you have these headsets, you have someone,

Figure 18 Interpreter Hyunsung Kim, Larry Young (MLB umpire supervisor, former MLB umpire), Félix Tejada (umpire from the DR), a Japanese umpire, and Carlos Rey (umpire from Puerto Rico) on a day off at the 2013 World Baseball Classic in Japan (Hyunsung Kim). Reproduced with permission of Hyunsung Kim.

you know, sitting beside the speaker and once the speaker says something the translator will translate. So it's like, you know, what the speaker says, and then the translation and so on.

But in the umpires' meeting, the head of the umpire crew, he just keeps talking. While you're translating, he's [saying] something else. But you have to grab on to that. So you can't really do a full translation of whatever has come out. You just need to briefly summarize it, just tell them the important stuff.

In Hyunsung's experience in other professional contexts, such as "a big conference," either someone physically set apart from the speaker—"talking in a booth" to audience members on headsets—would interpret simultaneously, or an interpreter "sitting beside the speaker" would conduct consecutive interpretation—that is, waiting for the speaker to pause and then interpreting the most recent "chunk" of the speaker's discourse.

Hyunsung implied that either option was more conducive to "doing a full translation" than his catch-as-catch-can strategy, in which he had to "grab on" to the gist of what the crew chief was saying even as he tried to "summarize . . .

the important stuff" that had preceded it. Empirical research on simultaneous versus consecutive interpretation suggests that each approach has pros and cons, depending on one's criteria for a good or successful performance (see, e.g., Gile, 2001; Russell, 2005; Lv & Liang, 2019). Be that as it may, Hyunsung certainly felt that simultaneous interpretation for the umpiring crew demanded a high "cognitive load" or "the portion of an interpreter's limited cognitive capacity devoted to performing an interpreting task in a certain environment" (Chen, 2017). In other words, since Hyunsung did not have unlimited cognitive capacity, the pregame meetings were especially difficult because factors *beyond* interpretation taxed his cognitive resources—having to interpret simultaneously, having to whisper to avoid interrupting the crew chief, the presence of multiple languages and forms of language brokering, and so forth.

Even so, Hyunsung embraced the challenge of interpreting for crew meetings, calling them "more intense" but also "more fun" than his intermittent language work during the games themselves:

> They made me wait in the video replay room. . . . And whenever the Korean umpire had some kind of misunderstanding or the manager of each team came out and . . . they wanted to argue about a call or if they didn't understand what the umpire was saying, then the umpire would call me, just give me some kind of hand signal, and I would go out and translate whatever they were talking about.

I commented that arguments and misunderstandings sounded like "high-pressure situations" for interpretation, but Hyunsung said that in-game interpretation was "a bit bland, actually, because there weren't any serious arguments. It was more making substitutions . . . . It wasn't that enjoyable on the field." Again, as with children who interpret for their families, the challenging and high-stakes nature of language work was inseparable from the "intensity" that made it rewarding (Reynolds & Orellana, 2009). Along with the pregame meetings, Hyunsung liked interpreting "daily conversations" for the umpiring crew, some of which required him to use his knowledge of Japanese or to stretch his repertoire in new directions. Hyunsung's Japanese speaking and listening ability was "very limited," in his words, but he relied on his Japanese literacy to broker everyday interactions for the Korean umpire, translating what was on the scoreboard, most critically, but also "tagging along" to restaurants and shops.

When Hyunsung found himself alone with the Dominican umpire—the only person on the crew with whom he did not share a language—he would ask the umpire to teach him basic baseball vocabulary in Spanish to prepare himself to mediate future interactions. Like the Spanish-speaking minor leaguers in

Chapter 2, Hyunsung found rich opportunities for language development in the in-between moments of games and practices, when not much seemed to be happening.

> There was one moment where the Puerto Rican umpire was in the game and the Dominican umpire was just watching the game and he had so many questions, and I was the only translator there, so I just had to use gestures . . . . I actually asked him to teach me some Spanish baseball terms. Like I'll just show him a picture of first base . . . you know, what is this, he'll say, "*primera base*" and pick that up and use it next time he asked something.

Hyunsung's omnivorous attitude toward other languages in this quintessentially "superdiverse" interaction—a South Korean interpreter and a Dominican umpire in a Japanese stadium, making do with gestures and a bit of Spanish—was not only responsive to communication needs in the present (i.e., being able to communicate with the umpire in that moment) but also oriented toward the future. Even a single Spanish phrase, he reasoned, was something he could "pick up and use next time."

Some encounters among the umpiring crew were challenging not because of the demands of simultaneous interpretation but because they exposed the "different cultural layers" to which Hyunsung referred above. In some cases, those "cultural layers" had nothing to do with traditional Korean or American practices; instead, they reflected the economic realities of transnational baseball as a global business. Baseball may transcend borders, but as earlier chapters have established, not everyone in the world is on equal footing with regard to the financial game. This is nakedly evident in the Latin American prospect pipeline to MLB.

As Hyunsung discovered, this uneven economic landscape also shapes interactions among umpires from the MLB "metropole" and the Asian and Latin American "periphery." When I asked about sources of misunderstanding in interpreter-mediated encounters, he cited "more technical terms . . . not related to umpiring." Rather, misunderstandings came about due to "how Major League Baseball works over there [in the US]" as opposed to the rest of the world:

> For instance, one time we had a meeting and they were talking about—I forgot the word. . . . Authentication. You know, like, during a game, they put some kind of hologram sticker with the number on game-used uniforms or gloves or whatever. And for umpires, they could authenticate a sports card or something they've used over there.

Authenticating game-used items, popular among collectors of baseball memorabilia—sold as they are or chopped up into relics and embedded in baseball cards—was apparently a "side hustle" for the MLB umpires at the WBC. MLB has an entire program devoted to the authentication of such items, a task now carried out by off-duty law enforcement officers who personally witness the items' use in MLB games, after which each item "receive[s] a tamper-proof hologram . . . with a unique alphanumeric combination."[5] However the umpires in question were involved, Hyunsung's point was that the conversation laid bare the differences between "how MLB works" and how baseball works elsewhere, as the MLB umpires invoked a cultural concept—a specific process of "authentication"—that had no parallel in the Korean umpire's experience, much less his language (or Hyunsung's):[6]

> And I had no idea what they were talking about. . . . From the beginning, [they] were just shooting technical [terms]. I just literally translated, I think, "authentication." Obviously the Korean umpire had no idea what they were authenticating.

Hyunsung's facility with Korean and English (among other elements of his repertoire) had not prepared him to get across the meaning of a practice that was as alien to him as it was to the umpire he accompanied to the WBC. Without understanding what the English-speaking umpires meant, Hyunsung resorted to translating the word *authentication* literally, but neither he nor the umpire had any idea what it meant in context. This anecdote puts the lie to the idea that "baseball is just baseball," even on the field; while some aspects of baseball transfer neatly across borders, the economics of the transnational game dictate that some on-field activities in one setting will be incomprehensible in others (e.g., using tamper-proof holograms to authenticate game-used relics for resale).

The language ideology that "speaking baseball" made linguistic and cultural differences irrelevant was also called into question in situations where foreign players lacked knowledge of the "unwritten rules" of Korean baseball, just as Latin American players like Richard Guasch and Ronald Acuña transgressed the tacit code of MLB comportment, wittingly or unwittingly (see Chapters 2 and 3).

The Meaning of a Mound Visit: Translating Baseball Behaviour in Public

In early June 2021, veteran left-handed pitcher Mike Montgomery opted out of his minor league contract with the New York Yankees to sign with the Samsung Lions of the KBO. Montgomery had been effective as a starter and reliever with several MLB teams but had struggled with injuries in the pandemic-shortened

2020 season. As in Dave Bush's case, Montgomery's Korean opportunity arose because one of the Lions' foreign pitchers had injured his shoulder, resulting in a "foreign buyout" and an expedited transition to the KBO.

Montgomery's Korean comeback was derailed on September 10, 2021, in the top of the fifth inning of a game against the league leading KT Wiz, for reasons that were also connected to "different cultural layers." Montgomery had an on-field tirade for the ages, even by the standards of MLB, which has elevated such rants to the level of performance art. (It is not a frequent occurrence for managers to pull bases out of the ground and throw them into the outfield or kick them toward the dugout, but it's not unheard of, either.)[7] After he was ejected from the game, he resisted his teammates' efforts to restrain him and launched the rosin bag at the umpire's back, where it exploded in a cloud of white dust.[8] His teammates pulled him toward the dugout, but as they hustled him away, Montgomery pulled off his jersey, balled it up, and threw it back onto the field.

Montgomery's outburst, which resulted in a twenty-game suspension, was apparently in response to the umpire's having approached the pitcher's mound to inform Montgomery that he had violated the KBO's twelve-second pitch-clock rule, which dictates that the pitcher is supposed to deliver the next pitch within twelve seconds of receiving the ball from the catcher. Montgomery's behavior begs for a "cultural" explanation precisely because it doesn't seem to make any sense (Agar, 2008). People often appeal to the culture concept to explain what is happening beneath the surface of events—some unspoken norm, understanding, belief, or expectation that does not reveal itself based on observation alone. Here, a whole series of linguistic and cultural phenomena came to bear on a single interactional moment: the moment when the KBO umpire walked to the mound to let Montgomery know he had broken a rule.

The rule in question does not exist in MLB, so its in-game application would have been relatively unfamiliar to Montgomery, even if he had been exposed to the rule in MiLB and spring training, where it has been piloted. However, that was far from the only factor in Montgomery's reaction. Hyunsung reflected on the "awkwardness" of player-umpire interactions in such situations, where the superficial resemblance between baseball games in different parts of the world obscures the different social meanings associated with verbal and nonverbal behavior:

> What's different over here is that in [US] Major League Baseball . . . when someone violated a rule [the umpires will] just call it. But over here in Korea . . . they want to make the others feel more comfortable, so what they do is they actually go out to the mound and . . . kind of explain to the pitcher like, "You just violated the rule."

Korean umpires, said Hyunsung, took on a mentoring role at times, giving novice catchers tips on how to position themselves behind home plate and alerting pitchers to potentially illegal motions, rather than calling a balk[9] right away, as an MLB umpire would. Montgomery, however, interpreted the umpire's attempt to mentor him in the finer points of Korean baseball as a confrontational act.

> And for a pitcher who came from the States . . . it could feel very awkward or sometimes he could feel that the umpire's trying to confront him. . . . A lot of the Korean fans and people here . . . didn't catch this but I was able to hear what Mike Montgomery was saying on the mound when the umpire went back. He said, "Nobody cares about you [being] here. Stay behind the plate."

Hyunsung suggested that what was at stake in the Montgomery incident was not primarily linguistic difference, in the sense of different codes like Korean and English, but a misunderstanding of what the umpire's embodied activity (walking to the mound and addressing the pitcher directly) indexed in the context of Korean baseball. By providing an explanation of Montgomery's transgression, the umpire may have intended to make the pitcher "feel more comfortable," but an American pitcher might interpret this behavior as confrontational, since MLB umpires do not customarily approach the mound to explain their decisions. On the recording of Hyunsung's comments, you can hear me laughing incredulously in the background, picturing the absurd scenario—from an MLB fan's point of view—of an umpire marching to the mound to respectfully inform the pitcher that he had run afoul of the law.

Montgomery's experience, like Dave Bush's, illustrates why "language brokering" is a more accurate descriptor than "interpreting" or "translating." "Translating" is something that an app can do for you efficiently and accurately; "interpreting" also carries a connotation of a straightforward transfer of meaning from one linguistic code to another. Language brokering, by contrast, focuses attention on the complex social and cultural negotiations that go into cross-linguistic interactions. The broker does not just have to deal with the referential meaning of someone else's words but must account for *all* the social meanings that are conveyed, spoken or unspoken, in interactions—in other words, the total linguistic fact (Morales & Hanson, 2005). Knowing Korean would not necessarily have helped Montgomery navigate the "cultural layers" of an unexpected mound visit.

Misreadings or misunderstandings go both ways in intercultural communication, however. In discussing the incident with Hyunsung, I detected a note of rueful compassion for Mike Montgomery. Hyunsung had been a language broker on both sides of similar scenarios, and whatever he thought of Montgomery's behavior, he took a critical view of what he characterized as the Korean public's ignorant response:

> But there's a lot of misunderstandings that happened in this incident. Obviously ... the Korean fans are just angry at this, you know, angry American like trying to look down on Korean culture. That's the general vibe by the media over here, but, you know, you got to look within that. It's actually something more complicated.

Hyunsung noted the hypocrisy of the Korean media's framing of Montgomery as yet another "angry American" without pausing to consider what might have been behind his actions, just as Montgomery apparently jumped to conclusions about the umpire's behavior. The social persona of the "angry American" is one that appears to be widely recognizable among Koreans, such that when Mike Montgomery lost his mind over a pitch-clock violation, fans and the media were quick to react: "Here we go again." In this context, the reputation of Americans, or American ballplayers, preceded Montgomery's arrival on the scene (Silverstein, 2005).

On closer inspection, the issue was not just that Montgomery did not share Korean norms for player-umpire interactions. The participant roles and framework for the entire situation—that is, the shared understanding of how people are expected to behave and communicate—might have been skewed from his perspective (Goffman, 1981). In US baseball, the role of managers in on-field disputes is to take the player's side or to "animate" the player's point of view, so that if anyone is ejected, it will be the manager and not the player. As with the occasionally spectacular base-throwing tirade, this is a form of verbal and embodied performance that does not change the umpire's decision but is meant to show the player that the manager "has his back" and is willing to defend his team's interests. For an MLB manager to abdicate this responsibility would be unthinkable—as unthinkable as the umpire walking to the pitcher's mound to confront a pitcher directly about a rule violation. Not so in South Korea, though:

> I think if it was in the States the manager probably [would go] out and ... support his players. He would argue with the umpire and get tossed. But over here, it's more reserved. If they feel like ... [their] player's doing something wrong, they don't tend to back you up. And they'll kind of play along with the umpire.

Hyunsung added that, in "a culture that stresses obedience and respect towards authority and seniority," managers and coaches might worry that umpires would retaliate for disrespect by allowing calls to go against their team in the future. "It's just how people are programmed here," he said, to the extent that one of Montgomery's coaches tried to dust the rosin off the umpire's uniform in the aftermath of the incident, in an effort to make amends on the team's behalf.

Thus, the participation framework of a KBO game, while outwardly like that of an MLB game, presumes a different alignment of participants with different associated roles. Unlike in MLB, managers are aligned with umpires in their allegiance to the underlying moral order, such that if a manager finds a player's behavior inappropriate, he will not come to the player's defense as would be expected in MLB. Again, outward similarities in the speech situations, expressed in the truism that "Baseball is just baseball," account for some of the pitfalls of intercultural communication. For Montgomery, Korean baseball appeared to be "just baseball," but in reality, it was a whole different game.

Dave Bush affirmed that language brokering went only so far in preparing US "imports" for behavioral expectations in Korea. Dave's interpreter would try to help fill in gaps in Dave's cultural knowledge; Dave, for his part, actively sought to make sense of Korean speech situations: "I asked a ton of questions, like, 'Hey, man, why are they doing this?' and he's like, 'Oh, well, here's why.'" Certain practices, however, were so "normal" from the interpreter's perspective that "he didn't really think about it," in the sense of anticipating what Dave might not know. This extended to interactions with teammates off the field, where Dave had to "follow along" with unspoken expectations around team building and pick up on unfamiliar interactional routines *within* team activities.

Team dinners were a notable instance. "In the US, when the game ends, we go into the clubhouse, we eat our food, you get dressed, you leave, and you go on your way." On the Wyverns, not only did players eat together after the game, but Korean cultural norms around commensality—food sharing—transferred to team dinners in surprising ways (Ochs & Shohet, 2006). Dave described the usual setup as "Korean barbecue style," with "the hot plate in the middle of the table" and players sharing food communally. Dave's initial difficulty had to do with who was expected to start eating and who could determine when the meal was over:

> One of the things I figured out eventually was that whoever the oldest person was . . . dictated the pace of the meal. So we all sit down, and whoever the oldest one was—and it didn't really matter what their status was as a player—but the oldest one was the one that we would wait for to be ready to eat. And then when that person was finished and everyone else was too, then that person kinda dictated, "Right now, it's time that you can get up and go."

So small things like that where it's like, "Right, let me just kinda follow along here, and you're the one who's leading the charge." And they included me in that too. If I was the oldest one, then they all looked at me to decide when the meal was over.

These "small things"—dimensions of communicative competence that transcended language—were not so small, after all. Dave framed his participation in team dinners as "figuring stuff out as quickly as I could" to "be respectful of what was important" to his teammates and because he "wanted to fit in." That may sound like an obvious course of action, but Dave's casual retelling undersells the complexity of his interactional work: holding back and "following along" as his teammates took the lead, minimizing his contributions until he "figured stuff out"—as children and other novices are expected to do in many cultural contexts—and understanding that he could not take for granted what was important to others (Rogoff, 2014). That his Korean teammates included him among the elders who could dictate the pace of a meal, without regard to on-field status, might be taken as evidence of their uptake, or recognition, of Dave's "respectful" behavior.

Desire and Difficulty: Ideologies of English Learning in Korea

For young Korean players making the transition to US baseball, one challenge was that the "very serious" approach to youth sports in Korea, which Hyunsung compared to "the Soviet Union style back in the seventies and eighties," left little time for other pursuits like extracurricular English learning. "Once you start a sport in elementary school . . . you don't really go to class; you just commit to that sport." Because of this, "you can't really expect high English skill from an amateur," in Hyunsung's experience as a scout. In recent years, the Korean government has tried to remedy this situation by requiring student-athletes to attend a certain number of class hours, as with college athletes in the United States, but such measures have not changed the underlying culture of sports.

Beyond the demands on Korean amateurs' time, however, widespread language ideologies about English and English learning in Korea colored Hyunsung's understanding of young players' language behavior. English in Korea is associated with "English fever," the feverish desire to attain English proficiency, which some have attributed to a "colonized state of Korean consciousness in which pursuing English is a 'natural' act that does not need to be questioned" and analyzed as an extension of socioeconomic class disparities in Korea (Cho, 2017, p. 19). English fever has manifested in English-only kindergartens, early study abroad, and an enormous market for private English tutoring, as depicted satirically in the film *Parasite,* driven by increasing competition within higher education and the workforce (Park, 2017). However, the desirability of English is coupled with a belief that learning English is especially difficult for Korean speakers—so much so that, in rare cases, Korean parents have resorted to elective tongue surgery for their English learner children, hoping that it will lead to native-like pronunciation of English /r/ and /l/ sounds (Shin, 2007, p. 78).

In accounting for young Korean players' difficulties with English, Hyunsung appealed to typological differences between the languages; in terms of word order, English is a subject-verb-object (SVO) language, while Korean is subject-object-verb (SOV). Because English was "mixed up" from the perspective of Korean speakers, he reasoned, they would find it more difficult to learn. In addition, as speakers often do, Hyunsung connected a structural feature of language—in Korean, the placement of the verb after subject and object—to a cultural tendency to "hear out the whole sentence . . . to fully understand," since "you have the verb at the end," in implicit contrast, perhaps, to the "angry American" tendency to act hastily (see, e.g., Zenker, 2014):

> I think I read this somewhere, that Korean is like the most difficult language for Western people to learn, and vice versa. Because the word orders—it's all mixed up. In English, you have the subject and the verb then so on, such and so on. But over here in Korean, you have the subject, and then you have such and such and so on, and then you have the verb at the end. So in Korean, you have to kind of hear out the whole sentence, what the other person is saying, to fully understand what they're trying to say. So it's a lot of adjustment for Korean young kids.

The question of what makes a language easier or harder to learn is not as straightforward as Hyunsung implied. Researchers in second-language acquisition have argued that "typological distance"—how different the first and second language are on a structural and functional basis—does correlate with "learning difficulties and learning pace" (Ramat, 2012, p. 1). Experimental work with constructed, or artificial, languages has also suggested that the grammatical features of certain languages may make them easier to learn and more likely to evolve in larger speech communities (Raviv, de Heer Kloots, & Meyer, 2021).

Even so, it can be tricky to establish which structures are more "difficult" for a given language learner (Ellis, 2008); it is also difficult to separate ideologies or beliefs about the *supposed* difficulty of certain languages from their structural features (Zentz, 2014). English might be objectively easier to learn for a Spanish speaker than a Korean speaker, since English and Spanish belong to the same extended Indo-European family, have similar word order, share vocabulary, and so on. But the Spanish speaker would also inhabit a different social context and develop a different relationship to English than the Korean speaker.

Hyunsung acknowledged that structural differences between Korean and English were not the only factor. Unhelpful language teaching strategies—namely, a focus on grammar to the exclusion of conversational proficiency—were also to blame and resulted in familiar outcomes; someone's performance in the English classroom or on standardized tests did not predict their success in "actually try[ing] to open a conversation" with English speakers. As Richard Guasch said in Chapter 2, "taking a class isn't the same as living [the language]." Hyunsung said:

> They do learn, they do have English classes as early as third grade. So it's almost nine years of learning English, but they focus too much on grammar, the structural side of a language. It's not just for English but other languages as well. They get very confused by that. I mean, this is not just baseball, but you have Koreans who score really high on the TOEFL test, but when you actually try to open a conversation, they get confused, and you have this block that kinda makes it tough for them to speak. They have a hard time trying to choose which vocabulary, which word to use in certain situations.[10]

Notwithstanding "English fever," young Korean ballplayers might find themselves in a similar situation to Latin American *peloteros* like Richard, with some exposure to English but little communicative competence upon arriving in the United States.

Linguistic Flexibility as a Resource in Taiwanese Baseball

Like Hyunsung Kim, Jacky Bing-Sheng Lee, a lifelong resident of Taipei and a play-by-play announcer for Taiwan's Videoland Sports Channel, took a roundabout path to professional language work in baseball. Jacky first encountered Major League Baseball through video games in elementary school. Shortly thereafter, when he started watching Taiwanese broadcasts of MLB games with Mandarin-speaking announcers, he recognized the players from their video game counterparts. This coincided with the ascension of right-handed pitcher Chien-Ming Wang to the US major leagues, creating what Jacky called "a perfect storm" for his burgeoning baseball fandom. Wang was the third Taiwanese player to make the leap to MLB and the highest-profile Taiwanese player by far. He debuted for the Yankees in 2005 and turned in two dominant seasons—in 2006, when he finished second in AL Cy Young voting, and 2007—before injuries intervened.

At this point, said Jacky, baseball became "the biggest thing in my life." Because of Chien-Ming Wang's presence on the Yankees, Jacky became a "super A-Rod fan"—an obsessive follower of the Yankees' brilliant third baseman Alex Rodríguez, who was "chasing the home run records" and who inspired Jacky, like many a baseball-addled youngster, to dive deep into statistics. In class, he would engage in under-the-table math to calculate how long it would take his hero to break Babe Ruth's and Hank Aaron's all-time home run records. "I still remember, when I was in class, I [would] count how many years [A-Rod] has to hit how many home runs to get to number 714, 755. All this stuff I'm doing on my own—math. It's quite funny."

Unlike in South Korea, sports were not seen as a serious pursuit for Taiwanese youth, according to Jacky, owing to an educational system that "value[d] tests and grades" above all else. Jacky credited this system for his initial motivation to learn English, saying that he wanted to impress his parents, teachers, and classmates that he was "good at something," without giving much thought to how English might benefit him in the future:

> It's our system. Our parents, our education system, value tests and grades very much, and we don't encourage students . . . or children to play sports, we don't encourage them to do stuff that is other than their schoolwork. For example, you want to learn music, you want to play sports, most of the parents would think that it is not good for their children to do [that] stuff. So it's a cultural thing, it's a societal thing. And I'm part of that culture, I was raised in that culture and that system, so that's why I was motivated to learn English. It started out as trying to get better grades, trying to, you know, impress my parents, impress my teachers, impress my classmates, that I'm good at something.

In high school, Jacky, not destined for MLB stardom, decided that he wanted to become a baseball play-by-play man and realized that "in Taiwan, if you want to do sports media, you have to be very fluent in English, so that you can, you know, translate all the information from the US, from other sports leagues, to Taiwan." This spurred him to "fortify [his] English ability" in high school, building on the "foundation . . . of my early stage of learning English at a very young age" and the "sense of accomplishment" that came from high achievement in English classes. Jacky did better than expected on the college admissions exam and was accepted to the prestigious National Taiwan University as a major in foreign languages and literature, whereupon he set about achieving his professional dream with the dedication, ingenuity, and unstinting focus typical of would-be major leaguers.

As with the English and Spanish learners in the preceding chapters, Jacky understood that his academic English studies, while useful, would not furnish his repertoire with everything he needed to become a baseball announcer. Specifically, he looked for ways to "cultivate" his knowledge of baseball English, which was not the focus of his classes at NTU, as well as American baseball culture:

> I started to listen to English baseball podcasts. That really helped me a lot in cultivating myself in the culture, in all the baseball jargon, all the Major League Baseball stuff, and also helping me continue to polish up my English throughout my college years. . . . It wasn't until I got into college that I started to, you know, put a lot of effort into reading English articles and consum[ing] media coverage in English.

Following his undergraduate years, Jacky entered NTU's master's program in interpretation and translation, where he interned with the Fox Sports Taiwan television network and completed a thesis on interpreters for foreign players and coaches in the CPBL (Lee, 2019). He also took advantage of opportunities to hone his own language brokering skills, volunteering at the 2017 Taipei Universiade, an international tournament for college athletes that he described as the "Olympics of universities." In his role as an interpreter at the baseball venue, Jacky helped Taiwanese media members who "couldn't speak English that well" and served as a liaison between international media and local staff.

The experience was instructive in several ways. It was Jacky's first encounter with the diversity of world Englishes, since English was the lingua franca for Universiade participants from many different countries. He recalled a conversation with a European coach whose "English accent was hard to understand, so even though he was speaking English, I was actually not quite sure what [he was] talking about." Like Hyunsung with the WBC umpiring crew, Jacky also began to grasp the constraints that certain participation frameworks imposed on language brokering. In Jacky's case, he discovered that postgame interviews were "very brief," with room only for minimal interpretation, because of what he characterized as local media's provincial attitude: "The [Taiwanese] media, they don't need that much information . . . . They only care about Chinese Taipei, our national team's performance, they [were] not really into other countries' performance in that event."

After graduation, Jacky continued working with Fox Sports Taiwan but lost his job when Disney, the network's parent company, decided to "close down the operation." He came into his current position with Taiwan-based Videoland thanks to an unexpected opportunity presented by the Covid-19 pandemic. In early April 2020, when MLB, the KBO, and NPB were still shuttered because of the pandemic, the CPBL resumed play, becoming "the first league to have professional [baseball] games" at a time when fans worldwide were desperate for action. "The TV stations saw this as an opportunity to promote the league," capitalizing on the lack of baseball elsewhere, and decided to broadcast CPBL games in English to appeal to non-Taiwanese audiences. Jacky was an obvious choice because of his fluid Mandarin-English bilingualism and his experience in sports broadcasting; he subsequently leveraged his temporary Covid-era announcing gig into a permanent position with Videoland:[11]

> I was lucky enough to be invited to do the English play-by-play of games [in 2020], so that experience has helped me to get the job that I have right now, because the person who persuaded me to join them, he watched my broadcast and watched the show I hosted, so he believed that I could do the play-by-play man job for the company.

Notwithstanding Jacky's luck, his initial experiences calling CPBL games in English amounted to a period of "very intense training" of "learn[ing] how to be a broadcaster on the fly" in a non-native language. Not only did he have to "overcome the language barrier," but he also had to become familiar with the conventions of play-by-play as a genre while making allowances for his relative lack of expressive control—the degree of control he could exert over his utterances—in English as opposed to Mandarin. Having to "think before [you] speak" is less than ideal in a real-time broadcasting situation, in which the announcer has to react quickly to "the things that happen on the field." As we have seen time and again, using another language "competently" also entails learning the communicative expectations associated with particular cultural contexts, speech genres, or interactional routines:

> I didn't have experience doing play-by-play for any kind of sports events. So my first broadcasting experience was actually broadcasting a game in English for CPBL games, and that was completely unexpected. Because in my imagination, my first experience should be broadcasting major league baseball games in Chinese.
>
> And it was very challenging because English is not my mother tongue, it's not my native language. I have to think before I speak. Even though I am very familiar with baseball jargon, baseball usages in English . . . it's still very challenging because doing play-by-play is all about reaction, it's all about being reactive to the things that happen on the field, and you have to be fast, you have to be

able to form a sentence very fast, and you have to be able to interact with the commentator ... and I didn't have any experience broadcasting.

As Videoland's official play-by-play man, Jacky attained his dream when he had the chance to do play-by-play commentary in Mandarin for the MLB playoffs. Providing commentary on US baseball for a Chinese-speaking audience—"what [he] was struggling for" since childhood—came as a relief after Jacky's trial by fire doing play-by-play for CPBL games in English, in that it involved less "mental effort" and allowed him to focus on the on-field action. Still, the Videoland job came with its own challenges. Broadcasting five days a week meant that Jacky could no longer treat each game as a "one-time major event," nor could he indulge in perfectionism with such a short time to prepare for each assignment. Taiwanese announcers, unlike those in the United States, do not have the "privilege" of specializing in a single sport because they are working in a much smaller market. As Jacky put it, "Your industry"—meaning the United States—"can support that kind of specialized broadcaster, but in Taiwan, if you want to be a sportscaster, you have to be able to broadcast all kinds of sports." Jacky's self-taught "baseball jargon" helped with baseball games, but not, for example, track and field competitions.

Language Diversity Hiding in Plain Sight

In a sense, Jacky's and Hyunsung's stories were the inverse of the stories of Latin American *peloteros* in Chapters 1 and 2. The latter worked tirelessly to develop their *potencia* or raw talent as baseball players and invested in language learning to the degree that it would allow them to "maximize their experience" as major leaguers in the United States. Jacky and Hyunsung, on the other hand, recognized bilingualism as a social and economic resource from an early age and honed their bilingual abilities to find a niche in the hypercompetitive ecology of transnational baseball (Ruiz, 2010).

But Jacky, Hyunsung, and young Latino prospects resembled each other in that their apparently straightforward bilingual repertoires—Spanish/English, Korean/English, and Mandarin/English—concealed multitudes, a fact that labels like "L1" and "L2" fail to capture. The elements that are visible in multilingual baseball interactions are not the full extent of someone's linguistic knowledge. To grasp how truly multilingual baseball is, it is critical not to erase the heterogeneity that exists even in contexts like South Korea and Taiwan, often imagined as ethnically and linguistically homogeneous (Irvine & Gal, 2000).

Jacky called the Taiwanese variety of Mandarin Chinese—the most widely spoken language in Taiwan, closely related to the Beijing dialect—his mother tongue and regarded English as his second-most-proficient language. His father and grandmother, however, were L1 speakers of "Taiwanese," Jacky said, meaning the Taiwanese variety of Hokkien, a Sinitic (Chinese) language that predates the arrival of the "Mainlanders" (Chinese Nationalists) and Mandarin in Taiwan by centuries.[12] Jacky's father learned Taiwanese Mandarin as a second language. His grandmother, on the other hand, never learned Mandarin but was a proficient speaker of Japanese, owing to her years in the Japanese colonial schooling system. Jacky described himself as knowing "some" Taiwanese, with stronger receptive (listening/understanding) than productive (speaking) competence, and a "baby level" of Japanese, which he had picked up only recently, thinking it would be useful for covering NPB games and developments.

In discussing the dominance of Mandarin and English-language media, Jacky acknowledged—with apparent regret—that it came at the expense of traditional Taiwanese ways of speaking, including Taiwanese Hokkien and Hakka, yet another Chinese language spoken by an ethnic minority, primarily in Taiwan's northwest: "People want to cater to the mainstream culture, mainstream language, so Taiwanese [Hokkien] and Hakka are being marginalized."[13] Indeed, research on language socialization in bilingual Taiwanese families supports Jacky's anecdotal account of a society-wide shift away from Hokkien and Hakka and toward Mandarin (Sandel, Chao, & Liang, 2006).

Before Mandarin, Hokkien, or Hakka were spoken in Taiwan, the island was home to Indigenous speakers of Austronesian languages—that is, belonging to the same family as Malay, Tagalog, Hawaiian, and Māori—about a dozen of which are still in everyday use among present-day Taiwanese Indigenous communities (Jan & Lomeli, 2022). Historically, Taiwanese Indigenous people have been renowned for their baseball prowess and as such have been coopted by various political agendas, as evidence of assimilation to Japanese colonial rule, as a symbol of opposition to the Chinese Nationalist government, and as emblems of an upstart league's "authentically 'Taiwanese' approach" to baseball, in contrast to the CPBL's "Chinese" approach (Morris, 2006, p. 79).

In Jacky's view, these "stereotypes" had little to do with Indigenous players' innate ability and more to do with the poor "socioeconomic situation" and historical marginalization of Indigenous people: "I think it's because of the stereotypes. . . . The society, they think collectively that aboriginal people are good at sports, they're good at outdoor activities," in a context where the mainstream "system" values academics more than sports, according to Jacky. Despite these stereotypes,

Indigenous Taiwanese baseball traditions have taken on a life of their own. Jacky referred to "a lot of famous baseball families . . . from those aboriginal tribes and communities" in the CPBL and Taiwan more generally. Thus, Indigenous children might "learn about baseball" from experienced relatives and "have access to all this baseball stuff." The two Taiwanese ballplayers who preceded Chien-Ming Wang in MLB were both Indigenous, as is catcher Kungkuan Giljegiljaw—formerly in Cleveland's minor league system, now in the CPBL—whom Jacky singled out as the first Indigenous player, to his knowledge, to use "his aboriginal name" as his official name, the name on the back of his jersey.

As in many transnational professional sports contexts, there is an awkward fit between the central position of racially minoritized groups—for example, the fact that "aboriginal identity is a big part of our baseball culture" in Taiwan, per Jacky—coupled with the problematic image of minority athletes as raw talent in need of discipline and the historical and continuing mistreatment of those groups (Besnier, 2015). Athletes walk a fine line between making their identities more visible (putting one's aboriginal name on the back of the jersey; *poniéndole el acento*, or adding an accent to one's Spanish name on the back of the jersey) and being wary of the ways in which visibility can become a trap (cf. Brayboy, 2003).

The linguistic and cultural diversity lurking beneath the deceptively homogeneous surface of Taiwanese baseball—to an outsider, anyway—brings to mind other examples of "invisible" diversity in transnational baseball, such as Elvis Novas, a hard-throwing right-handed relief prospect I met at the Royals' Dominican academy. As we eased into English conversation practice, he mentioned offhandedly that he hadn't found learning English too difficult because he was already bilingual. Elvis was Dominican but hailed from Jimaní, a small city on the border with Haiti, where as a child, he learned Kreyòl (Haitian Creole) on trips to the open-air market with his grandmother. On visits home from the academy, he said, he still used the language to communicate with his friends.

"My Translator Is My Voice": Language Brokering and Coaching across Borders

Jacky remarked that Taiwanese professional teams prioritized interpreters who were knowledgeable about baseball over those who might be more proficient in English but lacked experience in the game. Jacky conducted his research on "the reality of being a sports interpreter in Taiwan" with CTBC Brothers, a CPBL team that regularly hired from abroad and understood "it [was] very important to have good communication." Because of this, Brothers had invested heavily in interpretation, but only one of the interpreters in Jacky's study had had formal training in interpretation and translation before joining the team:

> Instead of people who are very fluent at English but know nothing about baseball, they want people who can speak English a little bit or maybe adequately but know a lot of baseball. So some interpreters are not that competent in their language abilities, but they're still there, and they are still doing quite a good job with their foreign coaches and players, they can communicate. They can, you know, facilitate their communication . . . with their emotions, with their facial [expressions], nonverbal cues, something like that.

Jacky mentioned John Foster, the CTBC Brothers pitching coach, as an example of an American import who had "started to fall in love with Taiwan" and "really settled down" in the country, moving his family abroad and sending his children to Taiwanese schools. A major reason for John's successful long-term tenure in the CPBL—at the time, he was in his fourth year coaching for Brothers—was the "very strong bond" he had formed with his interpreter. Jacky found that the interpreter "actually didn't like the job very much" because of the long hours, substandard pay, and lack of personal time, and had considered quitting on several occasions, "but the reason why he continued to stay with the club, continued to do this job, is because of Mr. John Foster. It's not a job for him now. It's part of his family. This is part of his life."

When I caught up with John, he was recovering from a dental procedure at his family's off-season home in Costa Rica. He reflected that his children, ten and eight, "have never been to school in the English language. They've only been to school in Spanish and Chinese. Pretty remarkable." John saw himself as unusual among "imports" to Taiwanese baseball in terms of his family's cultural immersion: "I think I'm one of the only ones who've actually brought their family over, like full-time . . . . We've really put ourselves into it." In addition to his children's schooling, John cited the family's use of Taiwanese government health insurance and "stay[ing] local with foods" as examples of their acculturation.

Born and raised in Stockton, California, John spent 1999–2008 bouncing around the minor leagues with the Atlanta, Milwaukee, and Kansas City organizations, with two brief stints in the majors and one winter in the Dominican Republic. Following his playing days, he accepted a job coaching youth baseball in mainland China through MLB's international arm, where he had no language support besides "an office person who spoke enough English" to get by. Like Dave Bush—who, as it happens, joined John to prepare the Chinese youth team for a tournament in Taiwan—John rose to the challenge of coaching abroad. He and his family "loved China" and, as he put it, "to be with Major League Baseball is not a bad thing" for one's career, even in the global hinterlands of the game.

After two years in mainland China, John was facing a demotion from manager to pitching coach and decided to seek greener pastures in the CPBL, figuring that the cultural differences between China and Taiwan would be minimal compared to coaching in Japan or Korea. As John recalled, "I came [to Taiwan] and basically made [CTBC Brothers] interview me and won myself a job." His combination of "a pretty good résumé and major league experience as a player," not to mention his track record of coaching in Asia, made him an attractive candidate. He was also fortunate, in a sense, that the Brothers' first-round draft pick had just had Tommy John surgery to reconstruct his elbow, an issue John was well equipped to deal with: "I had already gone through [the surgery], and they were asking, can I rehab him? Do I feel confident in that? I was like, absolutely. That is my thing."

John enthusiastically affirmed Jacky's account of his close relationship with his interpreter, Brian Tsai, with whom he had worked for his entire time with Brothers—"right from the beginning, first day." In addition to speaking English proficiently, Brian had completed a master's degree in sports management in the United States before his visa expired and he returned to Taiwan. In other words, said John, "I got really lucky.... I have the advantage of having somebody who's pretty dang smart." John described their partnership as "smooth sailing ever since we got [to Taiwan]." However, building and sustaining a "smooth" language brokering relationship required thoughtfulness and a good deal of behind-the-scenes work.

"I'm Gonna Treat Him Like a Person and We're Gonna Do This Together": Humanizing and Sharing Language Work

John explained the success of his relationship with Brian in deceptively simple terms: "You gotta treat 'em like a human and treat 'em like a person and then really educate each other, find out more about that person." In doing so, he identified two interlinked processes that contributed to the long-term viability of the partnership.

First, John emphasized the importance of *humanizing* Brian in his role as a language broker, pointing to the danger of treating interpreters as mere animators or conduits for others' voices. One remedy, especially considering the round-the-clock nature of CPBL interpreters' work (to which Jacky alluded above), was not to take Brian for granted or to assume that he would always be available. "He's not my servant. He has a life, too," John commented. "So I made it a point, in the beginning, I'm only gonna ask him for stuff if I really need it." John distinguished between interactions for which Brian's presence was essential—for example, "when I'm on the field and in the clubhouse," and at the immigration office, where "something [could] get lost"—and lower-stakes encounters where John could muddle through with support from Google Translate, by relying on apps like Uber Eats, or just "try[ing] to figure it out." As a coach, John expected the same from his non-Taiwanese "import pitchers"—that they would learn to be relatively self-sufficient and not rely on their interpreters to broker every interaction.

In a similar vein, John strove to treat Brian as an equal partner in language brokering interactions rather than a translation machine: "My translator is my voice. I am nothing without him. So I treat it that way." John approached intercultural communication as an opportunity for mutual learning, giving Brian rich information about the linguistic and cultural context of John's utterances even as Brian educated him about life and baseball in Taiwan. This multidirectional process of language socialization, with Brian and John learning from each other, was one element of treating Brian as a fully human being, instead of a "translator" or "servant." It also set the stage for future interactions to be "like butter": through their shared commitment, John and Brian improved their ability to work as a team, despite the differences in their repertoires.

> I can't just explain something in English, but he doesn't fully understand it, and then he can't get that point across unless he understands it. So I believe it's just as important for me to educate him on why we're doing it, how we're doing it, when do we do it, and really get the background of it, so he fully understands everything that we're talking about. So that way when it comes up, or when we talk about it more, it is like butter.

In light of Jacky's point at the beginning of this section—that CPBL teams valued baseball knowledge over fluid Mandarin-English bilingualism, where interpreters were concerned—such interactions yielded many "teachable moments" for Brian, as he gained detailed knowledge about baseball English and began to "understand baseball more and understand baseball mechanics," according to John.

Audience Design in Taiwanese and Chinese Baseball: Managing Language and Managing People

In addition to helping Brian understand baseball mechanics and terminology, John found that he had to adjust his own speech to make sure that he got his point across in interpreter-mediated interactions. This involved "a lot of trial and error and . . . really paying attention to what I'm saying and looking at the outcome and realizing, I need to explain that a little differently," John said. Learning to communicate effectively with interpreters was a key dimension of English speakers' language socialization in Taiwanese baseball. As opposed to Hyunsung's experience with real-time language brokering at the WBC, where the umpire did not modify his speech, making it impossible for Hyunsung to interpret "fully," John and fellow coach Nick Additon quickly came to understand that interpreter-mediated interactions went more smoothly if the English speakers designed their utterances with the audience and speech situation in mind (Bell, 1984). In other words, as the "import" coaches gained experience working with interpreters, they started to anticipate potential difficulties and adjust their speech proactively (Bakhtin, 1984).

Nick observed that certain situations—for example, making a speech to the entire team—demanded that he be especially mindful of how quickly he was speaking, how long his turns at talk were, and what he wanted to get across in his next turn:

> [The interpreters are] speaking a little bit broader. So really breaking down my sentences and slowing myself down, speaking for a minute, and then letting them speak and gathering my thoughts, and speaking again and letting them speak to me, especially like a speech when you're talking to a whole team—that, to me, was one of the bigger things that I had to learn how to do, was just slow down, make it simple, let the translator speak, and then speak again.

The "trial-and-error" process that led Nick and John to tweak their contributions for the interpreters and Mandarin-speaking audience, while it entailed a steep learning curve, also, in John's words, "made me a better coach . . . because I had to explain stuff a little bit more in depth and a little bit from the bottom to the top."

Even so, the constraints varied from one context to another. In Taiwan, with a rich baseball culture and a long history of the game, foreign players and coaches could still count on "the baseball language that transfers everywhere," as Nick put it, meaning the interactional norms and expectations that were widely shared in the transnational game. One example was the "embarrassing" case of breaking a bat in batting practice. "If you hit [the ball] on the sweet spot of the bat, you're not gonna break it," but if you take a bad swing and break the bat, the noise is unmistakable and "everybody on the field knows." Not just that, but everybody also understands the teasing that ensues, independent of the language(s) being spoken, said Nick:

> Whether you're in America, the Dominican, Mexico, Taiwan, or Korea, if somebody breaks a bat in batting practice, the whole field is yelling, talking to them, you know? And saying, "Go get another bat! Nice swing!" And it's just funny the way that works and it transfers.

As in Latin American baseball, English borrowings also pop up in Asian baseball, owing to the game's US origins and the globally dominant position of MLB. During Nick's time in the KBO, he noticed that Korean players would use an oddly familiar-sounding phrase when someone threw a good pitch: "I thought . . . man, that sounds like the guy just threw a 'nice ball.'" He asked his teammates if it was Korean, but it turned out that they were saying "nice ball" in English—an understandable, though non-native-like English phrase, which the Korean players had adopted as a bit of in-group slang, the way English speakers in MLB use Spanish *cambio* for "changeup." Tossing in a word or phrase from another language, especially English, can communicate "coolness," worldliness, or prestige, even if you are not using it the way a native speaker would (Blommaert, 2010).

The flip side of Taiwan or Korea was mainland China, which has "virtually no history of baseball," according to Dave Bush, but where Dave, like John Foster, started his coaching career as part of MLB International's efforts to promote the game in nontraditional contexts. Dave had already played in Korea and went on to coach in a range of international settings, including Australia and Johannesburg, South Africa, where he coordinated a month-long camp for "kids from all over the [African] continent." Still, he said, "from a coaching and language perspective, the [mainland] Chinese team was probably the most difficult."

Dave described Chinese baseball culture as "raw": "They just don't grow up playing it, so even trying to find a way to communicate in baseball was difficult." In interpreter-mediated interactions, the interpreter was "probably not a baseball person," making Dave's job doubly challenging, particularly in "situations where there's not a lot of time to translate." Like Nick and John, Dave learned to adapt his speech to work within these constraints:

> The most important thing I learned from that process was whatever I had to say, it's gotta be clean and quick and crisp . . . which, you know, when you stand on the mound, you only have about 30 seconds to get the whole thing done, right? So it's like, what can I say in 10 seconds . . . so that [it] can get relayed and then I can answer any questions and go back through the process. . . . The process was, "All right, how can I get this done? What do I really have to say? What's really, really important right now? 'Cause that's all I have time for."

Mainland Chinese baseball was what some second-language acquisition researchers would call a "context-reduced environment," relative to Taiwan and Korea. Without the "knowledge of baseball that transfers everywhere," to paraphrase Nick, Dave's interlocutors did not have the *context* to make sense of what he said (Cummins, 1983).[14]

Dave contrasted his struggles to communicate in China with his relationship with Hirokazu Sawamura, who made his MLB debut with the Red Sox in 2021 as a 34-year-old, 10-year veteran of NPB. As the Red Sox pitching coach, Dave "tried to learn a couple simple words" of Japanese to put Sawamura at ease but had "no ability to communicate with him about pitching" in the pitcher's L1. Initially, an interpreter was always present, and Sawamura made an effort to learn some English, but Dave recalled that their interactions went smoothly mostly because of Sawamura's maturity and long experience in Japanese baseball. Dave singled out Sawamura's knowledge of pitching craft and his comfort level with Dave, who had been in the pitcher's shoes in Korea:

> I think he played ten years or more in Japan. . . . Pitching-wise, there was a lot of understanding of concepts and ideas and deliveries that was pretty mutual. So I think the baseball part was a little bit easier with him, just 'cause he is older and more mature and knew what he wanted to do. . . . And I think he appreciated the fact that I played overseas and had been in a similar situation.

By the middle of the 2021 season, Sawamura felt comfortable enough communicating with Dave that when he was called on to pitch, he told his interpreter to go straight from the bullpen to the dugout instead of joining him on the mound for a tête-à-tête with the coach. "Sawamura was very determined to be able to have that conversation on his own or at least to understand what was being asked of him" in relief appearances. The interpreter could step in if needed, but Sawamura did not want to rely on him to broker every interaction—like Michel Gelabert, who wanted to be able to fend for himself in postgame interviews (see Chapter 2), and Nick Additon, who valued building relationships with Taiwanese players in Mandarin rather than through a bilingual go-between.

A final aspect of "audience design" in Asian baseball had to do more with "managing people," as John put it, than managing language per se. As a coach in Taiwan, John also saw himself as a "buffer" for Latin American players who ended up on the Brothers. On the one hand, John said, Latino *peloteros* "tend to adjust pretty easily because they've always played in a foreign land." The voices of players in Chapters 1 and 2 attest to the truth of John's statement: being socialized into an unfamiliar linguistic and cultural context is nothing new to Latino players who have worked their way through the Dominican academy system and the US minor and major leagues.

One such player was Aríel Miranda, a left-handed starter who began his professional career in Cuba's Serie Nacional at the age of eighteen, debuted in MLB in 2016 when he was twenty-seven, and followed his major league years with stints in Japan, Taiwan, and Korea, winning the KBO's most valuable player award in 2021 and breaking the league's single-season strikeout record. Miranda was a "class act" and "such a professional man," according to John, and he must have been exceptionally adaptable to succeed at a high level in so many different countries and leagues.

With Miranda, however, and with other Latin American imports to Taiwan, John found himself not so much mediating players' interactions as managing their expectations in two general areas. Both areas related to the CPBL's status as a "step down" in quality from MLB, NPB, and the KBO. First, John strove to instill respect for the Taiwanese game and high behavioral expectations in players who were descending a professional level, cautioning them, "Don't do anything here that you wouldn't do while you were playing for the Yankees." In his view, it was crucial that "imports" recognize the significance of the CPBL to Taiwanese society and act respectfully, as opposed to carrying themselves like the "hired guns" Nick referred to above.

Second, John had the difficult task of advocating for his foreign players—making sure they were well cared for and comfortable in an alien setting—while tempering their expectations of the CPBL experience, since players who were expecting MLB-caliber facilities and treatment were likely to be disappointed:

[The CPBL] is a couple steps down in field quality, how they treat you, and stuff like that. So my deal is, I'm like the buffer. I don't want them to be uncomfortable at all, and I'll go to battle for them all day long and do anything that I can to make sure they're comfortable within means, where they're not being prima donnas and trying to be spoiled.

John's dilemma—going to battle for his foreign players but not allowing them to be prima donnas—echoed comments from player-development staffers and education personnel in earlier chapters, who fretted about how much support to give their young Latin American prospects and how much independence and initiative to demand from them.

"It's Not the Way We Were Made to Communicate": Getting by in Mandarin as a CPBL "Import"

The "sad part" of John's story—his words—was that because of his spectacularly successful partnership with Brian, he "[hadn't] had to learn one bit" of Mandarin Chinese in his four years in Taiwan. This was not completely accurate; John allowed that he knew "how to order coffee [and] how to get a bag and tell guys to hurry up" as a coach, but he called his Mandarin "really, really brutal." When we spoke, he had just signed another two-year deal with CTBC Brothers and had promised his trilingual children that he would work hard on learning Chinese over the length of his contract. Dave Bush, likewise, commented that he'd learned more Spanish as the Red Sox pitching coach than he had Korean while playing in the KBO. With the benefit of hindsight, he regretted the missed opportunity: "If I were gonna go back now, I probably would put a little more effort into the language part. At the time, [there] was so much effort going into playing and so much effort going into living."

John and Jacky both directed me to Nick Additon, John's fellow coach on the Brothers, as an example of an American "import" who had learned "a lot of Chinese" after pitching for four seasons in the CPBL and making the transition to coaching in 2020. His player page makes Elvin Liriano look sedentary by comparison. Nick was drafted out of high school by the St. Louis Cardinals in 2006 and played for four MLB clubs in the minor leagues on and off until 2017.[15] From 2012 on, he said, "I played in the Dominican for five winters. I played in Mexico for one winter, Korea for one season and now I've been in Taiwan for seven years." At the time of our conversation in late January 2022, Nick had just returned to Taiwan for spring training and was enduring his mandatory two-week quarantine in a hotel room.

When I explained the topic of the book, Nick prefaced his story with, "I don't wanna sound cocky by any means, but you're talking to the perfect guy, because I'm fascinated by language." Nick was aware that other imports saw him as exceptional: "Everybody that comes here now is like, 'Man, how did you learn this much Taiwanese?'" In explaining his journey as a Chinese learner, Nick invoked his first season playing winter ball in Mazatlán, Mexico, about ten years prior. One of his teammates was "American through and through, but he could communicate with the guys" in Spanish, which Nick found as "unbelievable" as others now find his Chinese proficiency. He asked his teammate in Mexico the same question: "How did you get like this?"

Very sensibly, his teammate recommended that Nick dive into "the real-life practice of [the language]" little by little:

> He [was] like, "Man, one word a day, one phrase that you use every single day and ... you'll learn it, right? And the first time you try to use it, you'll hesitate with it, and it won't be easy, but then every time you use it, it just gets more and more ingrained."

Nick may have been fascinated by language, but he also embraced his teammate's unsentimental, fearless approach to picking up words and phrases he could use in everyday situations, bringing it with him to Taiwan. Like others in this book, Nick remarked on the difference between "applying [the language] in your everyday life" and studying language in a classroom setting, where "it's just so hard for it to stick." However, as I reflected on what allowed Nick to succeed at the "unbelievable" task of learning Chinese, a few telling features of his relationship to language and bilingualism emerged.

First, Nick came to see bilingualism as basically unremarkable, in implicit contrast to the widespread US bias toward monolingualism as the normal human state of affairs (Kellman, 2022). Although Nick did not grow up bilingual, he grew up in South Florida, an area where—recalling Emily Glass's comments in Chapter 3—in his peer group, "there would be like a grandparent from Cuba or the Dominican that lives in the house that would talk to the kids." Notwithstanding signs of an intergenerational shift from Spanish to English in South Florida, the region has stayed profoundly multilingual to a degree that is rare, if not unmatched, in the United States, which may have influenced Nick's orientation to other languages (Carter & Lynch, 2015).

Second, like many successful language learners, Nick had a realistic view of what he hoped to achieve in Chinese, aiming for "interactional competence"— the ability to hold his own in conversations—and not "native-like" proficiency (Kramsch, 1986). This required linguistic flexibility and the willingness to take risks. It also meant that Nick understood what he needed the language *for*—in what situations, with which people, and on which topics he needed to be able to speak Mandarin: "I'm just learning phrases that apply to me." After several years of practice, he said:

> Now anything that I want to express to you in Chinese, I could manage to say. Now, will it be grammatically correct and perfectly detail-oriented? No, absolutely not. But, that being said, I think the players really appreciate it.

Third, Nick assumed that he *could* learn Chinese. Refer to the Korean ideologies about English learning that Hyunsung Kim echoed earlier in this chapter; rather than starting from an ideological base of the inherent difficulty or impossibility of learning Mandarin, Nick believed that he could learn the language by following the same methodical route he had taken with Spanish. He acknowledged that differences between English and Chinese—especially in terms of phonology, or the system of sound-meaning correspondences—could be challenging for an L1 English speaker, modeling the distinction between departing, level, and rising tones.[16] Still, he said, "the players don't mind if you're messing up their language." The effort counted for more than proper pronunciation in the players' eyes:

> Here in Chinese, the words are so difficult to pronounce because there's different tones. . . . *Ma* could [have] four different meanings, whether you say it *mà* or *mā* or *mǎ*, right? So anyway, it's very, very difficult. The players, they just care that you're trying, you know?

Like other successful learners profiled in this book, Nick came up with strategies to get enough input, and the right kind of input, to continue developing as a Chinese speaker. "I don't know if you know what *Peppa Pig* is. I would imagine you do," he said, from one father to another (I did). Watching a cartoon intended for young children—thus, with simplified input—in Mandarin helped Nick build up his knowledge of the language slowly over time and gave him a chance to experience Chinese passively as "background noise," as opposed to the cognitively taxing experience of listening and responding to people around him:

> I've started watching some cartoons in Chinese, and like, *Peppa Pig*, it's very slow and it's very basic. And just having that in some headphones once a day kind of creates that background noise where you're just constantly hearing and paying attention rather than thinking about what you're gonna say.

Finally, Nick believed strongly in the value of communicating with Taiwanese players directly in Mandarin instead of having to rely on an interpreter. He spoke perceptively about his discomfort with interpreter-mediated interactions and what he saw as the superiority of "car[ing] enough to have a surface-level conversation in [the players'] native language," even if he still needed the interpreter's support to "go deep" with players.[17] "I don't like using my translator," he said, especially as a coach, "because it's the connection with the players, it's the relationships that I build":

> It's so hard to just communicate [with] a translator, even if you have the best translator in the world. I communicate to the translator, translator communicates to the player, player back to the translator, translator back to me. It's not the way we were made to communicate. It's not the way we were made to build relationships. . . . [The interpreter will] correct me when my Chinese is a little bit off . . . [and] when I want to go deep, that's when it gets difficult and I need to bring in the translator, but at least I've already set the standard with the player.

Peppa Pig and expressions of caring aside, Nick's socialization into Mandarin had a heavily gendered character. A professional baseball clubhouse is "a room full of alpha males," in his words, and building relationships in Chinese with teammates (as a player) or players (as a coach) involved performing a specific type of masculine identity in a language he was just beginning to learn. In Nick's experience, the "running joke" that "everybody learns the bad words in a language first" had a basis in reality, at least for ballplayers, in that swearing effectively in your L2 communicates that you "can handle [yourself] on a baseball team full of grown men." His account evoked Parker Dunshee's story about jumping into a clubhouse conversation in Spanish for the first time (in Chapter 3) and the timely "*¡Coño!*" from the A's coach (in Chapter 1):

> The minute you say a bad word in the right moment, in the right context, people look at you like, "Oh, dang, he's got it." . . . All you're doing is hanging out with the boys. You know, it's not like you're at church.

As a coach, Nick felt that his expanding Mandarin repertoire gave him additional insight into Taiwanese baseball culture. The connection (or lack thereof) between language and worldview has traditionally been the subject of much debate among linguists and anthropologists (Hill & Mannheim, 1992). Whether or not there exists a relation between the structural features of languages and people's thought patterns and cultural practices—the so-called strong version of the "Sapir-Whorf hypothesis"—language learners certainly *attribute* changes in cultural understanding to their acquisition of features of the L2 (Pavlenko, 2016; see also Zenker, 2014).

As learners notice linguistic disparities between the L1 and L2, they may posit "cultural" reasons for—or speculate about the consequences of—those differences. That theoretical linguists would see these speculations as baseless is beside the point. In Nick's case, reflecting on differences between Mandarin and English became a tool for looking more deeply into the differences between Taiwanese and American baseball. For example, when Nick realized that Mandarin lacked a synonym for a common English word, he claimed that it alerted him to a *cultural* dimension of coaching in Taiwan—namely, that players had to be reminded not to be too hard on themselves:

> It's funny, like, what does and what doesn't transfer in Chinese. There's no word for "judge," to judge somebody. . . . It's a weird thing here, because I found coaches over-judged their players when they don't have to. . . . The Taiwanese coaches are judging everything that [the players are] doing, every little movement, until you get to superstar status. . . . Now there is a word for "criticize." . . . "Criticize" is kind of judging, but . . . you can judge in a good way, you can judge in a bad way, but "criticize" is really just a bad thing. . . . And second of all, [with "criticize"] you're actually speaking it where judging is kind of just thinking it.
>
> So when I asked my translators about that word . . . and "to criticize" is *pīpíng*, I'm always saying, like, "Stop judging yourself. You guys need to stop. Like, in practice, just be free and don't get upset because you made the mistake."

The absence of a synonym for "judge" in Mandarin prodded Nick to analyze the differences between judging and criticizing—specifically, that criticism, unlike judgment, is always a negative evaluation and that it is expressed outwardly—and to consider how this salient linguistic difference might encode a cultural tendency to be hypercritical (or "over-judging"). Nick's growing knowledge of Mandarin, in other words, equipped him to imagine how things looked from the Taiwanese players' perspective and to intervene fruitfully in the process of player development.

Nick, like the other coaches, players, interpreters, and scouts profiled in this chapter, used bilingualism to give himself a competitive advantage and find a niche—multiple niches, actually—in the transnational game, using his US minor league experience as a springboard for a decade-long career in Latin America and Asia as a player and coach. But Nick's relationship to bilingualism was not couched in solely instrumental terms. That is, he did not treat language *only* as a resource for social and economic advancement. Language learning, brokering, and everyday use were "fascinating" topics, worthy of a lifetime of study and reflection, and afforded Nick the opportunity to overcome barriers to mutual understanding in intercultural encounters, "maximizing his experience" in ways that paralleled the *peloteros*' stories in Chapters 1 and 2.

At other times, and for other people, bilingualism exposed the disparities between transnational baseball contexts—as with Hyunsung's struggle to make sense of "authenticating" game-used memorabilia and Dave's efforts to connect with players in mainland China—and prompted commentary on what might *not* be the same from one clubhouse or diamond to another.

Conclusion

"Learn Baseball Language. It's Pretty Simple": Language Panics and Verbal Hygiene in Major League Baseball

On the evening of June 6, 2017, the New York Yankees hosted the rival Boston Red Sox for an early-season matchup in the Bronx. Masahiro Tanaka, the starting pitcher for the Yankees, had established himself as a dominant force in Nippon Professional Baseball (NPB), the highest-level league in Japan, from the age of eighteen. In 2014, the Yankees outbid other MLB teams for the 25-year-old's services, agreeing on a 7-year contract worth $155 million. By the time of the Red Sox game, Tanaka had justified the Yankees' investment with three-and-a-half years of solid if unspectacular performance.

Tanaka got into trouble in the fourth inning, giving up back-to-back home runs that put the Red Sox up 4–1 and prompted a mound visit from Larry Rothschild, the Yankees' pitching coach, accompanied by Shingo Horie, Tanaka's interpreter. The major leagues adopted a rule allowing interpreters for mound visits before the 2013 season, reflecting the linguistic diversity in the league. MLB, like the United States, has no official language, and league officials speculated that the rule would benefit "not only Japanese, South Korean and Taiwanese pitchers, but also speakers of Spanish, Dutch and Italian" (Waldstein, 2013).

As we have seen, the role of pitcher requires a good deal of in-game communication—with the catcher (which pitch to throw, the desired location, whether to switch up the signs—per Parker Dunshee in Chapter 3), infielders and outfielders (defensive positioning and managing runners on base), and coaches. MLB's pro-interpreter rule change was especially relevant to pitchers from Asia like Tanaka, who are usually experienced professionals before they debut in the United States and do not often undergo an extended period of English learning beforehand (like Hirozaku Sawamura in Chapter 4 and unlike the Latin American prospects in Chapters 1 and 2).

As the Red Sox broadcast team worked to fill the dead air, Dave O'Brien, the play-by-play guy—the member of the announcing team tasked with narrating ongoing action, like Jacky Bing-Sheng Lee in Chapter 4—commented, "With Tanaka, they bring out a translator." O'Brien's partner, the late Jerry Remy, the analyst or color commentator (the person who provides insight and commentary on the game) responded, "I don't think that should be legal." "Seriously?" asked O'Brien, his intonation suggesting mild incredulity. "I really don't," said Remy. "What is it you don't like about that?" O'Brien countered.

"Learn baseball language," Remy suggested. "It's pretty simple. You break it down pretty easy between pitching coach and pitcher after a long period of time." O'Brien offered a different take on the intelligibility of cross-linguistic mound visits: "I would say that probably they're concerned about nuance being lost in some of these conversations," since small differences in a pitcher's approach and execution can have huge impacts on outcomes. While watching a recent Toronto Blue Jays game, I wondered what poor Jerry Remy—a longtime Red Sox infielder prior to his broadcasting career—would have thought about a mound visit that appeared to involve at least three languages: Japanese-born pitcher Yusei Kikuchi was talking to the Jays' pitching coach[1] with his interpreter, while Dominican first baseman Vladimir Guerrero, Jr., narrated the proceedings for Venezuelan catcher Gabriel Moreno, who had just been promoted from the minor leagues.

Remy's comments were an example of a minor "language panic," an expression of moral beliefs about language that encodes underlying concerns and anxieties, such as the changing demographics of a country and the possibility that norms for language use might change as a result (Cameron, 1995). Predictably, Remy's comments provoked a moral panic in response, as the Red Sox and their regional sports television network distanced themselves from what was widely regarded as an out-of-touch perspective. Equally predictably, local news pundits and social media commenters were furious that the team had failed to defend their announcer in what some dismissed as a "PC-driven flap,"[2] political correctness—that is, the perception that individuals are expected to police their speech to avoid giving offense—being an evergreen source of moral panics in liberal democracies (see, e.g., Cameron, 2006; Zentz, 2021). Remy "sincerely apologize[d] to those who were offended," with a neat rhetorical flourish that placed the onus for the controversy on the offended ones. History does not record what, if anything, Tanaka had to say about the incident.

In the preceding chapters, I've focused on how professional baseball players, coaches, scouts, interpreters, language teachers, and others *live* bilingually. I've showed how people experience bilingualism in transnational baseball on a day-to-day basis and over the long term of their lives and careers. But multilingualism in baseball is not just an accepted fact of life. As in many non-baseball contexts, it is also fodder for commentary, evaluation, and judgment. In Chapters 1 and 2, moral evaluations were layered onto assessments of individual players' language proficiency. Someone's bilingual ability could be taken as evidence that he was "proactive," "not worried about making a mistake," or a good teammate; on the other hand, someone's struggles with language could feed the perception that he was a "bad boy."

This is not just a matter of language-based judgments about individual players or even groups of players, recalling the negative beliefs about Dominicans discussed in Chapter 1. Very often, it is not even *about* language in the final reckoning. US politicians' comments about bilingualism, approving or disapproving, evoke reactions related to demographic change, immigration, and the meaning of "being American"—as when George W. Bush opined that the national anthem should be sung in English, in response to "Nuestro Himno," the Spanish-language version, or when Barack Obama remarked that English-speaking parents should be more concerned with how their children could become bilingual than with immigrants' supposed resistance to learning English.

The idea that English monolingualism is a core feature of American national identity, and that a slide into plurilingualism will lead to "Balkanization," or undermine national unity, is even older than this 1917 quotation from Theodore Roosevelt:

> We must have but one flag. We must also have but one language. . . . We cannot tolerate any attempt to oppose or supplant the language and culture that has come down to us from the builders of this Republic. . . . The greatness of this nation depends on the swift assimilation of the aliens she welcomes to her shores. Any force which attempts to retard that assimilative process is a force hostile to the highest interests of our country (Quoted in Crawford, 2004, p. 66).

The fundamental contradiction, as discussed in "Introduction," is that "the evidence of societal plurilingualism is everywhere about us," yet the US "nation-state [is] perpetually trying to constitute of itself an officially unified society with a uniform public Culture" (Silverstein, 1998, p. 284). An abundance of evidence, in other words, is not sufficient to undo a language ideology that regards monolingualism as "natural" and multilingualism as deviant or extraordinary.

At times, major league teams have struggled to square the increasingly diverse game with the persistence of beliefs that players "making American dollars" (to paraphrase Bud Norris; see Chapter 3) should speak English and only English. In 2021, Seattle Mariners president and CEO Kevin Mather resigned after a video emerged of derogatory remarks he had made about charismatic prospect Julio Rodríguez's English—which the team had eagerly promoted as an example of successful adaptation to MLB—to a Rotary Club gathering in Bellevue, Washington (Salvador, 2021). The Dominican-born Rodríguez responded with a meme of Michael Jordan, onto which Rodríguez had pasted a photo of his own face, saying "and I took that personally."[3] (At the same event, Mather also implied that Japanese pitcher Hisashi Iwakuma's English had suspiciously improved after the Mariners told Iwakuma that he would have to pay for his own interpreter.)

As with politicians' statements about language, highly visible bilingual moments in professional baseball are opportunities to reinforce or contest this "monoglot standard" ideology. That is why, in "Introduction," I called it a "radically conservative" move for Steve Blass and Bob Prince to respond to Roberto Clemente's public use of Spanish as expected and unproblematic. In doing so, they acted as though Spanish belonged in the landscape of US professional baseball—a radical stance in contrast to attitudes like Remy's and a conservative one in that it affirmed what we have seen is true: that languages other than English have been present in American baseball from its inception.

In this concluding chapter, I consider the Remy-Tanaka incident alongside two other anecdotes about Japanese-born players in MLB. My goal, in part, is to explore how multilingualism is construed in "mediated discourse" about the game—on television broadcasts and in sports journalism—and how such texts are related to forms of social action in professional baseball (Scollon & de Saint-Georges, 2013). "Text," here, does not refer only to written texts; a text in this sense can be any use of language connected to a particular context. Remy's disapproving comments about Tanaka are a good example: the "text" in that case—"I don't think that should be legal," and so on—arose from social interaction between Remy and O'Brien, which relied on the interaction between Tanaka, Horie, and Rothschild. Once Remy's text was out in the world, it could be circulated among writers, fans, the Red Sox brass, their corporate partners, and others and used as a basis for *additional* forms of social action—for example, condemning Remy's comments, defending him and criticizing "political correctness," or advocating for changes to MLB's interpreter policy.

The point is that commentary on multilingual baseball affords opportunities to take action on social issues, baseball-related or not. But mediated discourse about multilingual baseball often bears little relation to the nimble, vibrant displays of bilingualism that were ubiquitous in Chapters 1 through 4. The wider universe of baseball discourse has some catching up to do with the everyday realities of the transnational game, it would seem.

"Be Very, Very Careful": Mockery and "Common Sense"

August 17, 2021, brought a midweek contest between the Detroit Tigers and the Los Angeles Angels, both middling teams, with records hovering around .500. This was a familiar situation for the Angels, who, despite employing Mike Trout, the greatest player of his generation, and spending prodigally in free agency, were as mediocre as they always seemed to be. However, there was one outstanding reason to be watching on that Tuesday night: Shohei Ohtani,[4] a Japanese player who, like Tanaka, had debuted in NPB at the age of eighteen and had subsequently been the object of a fevered bidding war among MLB teams, coming to the United States and the Angels when he was twenty-three. The comparison ends there. Tanaka emerged as a reliable starting pitcher, but Ohtani exploded onto the American baseball landscape like an incandescent meteor, displaying ace-level pitching ability and incredible prowess as a hitter.

After his first tantalizing seasons were derailed by injuries and an elbow reconstruction, Ohtani stayed healthy in 2021 and, in the first full season following the Covid-19 pandemic, was among the best pitchers in MLB while also leading the American League in home runs and ranking among the top ten most valuable offensive players. No one since Babe Ruth—on the short list of the best two or three players of all time—had simultaneously pitched and hit with anything approaching competence, never mind dominance. For that matter, Ruth did it in a different era, when players' physical abilities were not nearly as impressive and players of color were largely barred from MLB.

The game was tied 2–2 when red-hot Ohtani, who was hitting that night, stepped to the plate with two outs in the sixth inning. It was a perilous moment for the hometown Tigers, whose play-by-play announcer, Matt Shepard, gloomily asked, "Now what do you do with Shohei Ohtani?" His broadcast partner Jack Morris, a Hall of Fame pitcher who spent most of his career with the Tigers, replied, "Be very, very careful." It wasn't what he said, though; it was how he said it—in what many viewers immediately heard as a "fake Asian" or mock Asian accent (Chun, 2016).

Listening to Morris's utterance, it is possible to isolate the phonetic elements, or sounds, that are noticeably different from his usual way of speaking English. Here are the relevant bits—as I hear them, anyway—transcribed in the International Phonetic Alphabet, which can represent just about anything the human vocal apparatus can produce.[5] "Very" comes out /bæri/ (like "betty"), as opposed to "standard" American English /vɜɹi/. The details of Morris's pronunciation of "very" came to attention when some listeners speculated that Morris had not been doing a mock Asian accent but was impersonating Bugs Bunny's nemesis Elmer Fudd. But Elmer Fudd, as others[6] pointed out, says "vewy" (/vɛwi/), not "betty" (/bæri/).

Likewise, Morris pronounced "careful" as /keuʷfʌʷ/ ("cayoofuw," roughly) instead of /kæɹfʌl/, as a speaker of "standard" American English would say it. In "very" and "careful," the features of Morris's speech that indexed a fake Asian accent were pronunciations of /r/ and /l/ sounds that were noticeably different or "foreign-sounding" in ways that mimicked the supposed inability of East Asian speakers to produce those phonemes with "native-like" proficiency when speaking English. Should anyone doubt the power and reach of such ideologies, linked to seemingly insignificant variations in sound, recall from Chapter 4 that some Korean children were forced to undergo tongue surgery because of beliefs surrounding those troublesome English phonemes (Shin, 2007, p. 78).

Condemnation came swiftly enough that Morris apologized (sort of) later in the same game "if I offended anybody, especially anybody in the Asian community for what I said about pitching and being careful to Shohei Ohtani . . . I certainly respect and have the utmost respect for this guy and don't blame a pitcher for walking him"—as though the issue were Morris's contention that the Tigers should pitch Ohtani carefully, rather than his use of a mock Asian accent. Morris was suspended from broadcasting duties for the remainder of the season.

Ohtani earned accolades for what some termed his "graceful" handling of the situation. Headlines from the postgame news conference emphasized Ohtani's statement, delivered through his interpreter, "Personally, I'm not offended, and I didn't take anything personally." In saying so, Ohtani may have displayed grace in overlooking a momentary verbal transgression, even one with racial undertones. But Ohtani, no fool, probably understood that he did not stand to benefit from inflaming the American sports media with accusations of anti-Asian racism based on a passing comment that many US English speakers would see as basically harmless.

What Ohtani said just after "I didn't take anything personally" was telling, though: "I have no say [over] what the players wanted to do or what they did. I mean, [Morris] is a Hall of Famer. He has a big influence in the baseball world so it's kind of a tough spot." At first, Ohtani seemed to be saying that he had no control over being walked, apparently in reference to Morris's non-apology. Then, Ohtani acknowledged Morris as "a big influence in the baseball world" and said "it's kind of a tough spot"—for whom? For the aging, white, English-speaking broadcaster struggling to catch up with the changing face of modern baseball? Or for the Japanese superstar in a no-win situation, unable to criticize accent mockery without bringing down the forces of US language-ideological "common sense"—reinforced by mainstream journalism and social media—upon his head?

"Common sense," in this context, means that people do not usually see their beliefs about language as "ideological" or originating from a certain perspective or social position. Rather, people tend to regard their linguistic beliefs as "common sense," or "just the way things are" (Milroy, 2006). With respect to the history of language ideologies in the United States (see "Introduction"), according to which anything other than "standard" English is anomalous and out of place, "common sense" would dictate that a momentary use of a mock Asian accent is not a big deal. Calling attention to why it *might* be a big deal would run counter to the language-ideological consensus among many MLB fans; it would require people to rethink assumptions about language that have been ingrained in American "common sense" for generations.

In any case, Ohtani pitched eight one-hit innings against the Tigers the following day. He also hit his fortieth home run of the season.

"What Is Your Favorite American Expression?": Contesting Foreignness

The third anecdote concerns Ichiro Suzuki, the first Japanese position player and one of the first Japanese players to play in US Major League Baseball. Over a distinguished career in the two highest-caliber leagues in the world, NPB and MLB, Ichiro accumulated a record 4,367 hits. Younger Japanese players like Yu Darvish and Yusei Kikuchi have described Ichiro as "a god"; Shohei Ohtani was inspired not only by Ichiro's greatness on the field but also by how the elder player handled the American media (Rivera, 2019). A famous example is a televised interview with Bob Costas, the dean of US sports broadcasters, from 2003, Ichiro's third season in MLB.[7]

Recalling the interview in 2019, the year Ichiro retired, Costas described him as "the first true Japanese superstar in American baseball" and one who "understood more English than he let on."[8] The encounter with Costas was Ichiro's first full-length interview in English, according to Costas, who remembered Ichiro's interpreter as a "very dramatic" Japanese actor, in contrast to the "very reflective" ballplayer. Some of the questions played on the American public's fascination with Ichiro's "exotic" background in jokey—for example, who would win a fight between King Kong and Godzilla?—or more substantial ways, such as cultural differences between Japanese and US baseball. (Ichiro cited displays of negative emotion in MLB that would have been unacceptable in Japan, like throwing helmets or breaking bats to express displeasure after a poor plate appearance.)

The most memorable part of the interview came at the end, when Costas again sought to capitalize on Ichiro's exceptional status as a new "import" to MLB and the United States, asking him, "What is your favorite American expression?" Ichiro "waved off the interpreter," Costas recalled. Ichiro, known for his stoic nature, laughed to himself, put his hand to his cheek—as though flustered or trying to remember something—and gazed downward, thoughtfully. Then, in careful, methodical English, he said: "August? In Kansas City. It's hotter than two rats in a fucking wool sock." Costas lost it completely as Ichiro smiled broadly. "That's my favorite," he concluded, adding, by way of explanation, "I have bad teammates."

On the occasion of Ichiro's 2019 retirement, RJ McDaniel reviewed press coverage from 2001 and reflected that "it is hard to find any accounting for Ichiro's arrival [in the US] that does not in some way emphasize his foreignness" (McDaniel, 2019). Newspapers joked that "Ichiro Suzuki" meant "Can't hit Pedro" (Martínez) in Japanese and commented on his "Fu Manchu" mustache and "diminutive" stature—all descriptors that reinscribed Ichiro's racial and linguistic difference as an Asian in the United States (and despite the fact that Kazuhiro Sasaki, another Japanese mid-career transfer, had been named American League Rookie of the Year the previous season) (McDaniel, 2019).

It's understandable that American fans would be interested in what made Ichiro different from other MLB players; it's also understandable that they would want to hear about his adaptation to life in the United States and learning of English. The problem, as with the media's treatment of Charles Bender (see "Introduction"), is that, while Ichiro was a generational talent on the baseball diamond, what *mattered*—at least initially—was that he was Japanese. In 1905, Bender said that he wanted to be known as a pitcher, rather than having his every on-field exploit viewed through the lens of his being Chippewa (and frequently repurposed by writers and cartoonists to assert stereotypes about American Indians). Nearly 100 years later, Ichiro, who had won seven straight batting titles in NPB, dealt with a similar tendency to depict him as Japanese first and a baseball player second.

Readers might be tempted to dismiss the hurt feelings of a player who went on to make upward of $167 million over a nineteen-year career in MLB. As with Charles Bender, however, the emphasis on Ichiro's foreignness was related to a world of discourse that was much bigger than Ichiro himself. Stereotypes about

Native Americans weren't invented when Bender made his professional debut; likewise, stereotypes about the supposed foreignness of Asian Americans—even US-born Asian Americans who are monolingual English speakers—existed long before Ichiro's time in MLB. However, such stereotypes were invigorated in journalists' mockery of his Japanese name and fascination with his "exotic" appearance and practices.

As legal scholar Natsu Taylor Saito and others have documented, Asian Americans have historically been linked to contradictory sets of stereotypes—"Hardworking, studious, unassuming, thrifty. Inscrutable, sneaky, competitive"—that painted them as never quite "American enough" and were used to justify differential treatment under the law (Saito, 1997, p. 71). Not surprisingly, researchers have found that the "perpetual foreigner stereotype" (Uba, 2012) is related to language learning and use—specifically, the relationship between perceptions of "unassimilable" Asians' "accents" (Lippi-Green, 2012) and their experiences of discrimination (Kim, Wang, Deng, Alvarez, & Li, 2011; Cargile, Maeda, Rodriguez, & Rich, 2010).

Each of the three anecdotes above concerns an apparently innocuous utterance that concealed a host of assumptions about language, race, immigration, and baseball—though, as I've tried to show, this only makes sense if we take account of a history and national language community that transcend baseball. In each situation, moreover, an aging, white, English monolingual member of the "old guard" confronted demographic and linguistic changes in the modern game. My intent is not to rake Jerry Remy or Jack Morris over the coals again. As individuals, they had to deal with the consequences of their speech, but from a linguistic anthropological perspective, they are mostly beside the point. Remy's contention that Masahiro Tanaka should "learn baseball language" nodded to a mostly unspoken but widely recognized set of norms and expectations for language use in the United States. Morris's mock Asian commentary on Shohei Ohtani's plate appearance indicated a lingering discomfort or fascination with Ohtani's foreignness, refracted through the lens of linguistic difference—specifically, non-native English pronunciation. In this, it resembled many of the stories about Ichiro Suzuki's transition to MLB. Morris did not imply that Ohtani should not speak Japanese or that he should not speak English with a Japanese accent. He just made Ohtani's Japanese identity, expressed in linguistic mockery or "ventriloquism," the salient fact of his person.

The third instance, however, when Ichiro memorably turned the tables on Bob Costas, is a reminder that "when we seize the chance to do something different" with language, it may bring forth "a critical moment, a point of significance, an instant when things change" (Pennycook, 2012, p. 131). Costas put Ichiro on the spot, but Ichiro was "ready to take advantage of [an] unexpected moment," coming up with the perfect, straight-faced response to the invitation to make a spectacle of his foreignness for an American audience (Pennycook, 2012, p. 131). Even when people find themselves hemmed in by circumstances—as is unavoidably the case—there is always the possibility of doing something unexpected (O'Connor, 2020) and harnessing a "critical moment" to confound others' expectations. Ichiro told Costas that his teammates were "bad" for teaching him his "favorite expression," but, to paraphrase Nick Additon (Chapter 4), "learning the bad words" is by no means tangential to intercultural communication in professional baseball. Ichiro knew he was being funny, but, whatever Bob Costas was expecting, those were, in fact, some of the words Ichiro needed to know to "handle himself" on an MLB team, as Nick said.

Ichiro's cagey bilingualism was the stuff of legend among fans and players. However, it was not always seen only as a trait that reinforced his foreignness. For example, in a late-career tribute, Latin American players shared their surprise at hearing Ichiro speak Spanish, often in relaxed moments that called for trash talking. After reaching base on an infield hit, Rays' first baseman Carlos Peña remembered, Ichiro looked over at Peña and taunted him: *"¿Qué coño tú mira(s)?"*—What the fuck are you looking at? Note Ichiro's use of lexical (*coño*) and phonetic (/s/ aspiration or deletion in *mira(s)*, as Peña reported it) features of Caribbean Spanish, as well as his use of a speech genre that is central to relationships and masculinity in baseball—trash talking or "chirping" at opponents, as Parker Dunshee put it (in Chapter 3) (Lefton, 2014).

The same article quoted Ichiro's former teammate Raúl Ibáñez on Ichiro's strategies for picking up Spanish phrases: "He'd overhear us Latin guys talking and he would imitate it exactly the way that we said it and then he'd ask, 'What does that mean?'" Ichiro thought it important to use Spanish as a form of affiliation with his Latin American counterparts because, the Japanese player said, "We're all foreigners in a strange land." When pressed on why he continued to use an interpreter for interviews in English, despite being "uninhibited" in his Spanish, Ichiro was unequivocal: "Those are two completely different things" (Lefton, 2014). Ichiro had no illusions about the difference between off-the-cuff, private exchanges with Spanish-speaking opponents and his public self-presentation in English interviews, where he refused to play along with the expectation that "it might be funny . . . to hear me bumble my way through," as he put it (Lefton, 2014). Maybe that's why Shohei Ohtani so admired his handling of the American media.

Ichiro was not the only Japanese player to spoof stereotypes of Asian foreignness. Utility infielder Munenori Kawasaki—a journeyman, not a legend like Ichiro—became a cult hero because of his interviews, in which he preempted Jack Morris-like sentiments with unapologetic, crowd-pleasing displays of Japanese identity. In May 2013, while playing for the Blue Jays, Kawasaki hit a walk-off double against the Orioles. Afterward, in an on-field interview, his teammate Mark DeRosa remarked, "I don't know what [Kawasaki's] saying all the time, but he sure gives a lift to this team." DeRosa spotted "Muni," as he was known, and waved him over, putting an arm around his shoulders: "This is your interview!"

Kawasaki raised his arms in triumph, made a slight bow of gratitude, grabbed the microphone from the sportscaster, and turned to the crowd. "Thank you very much. My name is Munenori Kawasaki. I am from Japan," he began, focused and confident, then bellowed, "I am JAPANEEEEEESE!!!" before handing the microphone back. It wasn't as though Kawasaki had just gotten off the plane; he had logged 115 plate appearances the previous season with Seattle and had been playing with Triple-A Buffalo before the Jays called him up. The crowd ate it up. DeRosa, laughing, said, "I can't follow that. I'm outta here," and walked away. At that point, Kawasaki opened a small notebook, to the interviewer's surprise: "You have some notes here. What do you have written in your book?" Muni took the microphone again and read a statement he had presumably written with help from an interpreter—loudly and painstakingly, word by word, in decidedly nonnative but comprehensible English: "My teammates gave me an opportunity, so I wanted to do something about it."[9]

Muni Kawasaki and Ichiro Suzuki were known for having different personalities—the former outgoing, the latter guarded—but both were determined to face the English-speaking media on their own terms. Muni, unlike Ichiro, did not wait for someone to pose a question predicated on his status as a "perpetual foreigner." He took matters into his own hands, literally, seizing the microphone and the moment to bring his Japanese identity into focus and using his English resources to do so, rather than leaving space for insinuations that he should "learn baseball language."

On that last point, two things bear mentioning: first, Kawasaki's written statement displayed his communicative competence in the postgame interview genre as practiced in US baseball, quite apart from his limited competence in English. Deflecting the glory from one's own deeds and giving one's teammates the credit is the classy but expected move in such situations. Second, it is significant that Kawasaki spent his entire MLB career in Seattle and Toronto, cities with a high degree of language diversity, large Asian populations, strong Japanese American heritage and trans-Pacific connections (in Seattle's case), and state-sanctioned bilingualism (in Toronto's). Recalling the discussion of multilingual Miami in Chapters 3 and 4, playing in such environs may have had a role in making Kawasaki's verbal flamboyance possible.

At the conclusion of the bravura performance recounted earlier, Kawasaki experienced another American postgame ritual: his teammates feted his walk-off in grand fashion, hitting him almost simultaneously with a cream pie in the face and a cooler of red Gatorade over the head.

Postscript

In November 2015, Yordano Ventura, a skinny 24-year-old from the Dominican Republic, took the microphone to address an estimated 200,000 fans during the Royals' World Series celebration, one year after the team had lost in heartbreaking fashion to Hunter Pence's Giants. Ventura was easy to hate if you weren't a Royals fan and he was not always easy to love, even if you were. He had a reputation as an intense, hotheaded pitcher and had been involved in several nasty brawls early in the 2015 season, some of which erupted after he hit opponents deliberately with fastballs approaching 100 miles per hour (Lourim, 2016). At times, you could argue that he was enforcing MLB's "unwritten rules"—however misguided—by retaliating on a teammate's behalf; at other times, he appeared to target opponents just because they had gotten hits. He jawed at foes incessantly on the field and online. Ventura's "antics" were prominently featured in the 2015 *USA Today* article (discussed in Chapter 3) that placed the blame for on-field hostilities on a supposed "culture clash" between players from Latin America and the United States.

It was a different story at the Royals' Dominican academy, however, where Ventura was revered as the paramount example of *potencia* fulfilled and lost. In January 2017, barely a year removed from the victory parade, Ventura was killed when his customized, Royals-themed Jeep overturned in the Dominican Republic. His final tweet read, "One month until Spring Training!"; he had tagged his Royals teammates, who would travel to the Samaná peninsula to serve as pallbearers.[10] A framed poster at the academy outside the classroom and the Fifty-First State Room featured Ventura mid-pitch with a caption proclaiming him "Forever Royal." I was curious to know more about Ventura's time at the academy, but when I brought it up, his death still seemed to be a raw wound for

Jeff Diskin. Jeff did mention that the team took the American prospects who visited the Dominican (see Chapter 1) on a pilgrimage to Ventura's gravesite in Las Terrenas, Samaná, on the other side of the country from the academy.

Early coverage of Ventura's career, before he reached the major leagues and gained notoriety as a headhunter, is short on details, but it isn't hard to piece together the picture. He apparently dropped out of school at fourteen and worked in construction until signing with the Royals (Gregorian). I wondered how many of the laborers I saw waiting for the *guagua* outside the Marlins' partially built academy dreamed of living and playing there someday. I also thought of Parker Dunshee's reflection that his Latino teammates might be "a little life or death on every pitch" because they had experienced poverty that was unimaginable to players from the United States and "that's what they have to do to make their dream a reality"—as Ventura did, briefly, against incredible odds (Figure 19).

At the World Series celebration, Ventura draped a Dominican flag over the championship trophy. Before he spoke, his teammate Christian Colón, who was born in Puerto Rico but attended high school and college in California, told the crowd: "I had to help this young brother out, but he's getting better with his English. He's just a little shy sometimes, but he'll be good here." "Oh, my God," Ventura began, hanging his head and looking sheepish and heartbreakingly young behind his sunglasses. The impression was completely at odds with the

Figure 19 Yordano Ventura brandishes the Dominican flag during the Royals' World Series victory parade, November 4, 2015 (Ed Zurga/Getty Images).

popular view of Ventura as a mercurial flamethrower, prone to stirring up trouble. He rose to the occasion, soldiering through a speech that was more or less the English equivalent of Hunter Pence's (in "Introduction"). It was the ultimate postgame interview. I recalled Jeff's encouragement to his English learners—"Put faith in the training that you've had. Put faith in the process"— and Johan Febrillet's contention that, as a teacher, "you feel as if you're part of [the players'] success" in such moments. Ventura's teammates beamed at him, laughing and shaking their heads as the crowd hooted encouragement. It was entirely reminiscent of the scene around Pence in the Toros del Este locker room.

Unlike Hunter Pence, however, Ventura was not an English-speaking veteran trying out Spanish in a low-stakes environment. He was a 24-year-old Dominican at the beginning of his career marshaling his bilingual resources to get something across to a sea of Midwesterners, many of whom were likely monolingual. Maybe the fans were getting comfortable with the idea that bilingualism is not a rare occurrence or a sign of social deviance, or maybe they were just focused on the championship. Either way, the crowd went wild.

This book opened with the story of Roberto Clemente's Spanish *bendición*, or blessing, to his family in Puerto Rico following the Pirates' victory in the 1971 World Series. The superficial similarities to Ventura's speech are striking— another phenomenally talented *pelotero* who died too soon, another celebratory bilingual performance in front of a huge audience, another chip in the edifice of "uniform public Culture" in Major League Baseball, so to speak (Silverstein, 1998). But Clemente, like Ichiro and Muni Kawasaki, treated the interview as a critical moment. He seized the opportunity to do something unexpected, taking advantage of the familiar ritual of the postgame interview to affirm emphatically that Spanish and Latinos had always belonged in baseball, in words that echoed across the Caribbean.

Ventura, on the other hand, did exactly what was expected of him as a young professional who had been socialized to use English strategically to interact with teammates and coaches, as well as to "maximize his experience" with a largely monolingual fanbase. In that sense, his speech was a classic instance of "double-voiced discourse" (Bakhtin, 1984), crafted in anticipation of what the organization and fans were expecting to hear. Ventura was speaking, but what came out was the culmination of a multiyear process of language socialization, a discourse itinerary that the Royals had plotted and Ventura had followed from the age of seventeen (Scollon, 2008). All the same, to paraphrase the A's staffer from Chapter 1, that doesn't mean it was easy.

The differences between the two speech events (Clemente's and Ventura's) point to generational differences in MLB teams' approaches to language diversity—in particular, the halting steps toward wider acceptance of bilingualism, and the way teams now seek to instill players like Yordano Ventura with the linguistic capital needed for "Next Level Success," as the Royals would have it. But, as with Tanaka, Ohtani, and Ichiro, the institutional embrace of language diversity does not mean that someone will not be mocked or criticized the moment he opens his mouth, very often in ways that deepen the divides multilingual players (and others) have to bridge.

No less than the bravery of a Clemente or a Ventura, the history and future of multilingual baseball hinge on the contributions of people like Steve Blass, who exuberantly, if implicitly, validated Clemente's *bendición*, Christian Colón, who gave Ventura the linguistic and emotional support he needed to make his victory speech, and the Parker Dunshees, Michel Gelaberts, Hyunsung Kims, and Nick Additons of the world, the unsung multitudes who commit themselves to acquiring and using "whatever level of whatever language they have" to live bilingually across the borders of transnational baseball.

Notes

Introduction

1. https://www.wesa.fm/arts-sports-culture/2021-08-30/pittsburgh-pirates-mark-50-years-since-historic-all-black-and-latino-lineup.
2. https://en.wikipedia.org/wiki/World_Series_television_ratings#Viewership_records_for_Games_1%E2%80%937.
3. https://www.youtube.com/watch?v=wxn2jNOqYLY.
4. https://www.baseball-reference.com/bio/Puerto-Rico_born.shtml.
5. Linguists use "utterance" instead of "sentence" to differentiate what someone said in a turn at talk from the grammar-oriented understanding of what makes a "complete sentence." "Phrase" has a different, more technical meaning associated with the way theoretical linguists model human beings' ability to generate understandable talk in specific languages. "Utterance" just means "what someone said at a particular moment."
6. For an overview of "historic patterns of language conflict" in the United States, see chapter 1 of Crawford (2000).
7. I use "bilingual" and "multilingual" interchangeably throughout—that is, "bilingual" does not imply that someone speaks (or spoke) only two languages.
8. https://www.newyorker.com/magazine/2020/06/01/how-baseball-players-became-celebrities.
9. https://sabr.org/bioproj/person/moe-berg/.
10. https://www.americananthro.org/ConnectWithAAA/Content.aspx?ItemNumber=2583.
11. https://www.census.gov/topics/population/language-use/about/faqs.html.
12. Burgos, Jr., speculates that the Grays' decision may have been inspired by King Kelly's success at cultivating an Irish American fan base through association with ethnic identity.
13. A similar process of strategic "Europeanization" of Mexican-origin culture and populations was taking place in non-baseball contexts. See, e.g., Vélez-Ibáñez, Plascencia, & Rosales (2019).
14. These three terms refer to the same group. According to the White Earth Nation's website, "Anishinaabe" is the original inhabitants' name for themselves, "Ojibwe" came about from early contact with Europeans, and "Chippewa" is an Anglicization of "Ojibwe" and the name many tribal members in the United

States prefer. "Anishinaabemowin" refers to the language (as can "Ojibwe" and "Chippewa"). Charles Bender always referred to himself as Chippewa, as far as I know.

15 Source appears to be Tholkes (1983).
16 Apparently from the Buffalo (NY) *Enquirer*.
17 In another bilingual twist, the "Naps" nickname originated with Hall of Famer Napoleon "Nap" Lajoie, "the first superstar in American League history" and a Cleveland icon, who was born in Rhode Island to French-speaking immigrants from Canada: Constantelos and Jones (n.d.).
18 The name change was the outcome of a contest in the same newspaper, which finally denounced the Chief Wahoo logo—though not the team name—in 2014, nearly 100 years later: Levenson (2014).
19 Spokane is part of the Southern Interior Salish branch of the Salishan language family, which comprises over twenty languages in the United States and Canadian Pacific Northwest: https://glottolog.org/resource/languoid/id/spok1245; Mithun (2001).
20 https://www.milb.com/spokane/community/spokanetribe.
21 see also Minasian (2016).
22 https://www.mlb.com/news/2019-mlb-players-weekend-nicknames.
23 Others have argued (persuasively, in my view) that treating linguistic boundaries merely as social constructions disregards research findings on the architecture of bilinguals' mental grammars, viz., MacSwan (2017).
24 These quotations are from Nick Additon, Parker Dunshee, and Dave Bush, respectively.
25 https://www.youtube.com/watch?v=yYEIZgpvFJc&t=964s.

Chapter 1

1 English speakers in MLB organizations call them "Latin" players, that is, players who hail from Latin America.
2 I saw this very phrase in an e-book about the Royals' "Pyramid of Success" philosophy that educational staff created for players. It was taken from former Royals general manager and president of baseball operations Dayton Moore's book *More Than a Season*.
3 The Royals' academy dates to 1986, though their current facility is much newer.
4 See, e.g., Doerr, 2009. Second-language acquisition researchers have made a similar point about "nativeness" and "native speaker" as constructed categories.
5 This role is invariably referred to as "translator" in baseball, but linguists tend to distinguish interpretation as having to do with spoken or signed language

from translation as having to do with written text. I'll stick with that distinction throughout the book so that the terminology herein is consistent with research on interpretation and translation.
6. Jeff added that the Royals also had a curriculum for their (US) American players covering "such land mines as social media, financial literacy, video games, diet, sleep, etc." Latin American players were expected to enroll in that program once they had completed English classes.
7. Another player at the Royals' academy also singled out Drake and Lil Baby as important to his process of learning English. I joked that if he kept listening to Drake, he'd end up with a Canadian accent.
8. 10 hits and 16 walks in 127 plate appearances, to be exact: https://www.baseball-reference.com/register/player.fcgi?id=fernan001yos.
9. https://blogs.fangraphs.com/a-thursday-scouting-notebook-5-6-2021/.
10. And, very coincidentally, the same team for whom Hunter Pence starred in their improbable championship season—see "Introduction."
11. A shift is a defensive tactic that involves infielders (and sometimes outfielders) moving to different spots on the diamond, based on the probability that a given batter will hit the ball to a given part of the field.
12. This happens when teams A and B agree to a trade, and team B is given a list of possible players and a length of time to scout those players before making their selection. It sometimes also has to do with the performance of the player headed to team A, that is, depending on how much and how well that player performs, team B might get to pick from a different list.
13. "Flair" appears to refer to attitudes and behaviors stereotypically associated with young (immigrant) Latino players and often contrasted with those of more traditionally minded US players, as discussed at length in Chapter 3.

Chapter 2

1. The list of players who are signed to major league contracts with an organization and are eligible to be called up to the 25-man roster, or the active roster, at any time.
2. Technically, *decenas*, or "tens" of people.
3. It's more complex than this brief discussion implies. The role of input, what type of input, and other factors in L2 acquisition are subjects of vigorous debate among applied linguists, but "communicatively embedded input" is central to essentially all discussions of the sociocultural basis for language learning. See Krashen and Mason (2020), Lichtman and VanPatten (2021).
4. https://www.census.gov/library/visualizations/interactive/racial-and-ethnic-diversity-in-the-united-states-2010-and-2020-census.html.

5 https://www.montanalegionbaseball.org/legionhistory.
6 Josh Barfield, now the Diamondbacks' director of player development. Interestingly, Josh was born in Venezuela, while his father Jesse, a native of Illinois and a stalwart outfielder for the Blue Jays and Yankees, was playing winter ball there.
7 When linguists say "grammar," we don't mean rules for using language "properly." We mean the structure that underlies language or the set of principles we learn gradually from exposure to language as children and carry around in our brain (Hopper and Traugott, 2003).
8 The empirical basis of time-on-task ideologies (i.e., whether they're true or not) is beyond the scope of this discussion. Suffice it to say that language acquisition is a complex process and scholars differ on whether and to what extent L2 input alone (in the absence of L1 scaffolding) supports language development, if L2 output also contributes to language outcomes and so on.
9 Widely used proficiency guidelines developed by ACTFL, formerly the American Council on the Teaching of Foreign Languages.
10 In linguistics, this is known as "accommodation"—the social process according to which speakers adjust their production to "converge" with interlocutors: Giles, Mulac, Bradac, and Johnson (1987).
11 Mondesi was born in California, where his father was playing for the Los Angeles Dodgers, but was raised primarily in the Dominican Republic.
12 It should be mentioned that many of the English loanwords are in free variation with Spanish-derived counterparts (i.e., either term can be used)—for example, *picher/lanzador* ("pitcher"), *quecher/receptor* ("catcher"), and *ampair/árbitro* ("umpire"). For an exhaustive corpus-based treatment of Spanish baseball vocabulary, see Chaston and Smead (forthcoming).
13 The rest of this quotation, following "she doesn't recognize me," has been translated from Spanish. This is significant because most of our conversation was in English, though Michel and I would switch to Spanish for some phrases or sentences. The following quotation (beginning with "No, on the contrary") is also translated from Spanish.
14 The word translated as "dialect" in reference to Dominican Spanish is *idioma,* which can mean "language" or "way of speaking." Richard used English "fake" in the middle of an utterance that was otherwise in Spanish: "Incluso tengo amigos que me dicen cubano *fake* porque no hablo como cubano, que yo soy dominicano."
15 Eric mentioned Canó and Nelson Cruz as two Dominican MLB players who loomed especially large in the minds of Dominicans on the Dust Devils, since at that time Canó and Cruz (in addition to being All-Stars) were both playing for the Seattle Mariners, the closest team geographically to the Dust Devils' home in Pasco, WA.
16 Prior to the 2022 season, MLB organizations were not required to provide housing for their minor leaguers, most of whom make a relative pittance, do not receive large signing bonuses, and work other jobs during the off-season.

17 "Heritage speakers" are connected to a language through ethnicity or family history. Heritage speakers may speak the language proficiently or, alternatively, speak very little or none of the language but identify with it as a marker of ethnic or national identity. In this case, Eric described the Spanish students as "native speakers," meaning that they were probably from Spanish-speaking immigrant families but may have had limited opportunities to develop the language in academic settings. See, e.g., Beaudrie and Fairclough (2012).
18 https://www.mlbtraderumors.com/2022/03/mlb-international-draft-rumors.html.
19 An independent league's teams are not affiliated with MLB clubs, as opposed to MiLB teams; "organized baseball" indicates MLB affiliates or professional leagues outside the United States.
20 Jeff clarified that, while ex-prospects who had signed professionally in the DR were not eligible to play Division I baseball in the United States, they could play at small colleges and universities belonging to the National Association of Intercollegiate Athletics (NAIA). He said that the team had had the most success working with colleges from the NCCAA or the National Christian College Athletic Association, of which Mid-America Christian University is a member.
21 The Royals were working to direct other released high school graduates to college baseball programs in the Dominican, where they would have five years of eligibility.
22 Feared Dominican slugger, most notably for the St. Louis Cardinals and the Los Angeles Angels (Klein, 2014).

Chapter 3

1 Until 2022, the catcher would use secret hand signs to suggest the next pitch to the pitcher, who could accept or reject the catcher's suggestions by nodding or shaking his head. A runner on second base is ideally positioned to see the signs and—if he can decode them—pass them on to the bench or the batter. In 2022, to cut down on sign-stealing, MLB approved the use of PitchCom, an electronic device that privately conveys signs from catcher to pitcher and is programmed with English and Spanish options: https://www.espn.com/mlb/story/_/id/33674768/mlb-allow-pitchers-catchers-use-anti-sign-stealing-technology-regular-season-sources-say.
2 *Chirping* means good-natured teasing or ribbing. Jesús Luzardo, drafted by the A's and now pitching for the Miami Marlins, was born in Perú to Venezuelan parents and raised in Florida.
3 "Language ideology" was originally used in a more restrictive sense to refer to speakers' beliefs, implicit or explicit, about the grammatical structure of their languages: Silverstein (1979). See also Hill (1985).

4   This isn't meant as a knock on McLouth's Spanish proficiency. I just don't have enough data to say for sure how proficient he is.
5   https://www.youtube.com/watch?v=ReDF79T4fcM.
6   Language paranoia refers to the fear that other people are talking about you in a language you cannot understand or that someone you did not think could understand has been eavesdropping on you: Haviland (2003). Per "Introduction" and "Conclusion," language paranoia is the other side of the "monoglot standard" coin, in that it can refer to fears that the dominant language is (paradoxically) perceived to be in danger: Silverstein (2015).
7   https://www.youtube.com/watch?v=3dPoiuvLhPM.
8   Not to be confused with Max Muncy, the all-star second baseman for the Los Angeles Dodgers.
9   AP classes are challenging courses that prepare high school seniors to take a nationwide test. Students who do well enough on the test can use their AP coursework for college credit.
10 Parker offered these examples.
11 See also the discussion of Nick Additon's South Florida upbringing in Chapter 4.
12 Eye black is face paint that players apply below the eyes to help diminish glare and see the ball better. "The big eye black" refers to the practice of smearing eye black more liberally than in the two traditional neat lines. For another eye black-related controversy involving language, see: https://sports.yahoo.com/blogs/big-league-stew/yunel-escobar-apologizes-gay-slur-eye-black-says-203605396--mlb.html.
13 "Discursive formation," per Michel Foucault, refers to a set of discourses (ways of using language), practices, and ideologies or beliefs that come to constitute a coherent body of knowledge about a social phenomenon, a group of people, and so on (Foucault, 2010).

Chapter 4

1   The team was renamed the SSG Landers in 2021 after being acquired by a different corporation.
2   In 2014, the rule was changed to allow three foreign players per team, who cannot be all pitchers or all position players. Beginning in 2023, KBO clubs will also be allowed to sign one pitcher and one position player to their farm (minor league) team.
3   A "beat writer" is a journalist assigned to cover a specific baseball team on a daily basis—writing game recaps, interviewing players and coaches, and so on.
4   Others have criticized the construct of superdiversity for an ahistorical stance that does not pay adequate heed to the power-laden processes by which speakers end up in "superdiverse" contexts, as well as a tendency to accept claims about idealized language varieties at face value. See, e.g., Flores and Lewis (2016).

5 https://www.mlb.com/official-information/authentication.
6 A nod to Wittgenstein's *Tractatus Logico-Philosophicus* (1922): "The limits of my language mean the limits of my world." They don't, strictly speaking, but in this case, the quotation is apropos.
7 https://www.espn.com/blog/playbook/fandom/post/_/id/3490/five-years-later-wellmans-tirade-endures.
   https://www.nbcchicago.com/news/sports/chicago-baseball/nats-manager-davey-martinez-slams-base-to-ground-after-epic-tirade-ejection-vs-cubs/2514480/.
8 https://www.cbssports.com/mlb/news/watch-former-mlb-pitcher-mike-montgomery-hits-umpire-with-rosin-bag-during-kbo-game/. A rosin bag is a small, beanbag-like bag filled with "a sticky substance extracted from the sap of fir trees" and used by pitchers to get a firmer grip on the ball: https://www.baseball-reference.com/bullpen/Rosin_bag.
9 A balk occurs when a pitcher is judged to have interrupted his delivery of the pitch. All runners advance one base as a penalty.
10 Test of English as a Foreign Language, widely used to assess international students' and professionals' English proficiency as a precondition of educational and work opportunities.
11 "Mandarin" here refers to the Taiwanese variety of Mandarin Chinese. I use "Chinese" interchangeably with "Mandarin" to refer to the same language unless specified otherwise. https://glottolog.org/resource/languoid/id/taib1240.
12 https://glottolog.org/resource/languoid/id/taib1242.
13 Even labels like "Taiwanese Hokkien" and "Taiwanese Hakka" understate the country's linguistic diversity since each of those languages has numerous subdialects and regional variations. See, e.g., Chen (2010).
14 The distinction between context-reduced and context-embedded language is somewhat outdated but still useful for capturing differences in environments for L2 learning and use.
15 https://www.baseball-reference.com/register/player.fcgi?id=addito001nic.
16 English utterances display a range of tones, or varying pitches, but differences in pitch are not "phonemic," unlike in Chinese (Sinitic) languages—that is, whether you pronounce "ball" with a high, low, rising, falling, and so on, pitch does not change the word's meaning. In English, intonation marks differences on the level of pragmatics and discourse (utterances and conversations), not words. For example, English speakers may vary their pitch to express the difference between statements and questions, to convey emotion, and so on, but not to distinguish one word from another meaningfully.
17 As the foregoing discussion of language diversity in Taiwan would suggest, the question of "native language" is tricky, and all the CTBC Brothers players probably didn't have the same native language. Nick was talking about the use of Mandarin as the most widely spoken language and the language of public discourse in Taiwan.

Conclusion

1. Massachusetts native Pete Walker, who did a stint with the Yokohama Bay Stars of the Japan Central League in 2004.
2. https://www.bostonherald.com/2017/06/08/speros-jerry-remy-deserves-sox-support-in-pc-driven-flap/.
3. https://twitter.com/JRODshow44/status/1363597321217314818.
4. The English transliteration of Ohtani's last name caused some confusion even before his arrival in the United States. The English-speaking media initially spelled it "Otani" but later started using "Ohtani" after the player's representatives revealed that it was spelled that way on his professional jersey in Japan. The confusion had to do with distinctions in vowel length that are phonemic in Japanese but not in English—that is, a long /o/ sound can cause a Japanese word to differ in meaning from an identical word with its short counterpart.
5. Readers should be able to get the gist of the argument without knowing the IPA, but for those who are interested: https://www.internationalphoneticassociation.org/content/full-ipa-chart.
6. Sports journalist Michael Smith, for one: https://www.youtube.com/watch?v=ltQKBy0LDHw.
7. https://www.youtube.com/watch?v=GtImIqR5neU.
8. https://www.youtube.com/watch?v=cE-pzE14ZX0.
9. https://www.youtube.com/watch?v=X2rStdh9SyQ.
10. https://twitter.com/YordanoVentura/status/819934739071172609.

References

Adams, K. L., & Brink, D. T. (Eds.). (1990). *Perspectives on official English: The campaign for English as the official language of the USA* (Vol. 57). Berlin: Walter de Gruyter GmbH & Co KG.

Agar, M. (2008). *The professional stranger: An informal introduction to ethnography.* Bingley: Emerald.

Agha, A. (2005). Voice, footing, enregisterment. *Journal of Linguistic Anthropology, 15*(1), 38–59.

Agha, A. (2007). *Language and social relations.* Cambridge: Cambridge University Press.

Ahearn, L. (2021). *Living language: An introduction to linguistic anthropology.* New York: Wiley-Blackwell.

Appel, M. (1999). *Slide, Kelly, slide: The wild life and times of Mike "King" Kelly, baseball's first superstar.* Lanham, MD: The Scarecrow Press.

Au, W. (Ed.). (2009). *Rethinking multicultural education: Teaching for racial and cultural justice.* Milwaukee, WI: Rethinking Schools.

Bakhtin, M. (1984). *Problems of Dostoevsky's poetics* (C. Emerson, trans.). Minneapolis: University of Minnesota Press.

Bauman, Z. (1996). From pilgrim to tourist—or a short history of identity. In S. Hall & P. du Gay (Eds.), *Questions of cultural identity* (pp. 18–36). Thousand Oaks, CA: Sage.

Beaudrie, S. M., & Fairclough, M. A. (2012). *Spanish as a heritage language in the United States: The state of the field.* Washington, DC: Georgetown University Press.

Bell, A. (1984). Language style as audience design. *Language in Society, 13*(2), 145–204.

Berkow, I. (1982, August 10). The two loves of Ted Williams. Retrieved from https://www.nytimes.com/1982/08/10/sports/players-the-2-loves-of-ted-williams.html.

Berman, E., & Smith, B. (2021). De-naturalizing the novice: A critique of the theory of language socialization. *American Anthropologist, 123*(3), 590–602.

Besnier, N. (2015). Sports mobilities across borders: Postcolonial perspectives. *The International Journal of the History of Sport, 32*(7), 849–61.

Blitzer, J. (2016, August 6). Retrieved from https://www.nytimes.com/2016/08/07/sports/baseball/eduardo-nunez-putting-accent-on-spanish-names.html.

Blommaert, J. (2007). On scope and depth in linguistic ethnography. *Journal of Sociolinguistics, 11*(5), 682–8.

Blommaert, J. (2010). *The sociolinguistics of globalization.* Cambridge: Cambridge University Press.

Blommaert, J. (2014). Infrastructures of superdiversity: Conviviality and language in an Antwerp neighborhood. *European Journal of Cultural Studies, 17*(4), 431–51.

Blommaert, J., & Rampton, B. (2015). Language and superdiversity. In K. Arnaut, J. Blommaert, B. Rampton, & M. Spotti (Eds.), *Language and superdiversity* (pp. 21–48). New York: Routledge.

Bourdieu, P. (1991). *Language and symbolic power*. Cambridge, MA: Harvard University Press.

Brayboy, B. M. K. J. (2003). Visibility as a trap: American Indian representation in schools. In S. Books (Ed.), *Invisible children in the society and its schools: Second edition* (pp. 35–52). Mahwah: Lawrence Erlbaum Associates.

Brotherton, D. C., & Barrios, L. (2011). *Banished to the homeland: Dominican deportees and their stories of exile*. New York: Columbia University Press.

Burgos, Jr., A. (2007). *Playing America's game: Baseball, Latinos, and the color line*. Berkeley: University of California Press.

Cameron, D. (1995). *Verbal hygiene*. New York: Routledge.

Cameron, D. (2006). Ideology and language. *Journal of Political Ideologies, 11*(2), 141–52.

Cargile, A. C., Maeda, E., Rodriguez, J., & Rich, M. (2010). "Oh, you speak English so well!": US American listeners' perceptions of "foreignness" among nonnative speakers. *Journal of Asian American Studies, 13*(1), 59–79.

Carlisle Indian Industrial School. (1896a). Charles A. Bender student information card. Retrieved from https://carlisleindian.dickinson.edu/student_files/charles-bender-student-information-card.

Carlisle Indian Industrial School. (1896b). *Descriptive and historical record of student for Charles Bender*. Retrieved from https://carlisleindian.dickinson.edu/student_files/charles-bender-student-file.

Carter, P. M., & Lynch, A. (2015). Multilingual Miami: Current trends in sociolinguistic research. *Language and Linguistics Compass, 9*(9), 369–85.

Chappell, B. (2021). *Mexican American fastpitch: Identity at play in vernacular sport*. Stanford: Stanford University Press.

Chaston, J., & Smead, R. (forthcoming). *The Spanish lexicon of baseball: Semantics, style, and terminology*. Lanham, MD: Lexington Books.

Chen, S. (2017). The construct of cognitive load in interpreting and its measurement. *Perspectives, 25*(4), 640–57.

Chen, S. C. (2010). Multilingualism in Taiwan. *International Journal of the Sociology of Language, 205*, 79–104.

Cho, J. (2017). *English language ideologies in Korea: Interpreting the past and present* (Vol. 23). Cham: Springer.

Chun, E. W. (2016). The meaning of Ching-Chong: Language, racism, and response in new media. In H.S. Alim, J. Rickford, & A. Ball (Eds.), *Raciolinguistics: How language shapes our ideas about race* (pp. 81–96). New York: Oxford University Press.

Collins, J. (1992). Our ideologies and theirs. *Pragmatics, 2*(3), 405–15.

Constantelos, S., & Jones, D. (n.d.). Retrieved from https://sabr.org/bioproj/person/nap-lajoie/.

Coupland, N. (2001). Dialect stylization in radio talk. *Language in Society, 30*(3), 345–75.

Crawford, J. (2000). *At war with diversity: US language policy in an age of anxiety.* Tonawanda: Multilingual Matters.

Crawford, J. (2004). *Educating English learners: Language diversity in the classroom.* Los Angeles: Bilingual Education Services.

Cummins, J. (1983). Language proficiency and academic achievement. In J. W. Oller (Ed.), *Issues in language testing research* (pp. 108–29). Rowley: Newbury House.

Davydova, J. (2021). The role of sociocognitive salience in the acquisition of structured variation and linguistic diffusion: Evidence from quotative be like. *Language in Society, 50*(2), 171–96.

Dawidoff, N. (1994). *The catcher was a spy: The mysterious life of Moe Berg.* New York: Pantheon Books.

de Certeau, M. (1984). *The practice of everyday life.* Berkeley: University of California Press.

Dehé, N., & Stathi, K. (2016). Grammaticalization and prosody: The case of English "sort/kind/type of" constructions. *Language, 92*(4), 911–47.

Diaz-Strong, D. X. (2021). "When did I stop being a child?" The subjective feeling of adulthood of Mexican and Central American unaccompanied 1.25 Generation Immigrants. *Emerging Adulthood,* 2167696821992141.

Doerr, N. M. (Ed.). (2009). *The native speaker concept.* Berlin: De Gruyter Mouton.

Donato, R. (1994). Collective scaffolding in a second language. In J. Lantolf & G. Appel (Eds.), *Vygotskian approaches to second language research* (pp. 33–56). Norwood: Ablex.

Dörnyei, Z., & Thurrell, S. (1991). Strategic competence and how to teach it. *ELT Journal, 45*(1), 16–23.

Duranti, A. (2009). The relevance of Husserl's theory to language socialization. *Journal of Linguistic Anthropology, 19*(2), 205–26.

Eig, J. (2010). *Luckiest man: The life and death of Lou Gehrig.* New York: Simon & Schuster.

Ellis, R. (1994). *The study of second language acquisition.* New York: Oxford University Press.

Ellis, R. (2008). Investigating grammatical difficulty in second language learning: Implications for second language acquisition research and language testing. *International Journal of Applied Linguistics, 18*(1), 4–22.

Erker, D. (2018). Spanish dialectal contact in the United States. In K. Potowski (Ed.), *The Routledge handbook of Spanish as a heritage language* (pp. 269–83). New York: Routledge.

Erker, D., & Otheguy, R. (2016). Contact and coherence: Dialectal leveling and structural convergence in NYC Spanish. *Lingua, 172,* 131–46.

Ettl Rodríguez, F. I., & Kandel-Cisco, B. (2021). Language-supportive coaching practices for athletes who are learning English. *Journal of Sport Psychology in Action, 12*(3), 155–66.

Fazio, L., & Lyster, R. (1998). Immersion and submersion classrooms: A comparison of instructional practices in language arts. *Journal of Multilingual and Multicultural Development, 19*(4), 303–17.

Fitts, R. (2020). *Issei baseball: The story of the first Japanese American ballplayers*. Lincoln: University of Nebraska Press.

Flores, N., & Lewis, M. (2016). From truncated to sociopolitical emergence: A critique of super-diversity in sociolinguistics. *International Journal of the Sociology of Language, 241*, 97–124.

Flores, N., & Rosa, J. (2015). Undoing appropriateness: Raciolinguistic ideologies and language diversity in education. *Harvard Educational Review, 85*(2), 149–71.

Foucault, M. (2010). *The archaeology of knowledge*. New York: Vintage.

García, O. (2011). *Bilingual education in the 21st century: A global perspective*. Malden: John Wiley & Sons.

Geertz, C. (1983). *Local knowledge: Further essays in interpretive anthropology* (p. 16). New York: Basic Books.

Gile, D. (2001). Consecutive vs. simultaneous: Which is more accurate. *Interpretation Studies, 1*(1), 8–20.

Giles, H., Mulac, A., Bradac, J. J., & Johnson, P. (1987). Speech accommodation theory: The first decade and beyond. *Annals of the International Communication Association, 10*(1), 13–48.

Gilroy, P. (2002). *After empire: Melancholia or convivial culture?* New York: Routledge.

Gmelch, G. (1992). Superstition and ritual in American baseball. *Elysian Fields Quarterly, 11*(3), 25–36.

Goffman, E. (1959). *The presentation of self in everyday life*. New York: Doubleday.

Goffman, E. (1974). *Frame analysis: An essay on the organization of experience*. New York: Harper & Row.

Goffman, E. (1981). *Forms of talk*. Philadelphia: University of Pennsylvania Press.

Goffman, E. (1983). The interaction order: American Sociological Association, 1982 presidential address. *American Sociological Review, 48*(1), 1–17.

Golash-Boza, T. (2017). Structural racism, criminalization, and pathways to deportation for Dominican and Jamaican men in the United States. *Social Justice, 44*(2–3), 137–62.

González, N. (2010). The end/s of anthropology and education: 2009 CAE presidential address. *Anthropology & Education Quarterly, 41*(2), 121–5.

Greenblatt, S. (1980). *Renaissance self-fashioning from Sir Thomas More to Shakespeare*. Chicago: University of Chicago Press.

Gregorian, V. Retrieved from https://www.kansascity.com/sports/spt-columns-blogs/vahe-gregorian/article343428/Yordano-Ventura-has-the-stuff-dreams-are-made-of.html.

Guitart, J. M. (1997). Variability, multilectalism, and the organization of phonology in Caribbean Spanish dialects. In F. Martínez-Gil & A. Morales-Front (Eds.), *Issues in the phonology and morphology of the major Iberian languages* (pp. 515–36). Washington, DC: Georgetown University Press.

Guthrie-Shimizu, S. (2012). *Transpacific field of dreams: How baseball linked the United States and Japan in peace and war*. Chapel Hill: University of North Carolina Press.
Hall, E. T. (1966). *The hidden dimension*. Garden City: Doubleday.
Harvey, C. (2022, April 7). Retrieved from https://www.espn.com/mlb/story/_/id/33690660/atlanta-braves-ronald-acuna-jr-acknowledges-rift-former-teammate-freddie-freeman.
Harwood, R. (2018, September 13). Retrieved from https://indiancountrytoday.com/archive/spokane-indians-change-jerseys-to-salish-language?redir=1.
Haviland, J. B. (2003). Ideologies of language: Some reflections on language and US law. *American Anthropologist, 105*(4), 764–74.
Heller, M. (2011). *Paths to post-nationalism: A critical ethnography of language and identity*. New York: Oxford University Press.
Hill, J. H. (1985). The grammar of consciousness and the consciousness of grammar. *American Ethnologist, 12*(4), 725–37.
Hill, J. H. (2001). Mock Spanish, covert racism, and the leaky boundary between public and private spheres. In S. Gal and K. Woolard (Eds.), *Languages and publics: The making of authority* (pp. 83–102). Manchester: St. Jerome Publishing.
Hill, J. H. (2008). *The everyday language of white racism*. Malden: Wiley-Blackwell.
Hill, J. H., & Mannheim, B. (1992). Language and world view. *Annual Review of Anthropology, 21*(1), 381–404.
Hopper, P. J., & Traugott, E. C. (2003). *Grammaticalization*. Cambridge: Cambridge University Press.
Hunter, I. (2021, August 8). Retrieved from https://dailyhive.com/vancouver/toronto-blue-jays-home-run-jacket.
Iddings, A. C. D., & Jang, E. Y. (2008). The mediational role of classroom practices during the silent period: A new-immigrant student learning the English language in a mainstream classroom. *TESOL Quarterly, 42*(4), 567–90.
Ignatiev, N. (2012). *How the Irish became White*. New York: Routledge.
Illich, I. (1973). *Tools for conviviality*. New York: Harper & Row.
Irvine, J. T. (2004). Say when: Temporalities in language ideology. *Journal of Linguistic Anthropology, 14*(1), 99–109.
Irvine, J. T., & Gal, S. (2000). Language ideology and linguistic differentiation. In P. Kroskrity (Ed.), *Regimes of language: Ideologies, polities, and identities* (pp. 35–83). Santa Fe: School of American Research Press.
Jaffe, A. (2000). Introduction: Non-standard orthography and non-standard speech. *Journal of Sociolinguistics, 4*(4), 497–513.
Jaffe, J. (2021, November 10). 2022 Golden Days Era Committee candidate: Minnie Miñoso. Retrieved from https://blogs.fangraphs.com/2022-golden-days-era-committee-candidate-minnie-minoso/.
Jakobson, R. (1960). Linguistics and poetics. In T. Sebeok (Ed.), *Style in language* (pp. 350–77). Cambridge, MA: MIT Press.

Jan, J. S., & Lomeli, A. (2022). Ethnic context, education policy, and language assimilation of indigenous peoples in Taiwan. *International Journal of Bilingual Education and Bilingualism, 25*(1), 355–66.

Kahn, R. (1986). *Good enough to dream*. New York: New American Library.

Kanno, Y., & Norton, B. (2003). Imagined communities and educational possibilities: Introduction. *Journal of Language, Identity, and Education, 2*(4), 241–9.

Kashatus, W. (2006). *Money pitcher: Chief Bender and the tragedy of Indian assimilation*. University Park: Pennsylvania State University Press.

Keane, W. (2010). Money is no object: Materiality, desire, and modernity in an Indonesian society. In R. Preucel & S. Mrozowski (Eds.), *Contemporary archaeology in theory: The new pragmatism* (pp. 347–61). Malden: Wiley-Blackwell.

Kellman, S. (2022, March). Linguaphobia and its resistance in America. *The Montréal Review*. https://www.themontrealreview.com/Articles/Linguaphobia-and-Its-Resistance-in-America.php.

Kelly, M. (2006). *"Play ball": Stories of the diamond field and other historical writings about the 19th century Hall of Famer* (G. Mitchem & M. Durr, Eds., p. 7). McFarland Historical Baseball Library, Vol. 9. Jefferson, NC: McFarland & Co., Inc..

Kelman, H. (1971). Language as an aid and barrier to involvement in the national system. In J. Rubin & B. H. Jernudd (Eds.), *Can language be planned? Sociological theory and practice for developing nations* (pp. 21–51). Honolulu: University of Hawaii Press.

Kim, S. Y., Wang, Y., Deng, S., Alvarez, R., & Li, J. (2011). Accent, perpetual foreigner stereotype, and perceived discrimination as indirect links between English proficiency and depressive symptoms in Chinese American adolescents. *Developmental Psychology, 47*(1), 289.

Klein, A. (2006). Dominican Republic: Forging an international industry. In G. Gmelch (Ed.), *Baseball without borders: The international pastime* (pp. 117–35). Lincoln: University of Nebraska Press.

Klein, A. (2014). *Dominican baseball: Old pride, new prejudice*. Philadelphia: Temple University Press.

Knafo, S. (2022, April 28). Retrieved from https://www.nytimes.com/2022/04/28/nyregion/frankie-light-youtube-polyglot.html.

Kramsch, C. (1986). From language proficiency to interactional competence. *The Modern Language Journal, 70*(4), 366–72.

Kramsch, C. (2006). From communicative competence to symbolic competence. *The Modern Language Journal, 90*(2), 249–52.

Krashen, S., & Mason, B. (2020). The optimal input hypothesis: Not all comprehensible input is of equal value. *CATESOL Newsletter, 5*, 1–2.

Labov, W. (2018). The role of the Avant Garde in linguistic diffusion. *Language Variation and Change, 30*, 1–21.

Ladegaard, H. J. (2018). Codeswitching and emotional alignment: Talking about abuse in domestic migrant-worker returnee narratives. *Language in Society, 47*(5), 693–714.

Laurier, E., & Philo, C. (2006). Cold shoulders and napkins handed: Gestures of responsibility. *Transactions of the Institute of British Geographers, 31*(2), 193–207.

Lee, B.-S. (2019). *Exploring the roles of staff interpreters in a professional baseball team in Taiwan: Taking the CTBC Brothers as an example.* Master's thesis. National Taiwan University, Taipei.

Lefton, B. (2014, August 29). Retrieved from https://www.wsj.com/articles/ichiro-suzuki-uncensored-en-espanol-1409356461.

Lemke, J. L. (2000). Across the scales of time: Artifacts, activities, and meanings in ecosocial systems. *Mind, Culture, and Activity, 7*(4), 273–90.

Letasky, J. (2020, June 19). Retrieved from https://406mtsports.com/baseball/arizona-diamondbacks-minor-leaguer-working-out-mentoring-billings-scarlets/article_31165038-ac56-5875-b5bc-6d1141a0233e.html.

Leung, K., Ang, S., & Tan, M. L. (2014). Intercultural competence. *Annual Review of Organizational Psychology and Organizational Behavior, 1*(1), 489–519.

Levenson, E. (2014, February 28). Retrieved from https://www.theatlantic.com/culture/archive/2014/02/brief-history-cleveland-plain-dealer-and-indians-mascot-chief-wahoo-logo-editorial/358692/.

Lichtman, K., & VanPatten, B. (2021). Was Krashen right? Forty years later. *Foreign Language Annals, 54*(2), 283–305.

Lippi-Green, R. (2012). *English with an accent.* New York: Routledge.

Long, M. H., & Adamson, H. D. (2012). SLA research and Arizona's structured English immersion policies. In M. B. Arias & C. Faltis (Eds.), *Implementing educational language policy in Arizona* (pp. 38–54). Buffalo: Multilingual Matters.

Longenhagen, E. (2020, February 12). 2020 top 100 prospects. Retrieved from https://blogs.fangraphs.com/2020-top-100-prospects/.

Lourim, J. (2016, June 8). https://www.baltimoresun.com/sports/orioles/bal-yordano-ventura-s-incident-with-manny-machado-wasn-t-his-first-incident-20160608-story.html.

Lv, Q., & Liang, J. (2019). Is consecutive interpreting easier than simultaneous interpreting?–a corpus-based study of lexical simplification in interpretation. *Perspectives, 27*(1), 91–106.

MacSwan, J. (2017). A multilingual perspective on translanguaging. *American Educational Research Journal, 54*(1), 167–201.

Makoni, S., & Pennycook, A. (Eds.). (2007). *Disinventing and reconstituting languages.* Buffalo: Multilingual Matters.

Maraniss, D. (2006). *Clemente: The passion and grace of baseball's last hero.* New York: Simon & Schuster.

Margerie, H. (2010). On the rise of (inter) subjective meaning in the grammaticalization of kind of/kinda. In K. Davidse, L. Vandelanotte, & H. Cuyckens (Eds.), *Subjectification, intersubjectification and grammaticalization* (pp. 315–46). Berlin: Walter de Gruyter GmbH & Co. KG.

Markusen, B. (2006). *The team that changed baseball: Roberto Clemente and the 1971 Pittsburgh Pirates.* Yardley: Westholme.

Martin-Beltrán, M. (2010). Positioning proficiency: How students and teachers (de)construct language proficiency at school. *Linguistics and Education, 21*(4), 257–81.

Massey, D. (2005). *For space.* London: Sage.

McCarty, T. L., & Nicholas, S. E. (2014). Reclaiming Indigenous languages: A reconsideration of the roles and responsibilities of schools. *Review of Research in Education, 38*(1), 106–36.

McDaniel, R. J. (2019, March 21). Retrieved from https://blogs.fangraphs.com/the-meaning-of-ichiro/.

Meek, B. A. (2006). And the Injun goes "How!": Representations of American Indian English in white public space. *Language in Society, 35*(1), 93–128.

Mendoza-Denton, N., & Boum, A. (2015). Breached initiations: Sociopolitical resources and conflicts in emergent adulthood. *Annual Review of Anthropology, 44*, 295–310.

Milroy, J. (2006). The ideology of the standard language. In C. Llamas, L. Mullany, & P. Stockwell (Eds.), *The Routledge companion to sociolinguistics* (pp. 153–9). New York: Routledge.

Minasian, I. (2016, September 26). Retrieved from https://tht.fangraphs.com/mlbs-ponle-acento-campaign-is-a-step-in-the-right-direction/.

Mithun, M. (2001). *The languages of native North America.* Cambridge: Cambridge University Press.

Moore, R. (2021). Michael Silverstein (1945–2020). *Language in Society, 50*(4), 493–507.

Morales, A., & Hanson, W. E. (2005). Language brokering: An integrative review of the literature. *Hispanic Journal of Behavioral Sciences, 27*(4), 471–503.

Morris, A. (2006). Taiwan: Baseball, colonialism, and nationalism. In G. Gmelch (Ed.), *Baseball without borders: The international pastime* (pp. 65–88). Lincoln: University of Nebraska Press.

Morris, P., & Fatsis, S. (2014, February 4). Retrieved from https://slate.com/culture/2014/02/william-edward-white-the-first-black-player-in-major-league-baseball-history-lived-his-life-as-a-white-man.html.

Mortimer, K. S., & Dolsa, G. (2020). Ongoing emergence: Borderland high school DLBE students' self-identifications as lingual people. *International Journal of Bilingual Education and Bilingualism*, 1–13. https://doi.org/10.1080/13670050.2020.1783636.

Nakagawa, K. Y. (2014). *Japanese American baseball in California.* Charleston: The History Press.

Ngai, M. M. (2017). The architecture of race in American immigration law: A reexamination of the Immigration Act of 1924. In I. H. López (Ed.), *Race, law and society* (pp. 351–76). New York: Routledge.

Nowicka, M., & Vertovec, S. (2014). Comparing convivialities: Dreams and realities of living-with-difference. *European Journal of Cultural Studies, 17*(4), 341–56.

Ochs, E., & Shohet, M. (2006). The cultural structuring of mealtime socialization. *New Directions for Child and Adolescent Development, 111,* 35–49.

O'Connor, B. H. (2020). Revisiting Americanist arguments and rethinking scale in linguistic anthropology. *Journal of Linguistic Anthropology, 30*(3), 284–303.

Ohta, A. S. (2005). Interlanguage pragmatics in the zone of proximal development. *System, 33*(3), 503–17.

Omi, M., & Winant, H. (1994). *Racial formation in the United States: From the 1960s to the 1990s.* New York: Routledge.

Orellana, M. F. (2009). *Translating childhoods: Immigrant youth, language, and culture.* New Brunswick: Rutgers University Press.

Ortiz, J. (2016, December 14). Retrieved from https://www.usatoday.com/story/sports/mlb/2015/09/30/mlb-bench-clearing-brawls-unwritten-rules-ethnic-backgrounds/73066892/.

Otheguy, R., García, O., & Reid, W. (2019). A translanguaging view of the linguistic system of bilinguals. *Applied Linguistics Review, 10*(4), 625–51.

Páez, J. (2020, December 6). Retrieved from https://www.fishstripes.com/22157016/marlins-education-program-english-spanish-classes.

Park, J. S. Y. (2017). Class, competence, and language ideology: Beyond Korean Englishes. In C.J. Jenks & J. Won Lee (Eds.), *Korean Englishes in transnational contexts* (pp. 53–72). Cham: Palgrave Macmillan.

Pavlenko, A. (2016). Whorf's lost argument: Multilingual awareness. *Language Learning, 66*(3), 581–607.

Peirce, B. N. (1995). Social identity, investment, and language learning. *TESOL Quarterly, 29*(1), 9–31.

Pennycook, A. (2001). *Critical applied linguistics: A critical introduction.* New York: Routledge.

Pennycook, A. (2012). *Language and mobility.* Buffalo: Multilingual Matters.

Powers-Beck, J. (2004). *The American Indian integration of baseball.* Lincoln: University of Nebraska Press.

Pratt, R. H. (1894–1895). Annual Report of the Carlisle Indian School. Retrieved from https://carlisleindian.dickinson.edu/documents/annual-report-carlisle-indian-school-1894-1895.

Ramat, A. G. (2012). Typology and second language acquisition. In C. Chapelle (Ed.), *The encyclopedia of applied linguistics* (pp. 1–7). New York: Wiley Online Library, John Wiley & Sons. doi: 10.1002/9781405198431.wbeal1233.

Raviv, L., de Heer Kloots, M., & Meyer, A. (2021). What makes a language easy to learn? A preregistered study on how systematic structure and community size affect language learnability. *Cognition, 210,* 104620.

Reynolds, J. F., & Orellana, M. F. (2009). New immigrant youth interpreting in white public space. *American Anthropologist, 111*(2), 211–23.

Richardson Bruna, K. (2009). "You're magmatic now": Language play, linguistic biliteracy, and the science crossing of adolescent Mexican newcomer youth. In

K. Richardson Bruna & K. Gomez (Eds.), *The work of language in multicultural classrooms: Talking science, writing science* (pp. 167–89). New York: Routledge.

Riess, S. (1980). Professional baseball and social mobility. *The Journal of Interdisciplinary History*, *11*(2), 235–50.

Rivera, M. (2019, March 19). Retrieved from https://www.espn.com/mlb/story/_/id/26297707/mr-ichiro-god-japanese-players-mariners-icon-japan-series.

Rogoff, B. (2014). Learning by observing and pitching in to family and community endeavors: An orientation. *Human Development*, *57*(2–3), 69–81.

Rosa, J., & Flores, N. (2017). Unsettling race and language: Toward a raciolinguistic perspective. *Language in Society*, *46*(5), 621–47.

Rosenberg, H. W. (2004). *Cap Anson 2: The theatrical and Kingly Mike Kelly: US team sport's first media sensation and Baseball's original Casey at the Bat* (Vol. 2). Tile Books.

Ruiz, R. (1984). Orientations in language planning. *NABE Journal*, *8*(2), 15–34.

Ruiz, R. (2010). Reorienting language-as-resource. In J. Petrovic (Ed.), *International perspectives on Bilingual education: Policy, practice, and controversy* (pp. 155–72). Charlotte: Information Age Publishing.

Ruiz, R. (2016a). English language planning and transethnification in the USA. In N. Hornberger (Ed.), *Honoring Richard Ruiz and his work on language planning and bilingual education* (pp. 77–92). Blue Ridge Summit: Multilingual Matters.

Ruiz, R. (2016b). Jesus was bilingual. In N. Hornberger (Ed.), *Honoring Richard Ruiz and his work on language planning and bilingual education* (pp. 213–18). Blue Ridge Summit: Multilingual Matters.

Ruiz, R. (2016c). Paradox of bilingualism. In N. Hornberger (Ed.), *Honoring Richard Ruiz and his work on language planning and Bilingual education* (pp. 182–90). Blue Ridge Summit: Multilingual Matters Ltd.

Russell, D. (2005). Consecutive and simultaneous interpreting. *Benjamins Translation Library*, *63*, 135.

Rymes, B. (2014). Marking communicative repertoire through metacommentary. In A. Blackledge & A. Creese (Eds.), *Heteroglossia as practice and pedagogy* (pp. 301–16). Dordrecht: Springer.

Saito, N. T. (1997). Model minority, yellow peril: Functions of foreignness in the construction of Asian American legal identity. *Asian Law Journal*, *4*, 71. (pp. 71–95).

Salgado, Jr., E. (2008). Retrieved from https://www.californiaindianeducation.org/sports_heros/big_chief_meyers/.

Salvador, J. (2021, February 22). Retrieved from https://www.si.com/mlb/2021/02/22/seattle-mariners-president-kevin-mather-resigns-after-comments.

Sandel, T. L., Chao, W. Y., & Liang, C. H. (2006). Language shift and language accommodation across family generations in Taiwan. *Journal of Multilingual and Multicultural Development*, *27*(2), 126–47.

Schieffelin, B. B., & Ochs, E. (1986). Language socialization. *Annual Review of Anthropology*, *15*(1), 163–91.

Schwartz, A. (2008). Their language, our Spanish: Introducing public discourses of 'Gringoism' as racializing linguistic and cultural reappropriation. *Spanish in Context*, 5(2), 224–45.

Scollon, R. (2008). Discourse itineraries: Nine processes of resemiotization. In V. Bhatia, J. Flowerdew, & R. Jones (Eds.), *Advances in discourse studies* (pp. 243–54). New York: Routledge.

Scollon, S. W., & de Saint-Georges, I. (2013). Mediated discourse analysis. In J. P. Gee & M. Handford (Eds.), *The Routledge handbook of discourse analysis* (pp. 66–78). New York: Routledge.

Shin, H. (2007). English language teaching in Korea. In J. Cummins & C. Davison (Eds.), *International handbook of English language teaching* etc. (pp. 75–86). Boston: Springer.

Silverstein, M. (1979). Language structure and linguistic ideology. In R. Clyne, W. Hanks, & C. Hofbauer (Eds.), *The elements: A parasession on linguistic units and levels* (pp. 193–247). Chicago: Chicago Linguistic Society.

Silverstein, M. (1985). Language and the culture of gender: At the intersection of structure, usage, and ideology. In E. Mertz & R. Parmentier (Eds.), *Semiotic mediation* (pp. 219–59). London: Academic Press.

Silverstein, M. (1998). Monoglot "Standard" in America: Standardization and metaphors of linguistic hegemony. In D. Brenneis & R. Macauley (Eds.), *The Matrix of Language* (pp. 284–306). Boulder: Westview Press.

Silverstein, M. (2005). Axes of evals. *Journal of Linguistic Anthropology*, 15(1), 6–22.

Silverstein, M. (2015). How language communities intersect: Is "superdiversity" an incremental or transformative condition? *Language & Communication*, 44, 7–18.

Stevens, G. (1999). A century of US censuses and the language characteristics of immigrants. *Demography*, 36(3), 387–97.

Tagliamonte, S. A., & D'arcy, A. (2007). Frequency and variation in the community grammar: Tracking a new change through the generations. *Language Variation and Change*, 19(2), 199–217.

Tatum, B. D. (2017). *Why are all the Black kids sitting together in the cafeteria? And other conversations about race.* New York: Basic Books.

Tholkes, R. (1983). Retrieved from https://sabr.org/journal/article/chief-bender-the-early-years/.

Tollefson, J. W. (2007). Ideology, language varieties, and ELT. In J. Cummins & C. Davison (Eds.), *International handbook of English language teaching: Part 1* (pp. 25–36). Boston: Springer.

Torres, M., & Rosenthal, K. (2022, January 20). Retrieved from https://theathletic.com/3080470/2022/01/20/a-failed-system-a-corrupt-process-exploits-dominican-baseball-prospects-is-an-international-draft-really-the-answer/.

Uba, L. (2012). *A postmodern psychology of Asian Americans: Creating knowledge of a racial minority.* Albany: SUNY Press.

US Census Bureau. (1900). Schedule No. 1—Population. Indian Population. White Earth Indian Reservation, Polk County, Minnesota. Enumeration District No. 340a, sheet 5.

US Census Bureau. (1940). Population schedule. S.D. No. 8, E.D. 53–5, Sheet No. 81-a.

US Census Bureau, Indian Census Rolls. (1905–1909). Retrieved from https://www.fold3.com/image/174050089.

Valdés, G. (1997). Dual-language immersion programs: A cautionary note concerning the education of language-minority students. *Harvard Educational Review, 67*(3), 391–429.

Valdés, G. (2001). *Learning and not learning English*. New York: Teachers College Press.

Vélez-Ibáñez, C. G., Plascencia, L. F., & Rosales, J. (2019). Interrogating the ethnogenesis of the Spanish and Mexican. *Aztlán: A Journal of Chicano Studies, 44*(2), 41–76.

Vitanova, G. (2005). Authoring the self in a non-native language: A dialogic approach to agency and subjectivity. In J. K. Hall, G. Vitanova, & L. Marchenkova (Eds.), *Dialogue with Bakhtin on second and foreign language learning: New perspectives* (pp. 138–59). Mahwah: LEA.

Waldstein, D. (2013, January 19). Retrieved from https://www.nytimes.com/2013/01/20/sports/baseball/baseball-set-to-allow-interpreters-on-pitching-mound.html.

Wei, Li. (2018). Translanguaging as a practical theory of language. *Applied Linguistics, 39*(1), 9–30.

Whiting, R. (2009). *You gotta have wa: When two cultures collide on the baseball diamond*. New York: Vintage Books.

Wilczek, F. (2021). *Fundamentals: Ten keys to reality*. New York: Penguin.

Wiley, T. G. (2000). Continuity and change in the function of language ideologies in the United States. In T. Ricento (Ed.), *Ideology, politics, and language policies: Focus on English* (pp. 67–85). Philadelphia: John Benjamins.

Willis, P. (2017). *Learning to labor: How working class kids get working class jobs*. New York: Routledge.

Wolfe, P. (2006). Settler colonialism and the elimination of the native. *Journal of Genocide Research, 8*(4), 387–409.

Wong Fillmore, L., & Snow, C. (2000). *What teachers need to know about language*. Washington, DC: Center for Applied Linguistics.

Zenker, O. (2014). Linguistic relativity and dialectical idiomatization: Language ideologies and second language acquisition in the Irish Language Revival of Northern Ireland. *Journal of Linguistic Anthropology, 24*(1), 63–83.

Zentz, L. (2014). "Love" the local, "Use" the National, "Study" the Foreign: Shifting Javanese language ecologies in (Post-) modernity, postcoloniality, and globalization. *Journal of Linguistic Anthropology, 24*(3), 339–59.

Zentz, L. (2021). "I AM HERE AND I MATTER": Virtue signaling and moral-political stance in progressive activists' Facebook posts. *Narrative Inquiry*, 1–26. https://doi.org/10.1075/ni.20117.zen.

General Index

f denotes an in-text illustration

ability, linguistic   54, 57
acculturation   83
African Americans   9, *see also* players, Black (African American); United States
African descent   45
agentes   69
AL Cy Young Award   154
Allentown (Pennsylvania)   137
American Indians, *see* Native Americans
American League   179, 182
   Rookie of the Year   182
American Legion   73
anthropology   19–22, 32, 39, 47, 55, 111, 171, 183
   emic (insider) categories and   22
Arizona   28–9, 31, 50–1, 61, 66, 72, 78, 85, 87, 112, *see also* baseball teams
Arizona State University   55–6, 72
Aruba   30
Asia   138–41, 147, 162, 175
   baseball in   20, 139–40, 165, 167
Asians, stereotypes and   185, *see also* United States
audience, *see* fans
Australia   126, 165

Bahamas   62
Baltimore   4
baseball (general)
   accent mockery and   179–81, 183, 189
   All-Stars   133
   announcers, Mandarin-speaking   154
   announcers, Taiwanese   158
   announcers and   156–8, 176, 179
   balks   149, 197 n.9

baseball language/talk   23, 86, 141, 147, 176, 183, 185
basemen   1, 8, 61, 113–14, 155, 176, 184
catchers   3–4, 13, 31, 34, 54, 56, 61, 105, 148–9, 160, 175–6, 194 n.12, 195 n.1
coaches   15, 19–20, 23, 31, 38, 41, 51, 53–4, 57–8, 69–71, 89–90, 95, 118, 132–3, 135, 139–40, 150–1, 156, 161, 164, 172, 175–6, 188
coaches, English-speaking   60, 66, 82, 89
coaches, Spanish-speaking   66, 90
culture and   3, 156, 172
'culture clash' in   134, 186
ethnicity and   6
fastballs   186
Hall of Fame   6, 80–1, 128, 179–80
hitters   5, 53, 179
home plate   148
infielders   31, 48, 49*f*, 51, 56, 175–6, 185, 193 n.11
Japanese American   20
journalists/media and   1–2, 7, 9, 12, 14, 14*f*, 29, 55, 85, 91, 113, 120, 133–4, 150, 155–6, 159, 180–1, 183–5, 196 n.3
language and   3, 6
Latin American   103, 165
linguistic difference and   9
managers   1, 36, 51, 57, 65, 85, 92–3, 127, 145, 148, 150–1, 162
multilingualism and   3–4, 28, 107, 176, 178, 189
outfielders   18*f*, 24, 31, 175, 193 n.11
pitchers   10, 12, 18, 34, 45, 54, 57, 68, 73*f*, 82, 85, 105, 107, 124, 134, 137–8, 147–50, 154, 175–6, 178–80, 182, 186, 194 n.12, 195 n.1, 196 n.2

race and 3, 6, 9
racism and 4–5, 61, 117, 180–3
relievers 147
scouts 15, 19, 28, 33, 43, 51–3, 99, 128–9, 134, 137, 141, 152, 172, 176, 193 n.12
social action and 178
social media and 42, 84, 130, 176, 181
starters 147, 167
symbolic competence and 60
time limitations ('time to succeed') and 76–7
umpires 14, 19, 23, 35, 63, 105–6, 109, 119, 121, 142–4, 144*f*, 145–51, 164, 194 n.12
umpires, English-speaking 147
umpires, Spanish-speaking 106
baseball teams
Águilas Cibaeñas 106
Arizona Diamondbacks 37, 71–4, 85–6
 Dominican academy and 72
Atlanta Braves 133–4, 137, 161 (*see also* World Series)
Baltimore Orioles 1–2, 106–7, 185
Billings Scarlets 73, 73*f*
Boston Red Sox 123, 126–7, 138, 166, 168, 175–6, 178
Buffalo Bisons 185
Cleveland Indians 13–14, 160
 Chief Wahoo and 13–14
Cleveland Naps 13–14 (*see also* Cleveland Indians)
Colorado Rockies 29, 46, 90–1, 128
CTBC (Chinatrust) Brothers 139, 161–2, 167, 168
Detroit Tigers 142, 179–81
Houston Astros 30, 33, 45, 81, 113 (*see also* World Series)
Kansas City Royals 27–30, 30*f*, 31, 34, 39–42, 47, 49–51, 54, 63, 66–7, 79–80, 83–4, 100–1, 106, 116–17, 127, 130, 133–4, 141, 161, 186, 187*f*, 188–9
 2019 minor league handbook (Spanish) 42

Arizona training facility (Surprise) and 28–9, 31, 50, 85
Dominican academy and 27–30, 30*f*, 31–5, 35*f*, 36*f*, 38–42, 46–51, 57, 61, 79, 83–4, 90, 95, 111, 117, 160, 186–7
Dominican Summer League 43*f*
Embracing Diversity program and 39 (*see also* postgame interviews; World Series)
KT Wiz 148
Las Vegas Aviators 105–6
Lehigh Valley IronPigs 137, 140
Los Angeles Angels 179
Los Angeles Dodgers 133
Miami Marlins 29, 47, 78, 100–1, 112, 128–30
 bilingualism and 127–30
 Dominican academy and 78, 95, 187
 Latino character of 128
Milwaukee Brewers 137, 161
Minnesota Twins 17, 113
Napa (California) Silverados 98
New York Giants 13 (*see also* World Series)
New York Mets 100, 106
New York Yankees 134, 147, 154–5, 167, 175
Oakland Athletics 36, 38, 40, 43, 50–2, 52*f*, 53–66, 69–70, 83, 99, 105–7, 111–12, 117, 119–20, 123, 126, 188
 Arizona training facility (Mesa) 50, 55, 58, 61
Philadelphia Athletics 13
Philadelphia Phillies 69, 137–8
Pittsburgh Pirates 1, 188 (*see also* World Series)
Providence Grays 9
Samsung Lions 147–8
San Diego Padres 46, 90, 96–8, 134
San Francisco Giants 24, 106, 186
San Rafael (California) Pacifics 98
Seattle Mariners 177–8, 185
SK Wyverns 137–8, 151
Southern Illinois Miners 98

General Index

Spokane (Washington) Indians   16, 16*f*, 17
St. Louis Cardinals   43, 106, 111, 168
Tampa Bay Rays   184
Texas Rangers   137
Toronto Blue Jays   17–18, 24, 137, 176, 185
   La Gente Del Barrio jacket   17–18, 18*f*
Toros del Este   24, 188
Tri-City Dust Devils (Pasco, Washington)   89, 92, 93*f*, 93–4
Troy Haymakers   8, 9*f*
Washington Nationals   71
basketball, Black players and   61
Beijing   159
Bellevue (Washington)   178
Bible   99
bilingualism   2, 15–19, 21, 23, 38, 59, 68, 80, 85, 105, 110, 114, 116–18, 121–2, 125, 127–9, 140, 158, 176, 178, 184, 188–9, *see also* Miami Marlins
   competitive advantages and   172
   education and   3, 128–30
   'elite' bilingualism (Valdés)   108, 120–1
   immigrants and   4
   Irish-English   6
   Korean-English   142, 158
   Mandarin-English   157–8, 163
   non-signed Latin American prospects and   86–96
   as outcome for players   68, 81
   paradox of (Ruiz)   108
   political comments and   177
   professional pride and   130
   proficiency and   81, 177
   social solidarity and   83
   Spanish-English   116, 158
   state-sanctioned   186
   transition to life in USA and   109
   as unremarkable fact   169
Billings   72
bodies, Afro-Latino   45
Boston   49
Bronx   175
buscones   29

California   8, 134, 140, 187
Canada   15
Caribbean Series (2021–22)   98
Carlisle Indian Industrial School (Pennsylvania)   11–13
Catholicism, Irish   7
Central Intelligence Agency (CIA)   4
China   126, 131, 162, 165, 173
   baseball and   165–6
Chipotle Mexican Grill   37–8
Cleveland Plain Dealer   14
clubhouses   31, 70, 72, 82, 97, 106, 108, 110–12, 115, 117–22, 126, 128, 132, 135, 171, 173, *see also* Major League Baseball (MLB); South Korea
codeswitching, linguistic   68
Cold War   141
Colombia   45, 64
conviviality, notion of   115
Costa Rica   161
COVID-19 pandemic   71–5, 85, 106, 126, 130, 147–8, 157, 179
Cuba   8, 30, 37, 45, 69–70, 87, 114, 122, 169
   defection from   69
   education system and   45
   'fake Cubans'   88
   national youth baseball team   69
   Serie Nacional   167
   US immigration system and   89
cultural brokers   120
cultural layers   146, 148–9
Curaçao   61

Detroit Free Press   142
difference, linguistic   183
Disney   156
diversity   59, 110–11, 143, 177, *see also* language diversity; superdiversity
Dominican Republic   24, 27–30, 34, 43–9, 52, 57, 61–4, 66, 69, 73–4, 81, 84, 86–8, 95–6, 98–100, 105–8, 121, 128, 138–9, 143, 145–6, 161, 165, 168–9, 186–7, *see also* baseball teams; players, Dominican; prospects, Dominican

baseball academies (MLB) and   29–30, 30f, 31–5, 36f, 46, 59, 66, 68, 70–1, 77–8, 101, 167
   baseball industry and   103
   Colombia and   45
   education system and   44–8, 103
   Guaymate   51
   Jimaní   160
   La Romana   24
   Las Terrenas   187
   Major League Baseball, relationship with   101–2
   Major League Baseball office (Santo Domingo)   128
   returning to from US after contract release   98–102
   Samaná peninsula   186
   San Antonio de Guerra   27, 30, 48
   Santiago   48–9, 102
   Santo Domingo   27, 29, 61, 121, 128
   zonas francas and   102
Dominican Winter League   24, 52, 106
Duolingo   49, 129
Durango (Mexico)   8

El Paso   5
El Salvador   30, 69
English   2, 4, 11–12, 14, 19–24, 28–9, 31, 33, 35, 37–40, 43–6, 49, 52–61, 63, 66–8, 70, 111–12, 114–15, 122–7, 131–2, 147, 149, 153, 157, 159, 161, 166, 169–72, 177–8, 181–2, 187–8, *see also* English as a second language (ESL); English learning and education; English proficiency; teammates, English-speaking
   American English   7, 123, 179–80
   American Indian English   13
   non-native pronunciation   183
English as a second language (ESL)   21–2, 28, 34, 46–7, 65, 76, 80, 90–4, 132
English learning and education   27, 33–4, 36, 38, 44–6, 50, 56–9, 67–82, 86–7, 89, 91, 99, 105, 107, 118, 125–6, 129, 132, 134–5, 137, 142–3, 153–7, 162–3, 182, *see also* English proficiency; socialization; Spanish
   American Council on the Teaching of Foreign Languages (ACTFL)   77–8, 194 n.9
   Athletes Learning English (ALEs)   74–6
   borrowings/loanwords and   165, 194 n.12
   coaches, relationship with   56–7, 73–5, 82, 85, 126, 141
   conversational English   71, 85, 118
   deficit view and   46
   failure and   95–6
   food and   36–7, 90
   functional English and   36
   grammaticalization   76
   immersion   55–6
   lingo   75
   naturalistic learning   74–5
   players' strategies for   48–9, 72, 129
   professionalism ('becoming professional') and   25, 28, 34, 39–42, 57, 64–5, 67–8, 70–1, 81, 83, 105, 113, 133–4, 147
   slang   75–6
   socioeconomic dimension of   89
   South Korea and   152–4
   Test of English as a Foreign Language (TOEFL)   154
   time limitations and   76–80
   time-on-task and   77
   Total Physical Response (TPR)   75
   transferable skills and   96, 100
   transitional skills and   37–8
   workplace English and   34–5, 38, 40, 79
English proficiency   56–7, 71, 73, 80, 87, 102, 126

fandom   141–2, 154
fans   2, 12, 14, 19–20, 24, 83, 134, 144, 157, 164, 167, 178, 181, 184, 186, 188
   American   81, 182, 184
   Chinese-speaking   158
   English-speaking   84
   Irish American   191 n.12
   Irish Catholic   7

Korean   149–50
  Mandarin-speaking   164
  monolingualism and   188
  racism and   4
  relationship with players and   83
  Spanish-speaking   17
first language (L1)   21, 76, 166
  disparities with L2 and   172
  English   55–6, 75, 82–3, 85, 108, 117, 125, 127, 129–31, 170
  non-Dominican Spanish   88
  Spanish   37–8, 122, 130
  Taiwanese   159
Florida   29, 61, 87, 128, 130, 139, 169
Fordham University   8
Fox Sports   107

Google Docs   40
Google Translate   142, 163
Great Depression   6
Guatemala   69
Gwinnett (Georgia)   137

Haiti   160
Han Chinese   44
Higher Standards Academy (HSA)   34, 36, 65–6, 74, 126
Hillsboro (Oregon)   85
Hispanics   72

immigrants, Latin American   128
immigrants, Latinx   46
Incheon   137–40
Indiana   108
Indianapolis (Indiana)   106
intercultural competence   139–40
International Phonetic Alphabet   179
interpreters   15, 17, 19, 23, 53, 74, 82–5, 125, 140, 143–6, 149, 151, 156, 160–6, 170–1, 175–6, 178, 180–2, 184–5
inversionistas   69
Ireland   6
Italy   9

Japan   12, 20, 143, 146, 167, 175, 182
  baseball in   20, 140–2, 166, 182
  identity and   183, 185

Nippon Professional Baseball (NPB)   140, 157, 159, 166–7, 175, 179, 181–2
Japanese Americans   186
Johannesburg   165

Kansas City   182
Korea, *see* South Korea
Kuwait   95

language brokers   73–4, 82, 110, 140, 142–4, 149–51, 156, 163, 172
language communities   111
language diversity   2–4, 15, 18–20, 22–3, 40, 89, 133, 158, 175, 186, 189, 197 n.13, 197 n.17, *see also* Spanish
language ideologies   3, 21, 45, 105, 107, 110, 147, 152, 170, 177, 181, 195 n.3
language panic   176
language paranoia   108, 196 n.6
languages, *see also* English; English as a second language (ESL); English learning and education; first language (L1); mother tongue; native language; second language (L2); Spanish; Taiwan
  Anishinaabemowin   10–11, 15, 191 n.14
  Cahuilla   15
  Cantonese   113
  Celtic   7, 15
  Dutch   62, 175
  Esperanto   10
  'fake' or 'mock' Asian   179–81, 183
  French   4, 9
  German   4
  Hawaiian   159
  Hebrew   4
  'Hollywood Injun English'   13
  'Irish'   7
  Irish Gaelic   7
  Italian   9, 175
  Japanese   83, 85–6, 140, 142, 145, 159, 166, 182–3
  Korean   18, 83, 127, 139–40, 142, 147, 149, 152–4, 165, 168
  Kreyòl (Haitian Creole)   160

Malay 159
Mandarin 54, 127, 140, 154, 157–9, 161, 164, 167–72
Māori 159
Mock Spanish 9, 15, 24
Native American (general) 15
Old English 76
Papiamentu 62
Romantic 9
Russian 4
Scots Gaelic 7
Spokane 16, 192 n.19
Tagalog 159
Taiwanese 169
Taiwanese Hakka 159, 197 n.13
Taiwanese Hokkien 159, 197 n.13
Yiddish 4
languages, accents and 7, 15, 17, 70, 87–9, 124, 156, 160, 179–81, 183, 193 n.7
Latin America 20, 28–9, 33, 43, 51, 57, 62–4, 99, 116, 123, 128, 140, 147, *see also* teammates, Latin American
Latinos 2, 6, 19, 23, 25, 65, 96–7, *see also* players, Latino
La Vida Baseball 2
Learning to Labor (Paul Willis) 90, 103
linguistic homesickness 87
linguistics 20–1, 194 n.10, *see also* English as a second language (ESL); first language (L1); mother tongue; native language; second language (L2)
  etic (outsider) categories 22

McDonald's 44
Maine 137
Major League Baseball (MLB) 1, 6, 17, 19–20, 23–4, 27–30, 33–4, 39, 44, 55, 59, 62, 65–6, 68–9, 79–80, 83–4, 86–9, 95–6, 99–103, 112–13, 121–2, 125, 128–31, 133–4, 142, 146–51, 154, 157–8, 160, 162, 165–7, 175, 179, 181, 183, 185–6, 188, *see also* Dominican Republic
  bonuses and 32, 42, 50–1, 54, 62, 64, 92, 119, 194 n.16
  clubhouses and 20, 110, 117, 125
  Korea and 141
  MLB International 139, 165
  negative emotions and 182
  Players' Weekend 18
  'Ponle Acento' campaign 17
  release from contract and 96–8
  socialization and 19
  'ticking clock' and 77–8, 99
  transition from 98
  transition to 68, 177–8, 183
  unwritten rules and 186
Manhattan 4
Mara Salvatrucha (MS-13) gang 69
Mazatlán (Mexico) 169
memorabilia, authentication of 146–7, 173
mental skills training 52f, 53, 58, 60, 94
Mesabi Range Community College 61
métis 10
Mexican Americans 6, 17, 19–20
Mexico 5, 9, 30–1, 69, 86–7, 139, 165, 168–9
Miami 128, 186
Mid-America Christian University (Oklahoma City) 101
Minnesota 10, 61, 123
Minor League Baseball (MiLB) 19, 37, 39, 43, 45–6, 63, 68, 77–8, 97, 99, 128, 138, 145, 147–8, 167–8, 172, 176, *see also* bilingualism
  AAA 36, 105–6, 137, 185
  'social location' of players in 91–2
  'ticking clock' and 77–8, 99
Missoula 72
Montana 72, 76
  Yellowstone County 72
mother tongue 21–2
MRIs 125

National Association 8–9
National Public Radio 94
Native Americans 5, 15, *see also* players, Native American; United States
  Anishinaabe 10
  boarding schools and 12
  Cahuilla 13
  Chippewa 10–11, 182, 191 n.14

Colorado River Indian Tribes   18
linguistic policies and   3, 11–13
Mission Indian Agency of Southern California   13
Ojibwe   10
Salish   17
'speaking Indian'   10, 15–16
Spokane Tribe of Indians   16
stereotypical views of   12–13, 14f, 14–15, 183
White Earth Indian Reservation   10–11
native language   21–2
Netflix   48, 129
New Jersey   142
New York, upstate   6
New York City   142
Nicaragua   1, 30–1
North Carolina   78

Office of Strategic Services (OSS)   4
Ohio   112

Panama   43–4, 98, 111, 134
Panama Canal   44
Panda Express   37
Parasite (2017 film)   153
Pasco (Washington)   89, 96
peloteros (general)   66–8, 72, 74, 80, 86, 92–3, 96, 98, 101–3, 131–3, 173, 188, *see also* players, Cuban; players, Dominican; players, Latin American; players, Latino
Peppa Pig   170–1
phonemes   180, 197 n.16
players, Afro-Latino   55
players, American   116, 127–8, 132–4, 150
  'angry American' stereotype   150
players, Black (African American)   1, 4–5, 8–9, 12
  ethnic labels and   9
  exclusion and   12
players, brown   8
players, Colombian   45, 54
  mental 'preparedness' and   45
players, Cuban   9, 45, 57, 69, 71–2, 86–9, 107
  'Castilian' heritage of   9
  peloteros   87
  whiteness and   9
players, Dominican   44–8, 50–1, 85–90, 94–5, 98–9, 106, 117–18, 176–8, 188
  deportation and   98
  exploitation of   94
  mental 'preparedness' and   45, 89
  peloteros   43, 98
  release from contract and   96–8
players, English-speaking   89, 105, 108, 112, 120, 126, 132, 188
players, Irish American   8
players, Japanese   175–6, 178–82, 184
  speaking Spanish and   184
players, Korean   138, 141, 152–3, 165, 175
players, Latin American   19, 28, 51, 57, 68, 74, 84, 86, 88–9, 91, 95, 103, 108, 114, 116–17, 120, 126, 131–2, 134–5, 138, 147, 167, 184, 192 n.1
  Americans, stereotypical views of   108
  divisions among   117
  dominance in Major League Baseball and   133
  peloteros   154, 158
  Spanish, superficial resemblances and   88
players, Latino   1, 5, 7–9, 17, 20, 39, 57, 61–3, 74, 91, 108–11, 120, 123, 126–7, 131, 188
  behavior, on-field and   133–5, 193 n.13
  communication with   62–4, 84, 126
  infantilization and   39–40
  language and   9
  mestizo roots and   9
  peloteros   38, 89, 167
  racial ambiguity and   9
  stereotypes and   63–4
players, Mexican   90
players, Native American   5, 7, 10–12
  racialization and   13
players, nonwhite   4, 44
  stereotypical views of   44
players, Panamanian   90

players, Spanish-speaking   37–8, 72,
    83–6, 100, 108–9, 119, 125–7,
    133–4, 145, 184
players, Taiwanese   44, 154, 167, 170,
    172, 175
players, Venezuelan   54, 64, 86, 88–90,
    106, 117–18, 124, 133, 176
PlayStation 4   125
pluralism   3
postgame interviews   83–5, 156, 167,
    184–5, 188
    Kansas City Royals and   84
    Spanish-speaking players and   83–5
potencia   32, 42, 44–5, 50, 55, 58, 71, 94,
    158, 186
prejudice   117
Princeton   4
prospects, American   187
prospects, Dominican   43, 45–6, 50–2,
    55, 57, 61
    educación and   45
    intellectual ability, stereotypical views
        of   45–7
prospects, Latin American   68, 109, 146,
    168, 175, *see also* bilingualism
prospects, Latino   27–8, 34–42, 67, 81,
    100, 111, 158
prospects, Spanish-speaking   28, 105
prospects, Venezuelan   63–4
Protestantism, Irish   7
Puerto Rico   1–2, 81, 84, 114, 127, 138,
    143, 146, 187–8

racialization   5
racism, *see* baseball (general); fans
Reno (Nevada)   105
Rosetta Stone (language software)   31,
    49, 127, 129
Rotary Club   178

St. John's College (Bronx)   8, *see also*
    Fordham University
St. Louis   7
San Diego   5
Sapir-Whorf hypothesis   171
Saudi Arabia   55
Seattle   185–6
second language (L2)   21–2, 46, 75, 77–8,
    85, 118–19, 123, 129, 131, 171

English   110
Spanish   88, 110, 113–14, 120–1
'typological distance'   153
Second World War   4
self-segregation   112, 116
socialization   109
    cultural socialization   70
    language socialization   39, 42–4, 54,
        59, 74, 83, 85, 132, 135, 159,
        164, 188
    professional socialization   91
softball, fast-pitch   20
South Africa   126, 165
South Korea   12, 85, 127, 131–2, 137–8,
    140–8, 155, 158, 165–8, *see also*
    English learning and education
    American Forces Korea Network
        (AFKN/AFN)   141–2
    baseball in   20, 23, 138, 141, 147–51
    clubhouses and   138, 151, 163
    ethnic homogeneity and   138
    Korea Baseball Organization
        (KBO)   126–7, 138, 140–2,
        147–8, 151, 157, 165, 167–8
    Korean Americans   140
    scouts and   137, 141
    umpires and   148–50
Spain   8–9
Spanish   1–2, 9–10, 19–25, 28, 34, 37–8,
    46, 52–4, 56–60, 63–4, 66, 68,
    72–4, 82, 84–6, 105–6, 108–15,
    117–19, 122–5, 127, 131–2,
    135, 145–6, 161, 169, 171, 175,
    177–8, 188, *see also* teammates,
    Spanish-speaking; United States
    American Spanish   125
    AP (high school) Spanish   122
    Caribbean Spanish   60, 86, 121,
        123–4, 184
    Central American Spanish   86
    classes, mandatory   126
    'classroom' Spanish   124
    conversational   117
    Cuban Spanish   87–8
    Dominican Spanish   45, 88–9, 119–24
    'ecology' and   86–9
    English loanwords and   86
    English native speakers, use of   110–
        26

as index of cultural difference   121
Mexican   86
North American Spanish   86
South American Spanish   86
Spanish learning, coaches and   126
Spanish learning and education   57, 69, 77, 82, 92, 107–8, 113–15, 118, 126–7, 130–2, 153–4, 156, 168, 170
Spanish proficiency   82, 109–10, 113, 117, 123–4, 126, 135
United States, linguistic change and   87–8
variation and   122
Venezuelan Spanish   86, 124
speech communities   111, 115, 120, 126, 153
Stanford   112
Stockton (California)   51, 58–9, 83, 161
superdiversity   143

Taipei   154, 156
Taiwan   6, 85, 141, 155, 158, 160–3, 165–9, *see also* players, Taiwanese
baseball in   20, 139, 164–5, 167, 171–2
Chinese Nationalist government and   159
Chinese Professional Baseball League (CPBL)   139–40, 156–63, 167–8
coaching in   172
diversity and   160
Fox Sports Taiwan   156
Hakka   159
Hokkien   159
Indigenous baseball players and   160
Indigenous people and   159–60
Japanese colonial rule and   159
Latin American players in   167
linguistic diversity and   22
Mandarin Chinese and   159, 164, 167–8
National Taiwan University   155–6
sports announcers and   158
Taipei Universiade (2017)   156
Videoland Sports Channel   154, 156–8

teammates, English-speaking   56, 107, 110, 117, 132
teammates, Korean   151–2
teammates, Latin American   125
teammates, Latino   132, 134, 187
teammates, Spanish-speaking   24–5, 74, 106, 113, 115*f*, 125, 132, 135
Tennessee   94
Texas   87, 112
Thousand Oaks (California)   119
Tijuana   5
tilde (diacritic)   17
Times Square   101
Tommy John surgery   124, 162
Toronto   185–6
total linguistic fact (Silverstein)   21
translators   39, 72, 82, 84–5, 137, 140, 142, 144, 146, 149, 161–4, 171–2, 176, 192 n.5, *see also* interpreters
Troy (New York)   6, 8

Uber Eats   163
Ukraine   4
United States   2–3, 8, 15, 20, 24, 27–8, 32–3, 35, 37–41, 47, 55, 61, 66, 70, 78–9, 83–4, 86–8, 99, 101, 103, 107, 110, 114, 121, 123, 140–1, 155, 158, 162, 165, 175, 182–3, 187, *see also* Spanish
1860 US Census   6
1887 Dawes Act and   10
1905–1909 Indian Census Rolls   11
1940 US Census   11
2016 US presidential election   134
African Americans and   44
Asian Americans, stereotypes and   183
Balkanization and   177
Catholic schools and   8
Census Bureau   6, 11
Civil War   6, 8
Congress and   3
English *vs.* Spanish speakers and   83, 108
European colonization and   3
food and   37
identity and   111, 177
immigration and   134

immigration law and 5
immigration system and 89
linguistic diversity and 23
linguistic pacification and 3, 12
monolingualism and 3, 107–8, 169, 177, 183, 188
multilingualism and 3, 169, 177
Native Americans and 3
neocolonialism and 103
Nuestro Himno 177
plurilingualism and 177
sports announcers and 158
transition/adjustment to life in 19, 43–4, 49, 51, 57, 66, 68–70, 79, 109, 132, 154, 179, 182
University of Arizona 94
USA Today 186

Vanderbilt 112
Venezuela 30–1, 62–4, 66, 84–8, 114, 132, 138, *see also* players, Venezuelan
economic problems of 88–9

ventriloquism 183
Victoria, Queen 7

Wake Forest University 106, 111, 123–4
Washington State University-Tri Cities (Richland) 92, 93*f*, 93–4
WhatsApp 62–4, 89
whiteness 5
white passing 5, 9
Why Are All the Black Kids Sitting Together in the Cafeteria? (Beverly Tatum) 112
World Baseball Classic (WBC) 142–7, 156, 164
World Series 1, 24, 67
  1905 (New York Giants) 12
  1971 (Pittsburgh Pirates) 1
  2015 (Kansas City Royals) 186, 187*f*
  2017 (Houston Astros) 114
  2021 (Atlanta Braves) 66
wrestling 142

YouTube 113, 121

Index of names

f denotes an in-text illustration

Aaron, Hank   155
Acuña, Ronald   133–4, 147
Additon, Nick   139–40, 164–73, 184, 189
Almada, Melo   6
Altuve, José   114, 115*f*

Babe Ruth   4, 155, 179
Barfield, Josh   73
Basch, Zak   40, 55, 84, 111–12, 116–17, 120–4
Bellán, Esteban   8
Bender, Charles "Chief"   10–12, 13*f*, 14–15, 182–3
Bender, Mary   11, 11*f*
Berg, Moe   4
Berra, Yogi   3
Besnier, Niko   44
Biden, Joe   31
Birlingmair, Reid   107
Blass, Steve   2, 178, 189
Bleday, JJ   130
Brayboy, Bryan McKinley Jones   15
Bregman, Alex   113–14, 115*f*, 117, 129–30
Bugs Bunny   180
Burdick, Peyton   130
Burgos, Adrian Jr.   5, 9, 17
Bush, Dave   126–7, 131–2, 137–41, 148–9, 151–2, 162, 165–6, 168, 173
Bush, George W.   177

Cabrera, Miguel   84
Canó, Robinson   17, 90
Casilla, Alexi   107–8, 110, 120
Clemente, Roberto   1–3, 9, 15–17, 23–4, 178, 188–9
Colón, Christian   187, 189
Cora, Alex   127

Correa, Carlos   81, 114, 115*f*
Costas, Bob   181–4

Darvish, Yu   181
Denbo, Gary   129
DeRosa, Mark   185
Diskin, Jeff   27–8, 33, 39–40, 45, 49, 54–5, 78–85, 100–2, 116, 119, 123, 127, 187–8
Dolphus, Deron   47, 78–80, 100–1, 103
Drake   49
Dunshee, Parker   105–11, 113, 117–19, 121–6, 129–33, 135, 171, 175, 184, 187, 189

Elmer Fudd   180

Febrillet, Johan   29–30, 32, 35, 36*f*, 41–2, 46–8, 50, 61–2, 66–8, 78–9, 90, 188
Feinstein, Dan   51, 57, 65, 78
Fernández, Yosmi   48–9, 49*f*, 50, 54, 71, 100, 129
Foster, John   161–8
Freeman, Freddie   133–4

Geertz, Clifford   19
Gehrig, Henry Louis, *see* Lou Gehrig
Gelabert, Michel   37, 71–3, 73*f*, 74–6, 82–3, 85–8, 100–1, 129, 166, 189
Giljegiljaw, Kungkuan   160
Glass, Emily   29, 78, 112, 128–30, 135, 169
Godzilla   181
Goldstein, Kevin   33, 45–6, 54, 81, 113–14, 118, 120, 130
Gómez, Lefty   6
González, Adrián   17, 20
Guasch, Richard   57, 68–71, 82–3, 85–9, 107, 118, 123, 147, 154
Guerrero, Vladimir Jr.   176
Gurriel, Yuli   114
Guzmán, Jorge   28, 50, 80, 82–3, 117

Harris, Kamala   31
Hernández, Carlos   84–5
Hill, Jane   9
Horie, Shingo   175, 178

Ibáñez, Raúl   184
Iwakuma, Hisashi   178

Jaffe, Alexandra   55
Jesus Christ   3
Jeter, Derek   128–30
Johnson, Eric   46, 89–96, 103
Jordan, Michael   178

Kahn, Roger   95
Kawasaki, Munenori (Muni)   185–6, 188
Kelly, Catharine   6
Kelly, Mike "King"   6–7, 7f, 8, 10, 13, 15
Kepler, Max   18
Kikuchi, Yusei   176, 181
Kim, Hyunsung   141–4, 144f, 145–54, 156, 158, 164, 170, 173, 189
King Kong   181
Klein, Alan   27, 33, 43, 91, 103

Lebron, Hector "Tito"   17
Lee, Jacky Bing-Sheng   154–63, 168, 176
Lil Baby   49
Liriano, Elvin   93–101, 137, 140, 168
Lou Gehrig   4
Luzardo, Jesús   20, 106

McDaniel, RJ   182
McLouth, Nate   107–8, 110, 113, 120–1, 123
Martinez, Nick   140
Martínez, Pedro   81, 91, 182
Mather, Kevin   177–8
Mayer, Marcelo   20
Meek, Barbara   13
de Mercado, Jill Long   34, 36–7, 65–8, 74, 77, 79–80, 95–6, 103, 126, 129
Mesa, Victor Jr.   130f
Meyers, John   13–15
Mikolas, Miles   140
Miñoso, Minnie   55
Miranda, Aríel   167
Mondesi, Adalberto   85

Montgomery, Mike   63, 127, 147–51
Moreno, Gabriel   176
Morris, Jack   179–80, 183, 185
Mosquera, Juan   43–4, 99, 103, 111–12, 120, 127, 134
Muncy, Max   119–20, 123
Murtaugh, Danny   1

Nava, Vincent   8–10, 13, 15
Norris, Bud   134, 177
Novas, Elvis   160
Núñez, Eduardo   17

Obama, Barack   177
O'Brien, Dave   175–6, 178
Ohtani, Shohei   179–81, 183–4, 189
Oliver, Al   1
Ortiz, David   81, 95

Patiño, Luis   54
Peña, Carlos   184
Peña, Francisco   105–7, 109, 111, 121, 124–5, 132, 135
Pence, Hunter   24–5, 186, 188
Peralta, Manuel   107–8, *see also* Casilla, Alexi; McLouth, Nate
Pérez, Junior   51–2, 58–60
Pérez, Salvador   54, 71
Polanco, Luis   36f
Powers-Beck, Jeffrey   5
Pratt, Richard Henry   11–12
Prince, Bob   1–2, 178
Puason, Robert (Bobby)   50–8, 64, 70–2, 75–6, 83
Pujols, Albert   103

Remy, Jerry   176, 178, 183
Rey, Carlos   144f
Rivera, Emmanuel   84
Robinson, Jackie   1
Rodríguez, Alex   155
Rodríguez, Julio   178
Roosevelt, Theodore   177
Rothschild, Larry   175, 178
Ruiz, Richard   3, 108
Ryu, Hyun-Jin   18

Saito, Natsu Taylor   183
Sánchez, Anibal   124

Index of names

Santiago, Mario   138
Sasaki, Kazuhiro   182
Sawamura, Hirokazu   166, 175
Scott, Connor   130
Shepard, Matt   179
Silverstein, Michael   21, 110–11
Somoza, Anastasio   1
Suzuki, Ichiro   181–5, 188–9

Tanaka, Masahiro   175–6, 178–9, 183, 189
Tatum, Beverly   112, 116
Tejada, Félix   144f
Thames, Eric   140
Trout, Mike   179
Tsai, Brian   162–4, 168

Valdés, Guadalupe   108
Ventura, Yordano   186–7, 187f, 188–9
Victoria, Luis   38, 54, 57–64, 83–4, 117, 119–20, 123, 134

Wang, Chien-Ming   154–5, 160
Wilczek, Frank   2
Williams, Ted   5, 50
Willis, Paul   90
Wilson, Horace   12

Young, Larry   144f

Zerpa, Angel   66–7

www.ingramcontent.com/pod-product-compliance
Lightning Source LLC
Chambersburg PA
CBHW070724020526
44116CB00031B/1541